F

A Fisherman's Anthology

Edited by
David Seybold

Illustrations by Joseph Fornelli

Seasons of the Angler

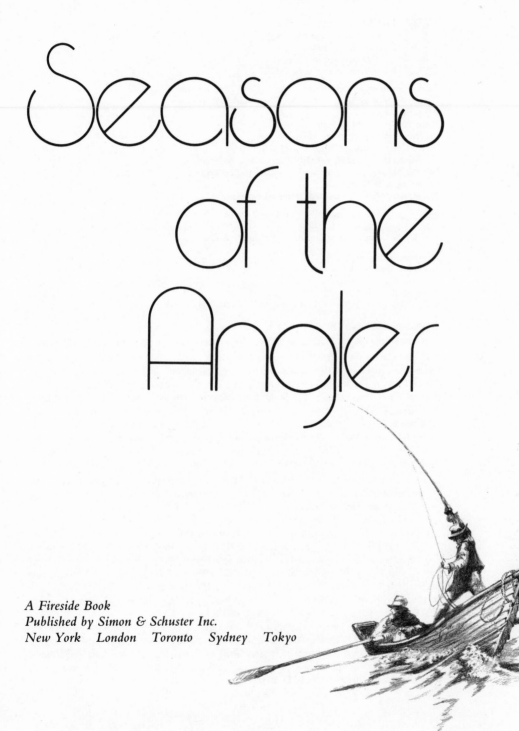

A Fireside Book
Published by Simon & Schuster Inc.
New York   London   Toronto   Sydney   Tokyo

Fireside
Simon & Schuster Building
Rockefeller Center
1230 Avenue of the Americas
New York, New York 10020

10 9 8 7 6 5 4 3 2 1 Pbk.

Library of Congress Cataloging in Publication Data

Seasons of the angler.
   "A Fireside book."
   1. Fishing—Literary collections.   2. American literature—20th century.
I. Seybold, David.
PS509.F5S43   1989   810'.8'0355   88-33489

ISBN 0-671-67509-5 Pbk.

For my mother,
Margaret Gove Seybold.

I would like to express my deep appreciation to Robert F. Jones, whose support and suggestions were of great value to me in the planning of this book.

DAVID SEYBOLD

Contents

Contents

The fisherman fishes as the urchin eats a cream bun—from lust.

T. H. WHITE,
England Have My Bones

Introduction

BOOKS ON angling abound in our literature. In fact, of all the sports it is the one most written about. Ever since 1676, when Izaak Walton's *The Compleat Angler* was published, there has been an effusion of books covering every aspect and nuance of angling. Yet notwithstanding the thousands of volumes extant, more books on angling are being published each year than ever before. And while many repeat old lessons, thoughts, and observances, there are enough fresh and innovative works to tell us that the art and practice of angling is forever changing.

Traditionally, books on angling occupy two distinct shelves, one literary, the other instructional, with the majority leaning toward the latter. The purpose of these "how-to" books is to keep anglers apprised of improved tackle, new techniques, and new outlets for their newly acquired knowledge. As popular and necessary as these books are, however, most are transient guides that lead anglers through only a brief period of time. They are the brains of angling, but, with few exceptions, they are no more than ephemeral. For even in so contemplative a sport as angling, there is change. Manufacturers make what laboratories create, fishermen refine and improve on yesterday's angling techniques, rivers and lakes become too well known, and waters where salmonids once thrived may now be home to coarse fish—all of which means there will always be a preponderance of instructional angling books.

In part it is the proliferation of how-to books that spawns the desire for more literary works, those which entertain while prompting reflection. Their importance lies in their ability to capture another, equally important aspect of the sport. Alongside the angler's ability to catch fish is his devotion, his contemplative reflection on *why* he fishes. There is a timelessness in all anglers' thoughts and perceptions, one that allows them to identify with experiences afield no matter how many years separate their lives. How-to books might represent the brains of angling, but these others reflect its soul. As the late Jim Deren of New York City's The Angler's Roost once said, "The romance of fishing isn't all just fish."

Seasons of the Angler is a collection of stories that largely disregards the how-to of angling in favor of the *involvement* of angling. As an angling book it offers little in the way of instruction, but does attempt to convey a history and philosophy. In choosing the pieces that make up the collection, I was interested less in fish and fishing than in fishermen. As in *The Old Man and the Sea*, I wanted stories that showed the effects of an experience on the protagonist. It mattered little whether a story told of boyhood days spent fishing for bluegills in small suburban ponds, or of long hours spent in the pursuit of trophy gamefish. I was not so much interested in what species of fish the protagonist was trying to catch, or what techniques or equipment he employed, as I was in a story that evoked a measure of the human experience in angling.

The result is a collection of many voices and experiences. They represent various forms and methods of angling—from ice fishing for yellow perch in Massachusetts to fly fishing for sailfish in Cozumel, from commercial salmon fishing in Alaska to guiding trout anglers on Montana rivers. There are short stories, memoirs, essays, and poems—all of which address the human experience in angling.

No anthology can avoid being a personal statement, and this one is no exception. It represents what I wanted most to see in such a book: well-written stories; a rich variety of experiences covering many regions of the world; an unusual combination of writers, some of whom are known for their angling stories while others are not even known to be anglers; and a blend of fiction and nonfiction that both entertains and prompts reflection.

Some readers may disagree with my selections; others will wonder how I could consider such a collection without including certain very well-known writers. Obviously there are many fine authors who could have contributed but chose not to, just as there were stories I had to turn back. This was due not to their lack of quality, but rather to how they contributed to the overall book.

Bringing forth this collection of new and previously unpublished stories (though a few have appeared in periodicals by now, all were written specifically for this collection) was, at times, confusing and even unsettling. Ultimately, however, it was exhilarating. Working with twenty-five writers from all parts of the country, tracking down those with peripatetic life-styles, going over deadlines and story changes was at times hectic but never unpleasant. And receiving stories that had never seen printer's ink or another editor's blue pencil called up the same emotions as when I hike into a remote pond and find native trout rising without another angler in sight.

The contributors agreed to write for *Seasons of the Angler* because they believed in the idea of an anthology that addressed the human experience in fishing. They became involved in the overall collection, constantly asking how it was progressing and whether there was anything they could do to help. My correspondence shows that this was so in every case.

It occurs to me, finally, that collecting the stories in *Seasons of the Angler* has a lot in common with being granted a rare opportunity to fish on a remote pond for native trout. The water is flat and reflective, the trout are rising in evocative enticement, and there is not another angler in sight. My casts are more fortuitous than skilled as I hook up with trout that are the color of the best sunset I've ever seen. They are strong and independent, and each has a singular spirit that makes me revere it more than all the others. In the tradition of angling etiquette, I net each trout, admire its individual artistry, and then carefully release it. I watch it swim away and hope it gives as much joy to others as it has to me.

DAVID SEYBOLD
New London, N.H.
August 1987

Seasons
of the
Angler

Synecdoche and the Trout

David Quammen

IT IS a simple question with a seemingly simple answer. "Why do you live in *Montana?*"

Repeatedly over a span of thirteen years you have heard this, asked most often by people who know you just well enough to be aware of the city where you grew up, the tony universities you attended, and a few other bits of biographic detail on the basis of which they harbor a notion that you should have taken your place in New York café society or, at least, an ivy-adorned department of English. They suspect you, these friends do, of hiding out. Maybe in a way they are right. But they have no clear sense of what you are hiding from, or why, let alone where. Hence their question.

"The trout," you answer, and they gape back blankly.

"The trout," they say after a moment. "That's a fish."

"Correct."

"Like lox."

"In some ways similar."

"You like to go fishing. *That's* why you live out there? *That's* why you spend your life in a place without decent restaurants or bookstores or symphony orchestras, a place halfway between Death Valley and the North Pole? A place where there's no espresso, and the *Times* comes in

3

three days late by pontoon plane? Do I have this straight, now? It's because you like to go *fishing*?"

"No," you say. "Only partly. At the beginning, that was it, yes. But I've stayed thirteen years. No plans to leave."

"You *went* for the fishing, but you *stayed* for something else. Aha."

"Yes. The trout," you say.

"This is confusing."

"A person can get too much trout fishing. Then it cloys, becomes taken for granted. Meaningless."

"Again like lox."

"I don't seem to fish nearly as much as I used to."

"But you keep talking about the trout. You went, you stayed; the trout is your reason."

"The trout is a synecdoche," you say, because these friends are tough and verbal and they can take it.

A biologist would use the term "indicator species." Because I have the biases of a journalist (working that great gray zone between newspaper reporting and fiction, engaged daily in trying to make facts not just talk but yodel), I speak instead of synecdoche. We both mean that a trout represents more than itself—but that, and more important, it also does represent itself.

"A poem should not *mean* but *be*," wrote Archibald MacLeish, knowing undeniably in his heart that a good poem quite often does both.

Likewise, a trout.

The presence of trout in a body of water is a discrete zoological fact that nevertheless signifies certain things.

It signifies a definite complex of biotic and chemical and physical factors, a standard of richness and purity, without which that troutly presence is impossible. It signifies aquatic nutrients like calcium, potassium, nitrate, phosphate; signifies enough carbon dioxide to nourish meadows of algae and keep calcium in solution as calcium bicarbonate; signifies a prolific invertebrate fauna (Plecoptera, Trichoptera, Diptera, Ephemeroptera), and a temperature regime confined within certain daily and annual extremes. It also signifies clear pools emptying down staircases of rounded boulders and dappled with patterns of late-afternoon shade cast by chrome-yellow cottonwood leaves in September. It signifies solitude so sweet and pure as to bring an ache to the sinuses, a buzz to the ears. Loneliness and anomie of the most wholesome sort. It signifies dissolved oxygen to at least four or five parts per million. It signifies a good possibility of osprey, dippers, and kingfishers, otters and water shrews, heron; and it signifies *Salmo gairdneri, Salmo clarki, Salmo trutta*. Like a well-chosen phrase in any poem, MacLeish's included, the very presence of trout signifies at more than one level. Magically, these creatures are literal and real. They live in imagination, memory, and cold water.

For instance: I can remember the first trout I ever caught as an adult (which was also the first I ever caught on a fly), and precisely what the poor little fish represented to me at that moment. It represented (a) dinner and (b) a new beginning, with a new sense of self, in a new place. The matter of dinner was important, since I was a genuinely hungry young man living out of my road-weary Volkswagen bus with a meager supply of groceries. But the matter of selfhood and place, the matter of reinventing identity, was paramount. My hands trembled wildly as I took that fish off the hook.

A rainbow, all of seven or eight inches long. A Black Gnat pattern, size 12, tied cheaply of poor materials somewhere in the Orient and picked up by me at Herter's when I had passed through South Dakota. I killed the little trout before it could slip through my fingers and, heartbreakingly, disappear. This episode was for me exactly equivalent to the one in Faulkner's "Delta Autumn," where blood from a fresh-killed buck is smeared on the face of the boy. *I slew you*, the boy thinks. *My bearing must not shame your quitting life*, he understands. *My conduct for ever onward must become your death.* In my own case, of course, there was no ancient Indian named Sam Fathers serving as mentor and baptist. I was alone and an autodidact. The blood of the little trout did not steam away its heat of life into the cold air, and I smeared none on my face. Nevertheless.

This fish came out of a creek in the Big Horn Mountains of north-eastern Wyoming, and I was on my way to Montana, though at that moment I didn't yet know it.

Montana was the one place on earth farthest in miles and in spirit from Oxford University where you could still get by with the English language, and the sun didn't disappear below the horizon for days in a row during midwinter, and the prevailing notion of a fish dinner was not lutefisk. I had literally never set foot within the borders of this place called "Montana." I had no friends there, no friends of friends, no contacts of any sort, which was fine. I looked at a map and saw jagged blue lines, denoting mountain rivers. All I knew was that, in Montana, there would be more trout.

Trout were the indicator species for a place and a life I was seeking.

I went. Six years later, rather to my surprise, I was a professional fishing guide under license from the Montana Department of Fish, Wildlife and Parks. My job was to smear the blood on other young faces. *I slew you. My bearing must not shame your quitting life.* Sometimes it was actually like that, though quite often it was not.

Item. You are at the oars of a fourteen-foot Avon raft, pushing across a slow pool on the Big Hole River in western Montana. An August afternoon. Seated in front of you is an orthopedic surgeon from San Francisco, a pleasant man who can talk intelligently about the career of Gifford Pinchot or the novels of Evelyn Waugh, who is said to play a formidable game of squash, and who spends one week of each year fishing for trout. In his right hand is a Payne bamboo rod that is worth more than the car you drive, and attached to the rod is a Hardy Perfect reel. At the end of the doctor's line is a kinked and truncated leader, and at the end of the leader is a dry fly which can no longer by even the most technical definition be considered "dry," having been slapped back and forth upon and dragged through several miles of river. With this match of equipment to finesse, the good doctor might as well be hauling manure in the back seat of a Mercedes. Seated behind you is the doctor's wife, who picked up a fly rod for the first time in her life two hours earlier. Her line culminates in a fly that is more dangerous to you than to any fish in Montana. As you have rowed quietly across the glassy pool, she has attacked the water's surface like a French chef dicing celery.

Now your raft has approached the brink of a riffle. On the Big Hole River during this late month of the season, virtually all of the catchable trout cluster (by daylight) where they can find cover and oxygen, in those two wedges of deep still water flanking the fast current at the bottom of each riffle. You have told the doctor and his wife about the wedges. There, *those*, you have said. Cast just across the eddy line, you have said. Throw a little slack. We've got to hit the spots to catch any fish, you have said in the tactfully editorial first-person plural.

As your raft slides into this particular riffle, the doctor and his wife become tense with anticipation. The wife snags her fly in the rail rope along the rowing frame, and asks sweetly if you would free it, which you do, grabbing the oars again quickly to avoid hitting a boulder. You begin working to slalom the boat through the riffle. The wife whips her fly twice through the air before sinking it into the back of your straw cowboy hat. She apologizes fervently. Meanwhile, she lets her line loop around your right oar. You take a stroke with the left oar to swing clear of a drowned log, and point your finger over the doctor's shoulder: "Remember, now. The wedges." He nods eagerly. The raft is about to broadside another boulder, so you pull hard on both oars and with that motion your hat is jerked into the river. The doctor makes five false casts, intent on the wedges, and then fires his line forward into the tip of his own rod like a handful of spaghetti hitting a kitchen wall. He moans. The raft drops neatly out of the riffle, between the wedges, and back into dead water.

Item. You are two days along on a wilderness float through the Smith River canyon, fifty miles and another three river-days from the nearest hospital, with cliffs of shale towering hundreds of feet on each side of the river to seal you in. The tents are grouped on a cottonwood flat. It is dinner hour, and you have just finished a frigid bath in the shallows. As you open your first beer, a soft-spoken Denver architect walks back into camp with a size 14 Royal Wulff stuck past the barb into his lower eyelid. He has stepped behind another fisherman at precisely the wrong moment. Everyone looks queasily at everyone else, but the outfitter—who is your boss, who is holding his second martini, and whose own nerves are already frazzled from serving as chief baby-sitter to eight tourist fishermen—looks pleadingly at you. With tools from your fishing vest (a small pair of scissors, a forceps, a loop of leader) you extract the fly. Then you douse the architect's wound with what little remains of the outfitter's gin.

Item. Three days down the Smith on a different trip, under a cloudless July sky, you are drifting, basking comfortably in the heat, resting your oars. In your left hand is a cold Pabst Blue Ribbon. In place of your usual tee shirt, you are wearing a new yellow number that announces with some justice: "Happiness Is a Cold Pabst." On your head, in place of the cowboy straw, is a floppy cloth porkpie in a print of Pabst labels. In the bow seat of your raft, casting contentedly to a few rising trout, is a man named Augie Pabst, scion of the family. Augie, contrary to all your expectations, is a sensitive and polite man, a likable fellow. Stowed in your cargo box and your cooler are fourteen cases of Pabst Blue Ribbon, courtesy. You take a deep gulp of beer, you touch an oar. Ah, yes, you think. Life in the wilderness.

Item. You are floating a petroleum engineer and his teenage son through the final twelve miles of the Smith canyon, which is drowsy, meandering water not hospitable to rainbow trout but good for an occasional large brown. The temperature is ninety-five, the midday glare is fierce, you have spent six days with these particular people, and you are eager to be rid of them. Three more hours to the take-out, you tell yourself. A bit later you think, Two more. The petroleum engineer has been treated routinely with ridicule by his son, and evidently has troubles also with his wife. The wife is along on this trip but she does not fish; she does not seem to talk much to her husband; she has ridden a supply boat with the outfitter and spent much of her time humming quietly. You wonder if the petroleum engineer has heard of Hemingway's Francis Macomber. You are sure that the outfitter has not and you suspect that the wife has. The engineer says that he and his son would like to catch one large brown trout before the trip ends, so you tell them to tie on Marabou muddlers and drag those billowy monstrosities through certain troughs. Fifteen minutes later, the boy catches a large brown. This fish is eighteen inches long and broad of shoulder—a noble and beautiful animal that the Smith River has taken five years to grow. The father tells you to kill it—yeah, I guess kill it—they will want to eat it, just this one, at the hotel. Suddenly you despise your job. You despise this man, but he is paying your wage and so he has certain entitlements. You kill the fish, pushing your thumb into its mouth and breaking back the neck. Its old sharp teeth cut your hand.

The boy is a bad winner, a snot, taunting his father now as the three of you float on down the river. Half an hour later, the father catches a large brown, this one also around eighteen inches. You are pleased for him, and glad for the fish, since you assume that it will go free. But the father has things to prove to the wife as well as to the son, and for the former your eyewitness testimony of a great battle, a great victory, and a great act of mercy will not suffice. "Better keep this one, too," he says, "and we'll have a pair." You detest this particular euphemistic use of the word "keep." You argue tactfully but he pretends not to hear. Your feelings for these trout are what originally brought you out onto the Smith River and are what compel you to bear the company of folk like the man and his son. *My conduct for ever onward must become your death*. The five-year-old brown trout is lambent, spotted with orange, lithe as an ocelot, swirling gorgeously under water in your gentle grip. You kill it.

I don't guide anymore. I haven't renewed my license in a handful of years. My early and ingenuous ideas about the role of a fishing guide turned out to be totally wrong: I had imagined it as a life rich with independence, and with a rustic sort of dignity, wherein a fellow would stand closer to these particular animals he admired inordinately. I hadn't foreseen that it would demand the humility of a chauffeur and the complaisance of a pimp.

And I don't seem to fish nearly as much as I used to. I have a dilemma these days: I dislike killing trout but I believe that, in order to fish responsibly, to fish conscionably, the fisherman should at least occasionally kill. Otherwise he can too easily delude himself that fly fishing is merely a game, a dance of love, played in mutual volition and mutual empathy by the fisherman and the trout. Small flies with the barbs flattened are an excellent means for allowing the fisherman's own sensibilities to be released unharmed—but the fish themselves aren't always so lucky. They get eye-hooked, they bleed, they suffer trauma and dislocated maxillae and infection. Unavoidably, some die. For them, it is not a game, and certainly not a dance. On some days I feel that it's hypocritical to profess love for these creatures while endangering and abusing them so wantonly; better to enjoy the thrill of the sport honestly, kill what I catch, and stop fishing when I have had a surfeit of killing. On other days I do dearly enjoy holding them in the water, gentling them as they regain breath and balance and command of their muscles, then watching them swim away. The dilemma remains unresolved.

"Yet each man kills the thing he loves," wrote Oscar Wilde, and I keep wondering how a person of Wilde's urban and cerebral predilections knew so goddamn much about trout fishing.

Why do you live in Montana? people ask. For the trout, I answer. Oh, you're one of those fanatical fisherman types? Not so much anymore, I say. It's just a matter of knowing that they're here.

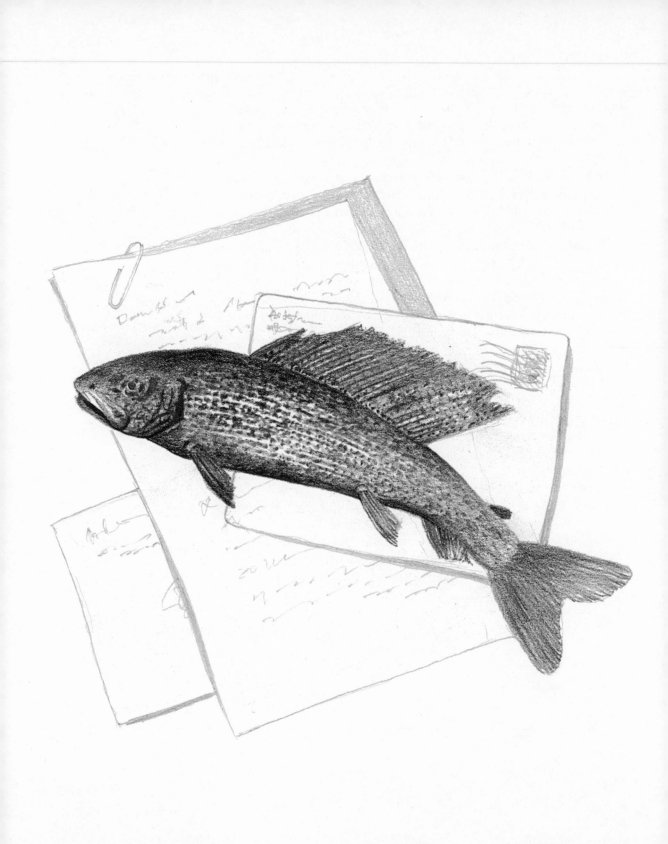

Fishing by Mail

Vance and Philip Bourjaily

THE FOLLOWING exchange of letters between Philip Bourjaily and his father, Vance, is the result of my asking them to contribute a story about shared angling experiences. One of my objectives was for them to provide, as I put it, "insights into the character of the angler in today's society."

—D.S.

Redbird, IA
April 21, 1986

Dear Dad:

I received this intriguing surprise in the morning mail. Not being the introspective sort, I have never given much thought to my place in society as a fisherman. Looking back over the years for some clue, all I can remember is falling into a lot of rivers, breaking several rod tips, not catching very many fish, and, on one famous occasion, hooking you in the nose with an errant backcast.

I don't know what I have learned from all this besides what a grown man with a trout fly stuck in his nose sounds like, nor do I see how I would have turned out differently if I'd spent my youth losing kites in trees instead of fishing tackle. But I will give the matter quite a bit of thought.

Love,
Philip

11

New Orleans, LA
May 6, 1986

Dear Philip:

Like you, I am ladled into a gentle stew of bemusement over the question of what our "act of fishing means to the society in which we live." On the scale of public nuisance to civic benefactor, we might be placed slightly higher than water skiers, if measurably lower than professional clowns. As inadvertent clowns we do pretty well, as your letter reminds me, earning as much laughter as, while giving less offense than, such brother amateurs as folk singers and guys who claim they know how to fix your car. We are probably about as neutral as stamp collectors, but I really don't know.

What I do know is the solution to our bafflement. Through some years of intermittent engagement with attempts at writing thoughtful nonfiction, I've found, often enough, that thought won't crystallize, and have learned to apply the following sneaky rule: *When in doubt, tell a story, reasonably true if possible.* Here is the reasonably true, particular story of my own earliest recollection of taking you fishing.

It was a Fourth of July weekend. You were three and a half. We went, with your mother and sister, to camp and to fish for trout in northeast Iowa, near Decorah, where the limestone creeks once held native brook trout. When the banks were cleared, many years ago, the water temperatures went up and the brookie population went down. Now the creeks are only suitable for the put-and-take stocking of rainbows and browns.

We drove up beside the creek on a car track for a mile or so and put up our tent where the water fell in a series of shallow rock pools. Your sister and I strung up fly rods and walked downstream to a fairly deep hole, where Anna started fishing with a salmon egg and I tied on some wet fly or other. I'm going to guess it was a Queen of the Waters, which seems regally attractive to me, although I don't recall that many trout shared that opinion.

It was extremely hot. The water was low and clear. After an unproductive hour, it occurred to me to dip a hand into the water. Even below the surface it felt lukewarm, nothing the fish would want to venture out into from whatever deep and shaded crannies they were basking in. I decided it was basking time for me, too, back at camp with a cold beer.

"It's too hot. The trout aren't active," I called out to your mother as we arrived. She was sitting on a rock, watching you and Moon, the Weimaraner, play in the shallow pool.

"But Philip's got one," your mother said. "That's a trout, isn't it? Show Daddy."

Whereupon you held up a live, comatose twenty-two-inch rainbow you were playing with and then plunged her back again into the tepid stream. The hatchery folks had stocked up heavily for the holiday weekend. The place we'd stopped seemed to have been one of the stocking points, and along with the usual seven- to twelve-inch fish, they'd apparently added at least one of the larger females, now retired from being inseminated and milked.

She was disoriented, I suppose, out of her hatchery tank, and over-heated, with no residual instinct to tell her she could swim away to coolness.

Yesterday afternoon, sitting in a big striped tent at the New Orleans Jazz Festival, eating barbecued alligator and listening to a woman named Carrie Smith sing a Bessie Smith blues called "Just Give Me One Smile," I couldn't lose the thought that I hoped we'd done right by that fat old lady trout—put her in a bucket and carried her to a deep hole where she might have found a cool place. I'm not sure we did that, I only hope we did. All I'm sure of is that she was the largest trout you or I ever caught.

Anyway, someone asked me what alligator tasted like, and I was able to tell her it's a whole lot like iguana.

Love,
Dad

Redbird, IA
May 12, 1986

Dear Dad,

I would have thought alligator tasted like snapping turtle, since they are both so bad-tempered, but that just shows what a provincial guy I am. I do remember how the large rainbow trout tasted: like the doughballs the hatchery workers at Manchester throw into those long concrete troughs full of fish. I know because we *ate* that fish. Three-and-a-half-year-olds don't always do the right thing by the fish they catch, but then, neither do a lot of adults.

Of course, you didn't raise me to be a trout tickler, and I believe it

13

was shortly after the trip to Decorah that you took me to the tackle shop at Abercrombie & Fitch and bought me a four-foot bamboo fly rod and matching Hardy reel. Few children have received such auspicious starts to their fly-fishing careers, but I'm sure that none of them have parlayed that early advantage into baser incompetence than have I.

This is not to say I haven't had my fly-fishing moments. I have. Some of them even involved catching fish, but the one that I remember as most inspirational does not, at least on my part. We were on a family car trip, either en route to, or returning from, Boulder, Colorado, in 1969. Stopping at a large national park, perhaps Rocky Mountain National Park, we parked at the first beaver pond and uncased our fly rods. Several people were arranged around the edge of the pond, sitting on coolers and camp chairs, watching bobbers unexpectantly. You and I began casting, which excited no little curiosity on the part of the assembled bait fishermen, particularly because my own style, while earnest, resembled a child defending himself from a swarm of buffalo gnats. Painfully aware that we were the center of attention, I yearned for the anonymity of a spin-casting rig and a hat less conspicuous than the jaunty Australian Digger model with flies stuck in the band that I wore in those days. It was what theological types call "a crisis of faith."

As if in answer, you caught a fish. Not a huge fish, just the sort of trout that anglers other than myself pull routinely from Western beaver ponds. To judge from the reaction of the other fishermen, however, it was a newsworthy event. Two teenagers who had been watching nearby came over to see your fish.

"Whadja catch him on?" asked one.

"This trout fly, son," you said, holding up a yellow-and-black McGinty for them to see. "You might want to find some smaller hooks for your night crawlers."

Someday, I thought, retrieving my own fly from a clutching willow, I'll be like that. Seventeen years later, I have not yet lived up to the beau ideal of the gracious purist you set for me. I do most of my fishing now for bass and catch them with ugly rubber grubs.

By the way, the subject of bass is a melancholy one this year. We had a long snowy winter, and when the ice melted off our farm pond in March, the wind blew a huge raft of winterkilled fish up along the dam. There were four-pound bass, bluegills the size of Frisbees, and walleyes (the ones we put in years ago and never saw again) bigger than the largest bass. A couple of local tournament fishermen I know wanted to come out fishing even after I told them about the winterkill. Tom and John told me that if there were fish to be caught in the pond, it was just a matter of figuring out how they were relating to the subsurface structure and then finding the right bait. I said glumly that as far as I knew the fish were relating to the structure by floating upside down over the top of it. After a long unproductive morning, they were ready to agree with me. We're going to catch some bass in a neighbor's pond and try restocking in a couple of weeks.

On a happier note, the morel mushrooms have come and gone in satisfying numbers, and Cousin Shaun bushwhacked a wild turkey as it flew down from its roost at the Hawkeye Wildlife Area just as shooting hours began. He smoked it and brought me a large piece of the breast, which tasted like smoked alligator.

Love,
Philip

New Orleans
May 20, 1986

Dear Philip:

This correspondence seems to deal as much with eating as it does with fishing, which is appropriate to the reminiscence I'm about to self-inflict. It goes back to the grandest of our fishing trips, to the Big Hole in Montana, with Dek Lardner and his boys.

Distrustful that any hand but my own should turn the spatula, I appointed myself camp cook—well, motel cook. And I will maintain that I started off with a real triumph when I presented the first day's catch flambé, pouring a jigger of Wild Turkey over the hot fish as they came from under the broiler, coated with butter, fennel, garlic, and slivered almonds. The flame when I lit a kitchen match to the pan not only astonished the company but was explosive enough to be satisfactorily alarming, and the trout (add lemon and Tabasco to taste) were absolutely great. As I hope you'll agree.

The next night we ate out. At noon on the third day, I realized a fantasy. I had always felt one could cook *truite au bleu sur rive*—I've probably got the second preposition wrong, and maybe the final noun as well. It's supposed to mean Blue Trout Streamside and, grammar notwithstanding, the method should be known to all:

1. As you catch your trout, keep them alive. 2. Heat a large pot

of water to boiling; add vinegar, salt, and small, peeled new potatoes. 3. When the potatoes are tender, remove pot from heat. Quickly kill and gut the trout, dropping them into the scalding water while they are still quivering. 4. In a couple of minutes, the skin separates, the flesh flakes and turns pale blue. 5. Remove and serve fish and potatoes, with butter, salt, and pepper. Best damn trout I ever cooked or ate (your agreement once again seems necessary), and what could I do to exceed it?

Well, the sophisticated chef takes advantage of fresh local produce in season, and what Montana produces most abundantly is sagebrush. The trout presented on the evening of the fourth day were marinated in white wine and heaps of sage leaves, sautéed meunière, and rivaled the green persimmon in mouth-puckering ability. Jamie and David Lardner volunteered to run down to the corner for hamburgers, and I don't believe even the motel cats would touch the trout.

There was only one other low-comedy moment for me in what was otherwise a hell of a fine trip, and I don't think I've ever confessed this one. Jamie, Steven, David, Dek, and you went off someplace arduous, and I elected to fish an easy stretch of water running through the next-door ranch, all by myself. Looked good, and I felt lazy. Up to that hour, we hadn't thought it would be practical to try to carry any fish back to Iowa, but here and now, it seemed to me, feasibility flickered. Whatever I might catch and clean I could hustle to the motel, pack in the ice chest, and it would reach Iowa with us five hours later. It was dusk, there was a hatch on, and I was motivated to fish hard. The hatch looked something like a size 8 Irresistible, and I had one of those deer-hair beauties. I was on the shallow side of a very long, swirling pool, with a rock wall opposite, curves for concealment, nothing behind me, and trout leaping in front. I cast to one, and now I had him, now I didn't. I hooked him fine, brought him halfway across the stream and almost to the landing net before he flipped off. I did it again. It happened again. Fish caught, fish lost. The only faster fishing I've ever seen was for tinker mackerel, which will fight to take a bare hook dropped into the midst of the school. In half an hour, I think I had thirty fish—a fish a minute—hit, take, and slip off. It was exciting, frustrating, and deeply puzzling. But no experienced angler will have to turn to some footnote at the end of this for a solution to the puzzle: Bourjaily *père* had neglected to check the hook on his beautiful size 8 Irresistible. The point and barb were broken off.

While I was thus learning humility, I believe you were completing your famous Big Hole hat trick, but I have never heard the details of it, and I need now to know that tale of success, in order to restore at least family pride.

I brood about your winterkill. Each time it happened when I was on the farm, I'd question whether I really wanted to restock. But, well, our walleyes lasted seven years, and some of those bass must have been close to the same age. And there must be further measures—windmills, maybe hay bales floated just before freeze-up to keep air going in. As long as the ponds were there, it seemed to me we had to keep trying.

Love,
Dad

Redbird, IA
May 27, 1986

Dear Dad,

I'm sorry to contradict your total recall, but my memories of motel dining in Montana are a little different: The Lardners and I were so sick of trout after a solid week of it that we mutinied and bought a couple of chickens, which you then stuffed with sage when we weren't looking. The great suspense of the evening was provided by Dek Lardner, who was visibly on the brink of blurting the punchline to his favorite joke (you know, the one about the camp cook that ends: "This tastes like moose-manure pie . . . but GOOD!") but, by sheer force of good manners, did not.

It is true that I did complete the Big Hole Grand Slam (or Big Hole Big Five, as those of us who spend our daydreaming hours in Africa like to call it). The five are rainbow, brookie, cutthroat, brown trout, and grayling, and the Big Hole is the only river in the Lower Forty-eight where all five can be found. While you were losing all those fish near the motel that day, the Lardner brothers and I drove several miles upstream to a place where the Big Hole, which was extremely low that year, winds slowly through a pasture with some red cows in it. Except for the mountains in the background, it looked a great deal like the trout streams in northeast Iowa that we used to fish.

David and Steven moved on upstream to fish, and Jamie, who was bored with catching trout, went looking for rattlesnakes. I found a small pool that looked good to me, plopped a red Humpy into the current above it, and immediately caught a ten-inch rainbow. I cast back to the same place and found myself fast to a mountain whitefish, a species that had apparently singled me out as being the only member of our party deserving of their attention on the trip. I caught another trout, then a whitefish, another trout, and so on. Noticing the Humpy was somewhat the worse for wear, I replaced it with a fresh one and made yet another cast to the head of the pool, and saw the surface dimple slightly around the fly, which was carried off daintily toward the bottom. I set the hook with my customary finesse—it's the same motion as pull-starting a reluctant lawn mower, but with more feeling—and the battle was joined. I made short work of the fish with the Heddon heirloom the Lardners had lent me for the week, a phone-pole-stiff nine-and-a-half-footer with checkered walnut grips. In five seconds the fish was swimming meekly at my feet. Neither trout nor whitefish, it was a beautiful purple-green fish with an oversized, flowing dorsal fin. Grayling, I realized, carefully unhooking the fly. I admired the fish for a minute and was relieved to see it swim away unhurt.

About this time, David and Steven rejoined me, creels bulging with large trout. I told them I'd caught a grayling. They looked at me blankly. I explained what it was. Steven then said: "Oh, yeah. We caught a bunch of those upstream, but we let 'em go. We thought they were suckers." *Sic transit gloria piscatori.*

Later, much later in fact, after we had locked the keys in the trunk of our rental car and recovered them by pulling out the back seat, we determined that I was the only member of our party to achieve the fabled Grand Slam. The margin of victory turned out to be a tiny cutthroat caught and released by me earlier in the week. Since there was no contest as to who had caught the fewest and smallest fish on the trip, I rarely brag about my accomplishments on the Big Hole, at least not to anyone who was there.

Tom and John came back to help me restock the pond a few days ago. Fishing was slow, and we caught only nine small bass among us. After a couple of hours, I drove the fish back to our pond to release them. As I approached the water's edge, I noticed several bluegills finning in place just under the surface. They withdrew to a prudent distance and watched balefully as I dumped the bass into the pond, wondering who I was and why I was adding bigger fish to the food chain. The largemouths scattered blindly, looking for cover, and the alarmed bluegills turned together and disappeared as if sucked up by a vacuum cleaner.

So, some fish seem to have survived the winter after all, and two of the bass I released were full of eggs. Life will go on in the pond despite my heavy-handed stewardship. John told me the local B.A.S.S. club improves cover in lakes by wrapping chains around Christmas trees for ballast, then dragging them out onto the ice in the winter so they'll sink to the bottom and provide hiding places in the spring. I think a ghost did that to Ebenezer Scrooge once, but it sounds like it's worth a try.

Have a good summer in India. What do they fish for there anyway?

Love,
Philip

En Route to India
London
June 2, 1986

Dear Philip:

Thank you for filling in the hole in the Big Hole, and I'm delighted to hear you have fish in the pond again. In answer to your question, the great freshwater game fish of India is the mahseer, for which I hope to be fishing next week. So far, no one here in London can tell me more than I already know, which is that the mahseer has the disposition of a very cross musky, grows to four feet in length and up to seventy pounds. According to the *Encyclopaedia Britannica*, the mahseer is a barbel, and so related to the carp, but is most emphatically not a vegetarian. Its "flesh, like that of the salmon, is much esteemed."

I have distilled my scant knowledge of the mahseer into the following verse:

> *We're off to Kashmir, to catch the mahseer,*
> *Whose teeth are as sharp as a headhunter's spear.*
> *We will bait with live cobras to conquer our fear,*
> *And his much esteemed flesh we will eat with cold beer.*

You and I have now, I judge, totally and irresponsibly evaded producing any insights into the role of the angler in today's society, but it's been fun writing. The fishing was fun, too—and why isn't that a pretty good insight right there? The fisherman finds enjoyment in a pursuit that is very close to harmless, more so than hunting, since you

19

can return the quarry undamaged by fishing barbless. You can even do this when you don't mean to at all, as Bourjaily *père* learned on the Big Hole.

Love,
Dad

Redbird, IA
June 9, 1986

Dear Dad,

I've enjoyed these reminiscences, too. In fact, trying to write some fish stories myself has prompted me to reread some old favorites. Looking through Ray Bergman's *Trout* the other day, I came upon a story about grayling that made me think about my own experience in a new light.

In 1933, Bergman made his first trip to fish for grayling in the Elk River in Colorado. He caught several, was not very impressed, and wrote an article for a fishing magazine in which he stated rather bluntly that grayling were nothing more than suckers and he couldn't see what all the fuss over them was about. Several fishermen wrote back to say that what he caught were whitefish, which look like grayling and in some places are even called "grayling," the Elk River among them. Chastened, Bergman went on another trip, this time to Yellowstone, caught a lot of grayling and became a big fan of the species.

Maybe you can already see what I'm getting at, but let me quote from A. Laurence Wells's *Observer's Guide to Freshwater Fishes*: the grayling is a "delightful fish which so closely resembles the whitefish, especially regarding the mouth and scales and is referred to, and justifiably so, as 'the lady of the stream' and sometimes the 'queen, or flower of the water.' " Since I know I caught both grayling and white-fish that day, and since David and Steven had never seen either before, it seems obvious to me that they made the same mistake Ray Bergman did in confusing the two. Therefore, I caught the only grayling on the trip, and some of the tarnish is removed from the Grand Slam. *Living Fishes of the World* puts the average grayling at twelve to sixteen inches, and mine was nothing if not average. I think he probably was closer to twelve inches than ten, as I used to think. Put up quite a tussle, too.

My shameless revision of the grayling story (I *believe* what I just told you) and our differing memories of camp cooking in Montana and other events lead me to the following conclusion: The act of fishing only begins with the catching of a fish. Over the years, we build on the original grain of truth until we've formed a pearl, which may bear little relation to the event that inspired it. While the IRS may frown if you try that on your tax return, it's a harmless enough vice if confined to fishing. In fact, it's almost mandatory, since the evidence is so often eaten, released, or lost. If fishing needs any justification, we can do so by deeming it an acceptable outlet for creating the small fictions about ourselves we would like others to believe.

Good luck as you pursue the wily mahseer, and I look forward to a highly readable, if only reasonably true, account of the quest.

Love,
Philip

Let Them Eat Cake

William Hjortsberg

ONE DAY, the ornithologists came by with a Mason jar full of frogs. The frogs were beautiful and tiny, bright as jewelry, their black bodies patterned with emerald lozenges. For the past week, the ornithologists' camper was parked under the coconut palms at the end of the dirt road not far from our house. When you peered through the fine plastic screen into the sunlit interior of their truck, numbers of captive hummingbirds hovered within. It was like some fantastic waterless aquarium filled with airborne tropical fish.

"We wanted to warn you," the ornithologists said, showing me the jar. "We saw your little girl playing on the beach. These are so pretty, they'd be very tempting if she found one." They were also deadly. Before the Spanish came, when Costa Rica still had an indigenous Indian population, hunters dipped the tips of their arrows in the slime that covers the backs of these frogs. Thus envenomed, the merest flesh wound would drop a scampering monkey out of the treetops, the poison bringing paralysis and death before the animal's body hit the ground.

The ornithologists returned to photographing hummingbirds, leaving me with the innocuous-looking frogs. Their intense beauty and deceptive innocence seemed to embody the Caribbean coast of Central America. Our house sat on the edge of a perfect crescent of white sand ringing a small cove six kilometers north of Puerto Limón. The setting was idyllic, perfect as a postcard. A pellucid sea curled in a rush of foaming surf onto the bone-white beach. Mast-high coconut palms

23

towered above the tin-roofed house. Just behind them was the jungle; lush, fecund, a living wall of impenetrable green.

The jungle was where the poison frogs lived. They were not alone. Their virulent companions included bushmasters, coral snakes, tarantulas, and scorpions. Here trees barbed with thorns ripped unsuspecting flesh, and enormous yellow hornets, known as Jack Spaniards, built fragile paper nests suspended from vines like booby-traps for the unwary. This was a world where it was impossible to tell friend from foe. Was the slender green serpent weaving across the window screen merely an innocent vine snake, or was it, instead, its lethal look-alike cousin?

We ventured into the jungle only to pick fruit in the company of Hugo, a Tico of Jamaican ancestry, who could scale limbless palm trees, hear the sibilant passage of snakes across a meandering trail, and select the proper roots and leaves to brew into a tonic for sore throats. We turned our backs on the land and became devoted acolytes of the sea.

The house at Playa Bonita was first glimpsed when the ocean was dead calm. Part of the decision to rent was based on the anticipation of unspoiled fishing. Here, it seemed, was unfished water. We would be the first hogs in the trough. But daydreams of delirious bonanzas faded abruptly upon our return from San José with our few belongings.

It must have had something to do with the phase of the moon, for the sea was only once again to be as calm during our six-month tenure as it was that first enchanted afternoon. Instead, a monstrous surf raged, the perfect cresting waves often reaching nine feet. A ferocious current tugged the unwary seaward. We, the initiated, rode it like seals out to a sand bar behind the waves. Here we waited on tiptoes, heads just above the surface, and watched for incoming sets. Our lives were given over to the ritual of body-surfing.

All the while, my custom Winston fly rod and Fin-Nor reel stood neglected in a corner while gaudy tropical spiders shrouded them in gossamer. Mildew camouflaged my tackle vest. Only fantasies of fishing remained untarnished. It is one thing to dream of fishing while snowbound in Montana; quite another story when the turquoise-and-azure Caribbean glistens at my doorstep.

Among our little gang of surfers, mostly local guys like Hugo, was a wiry French-Canadian named Marcel, who lived in a single-room shanty at the far end of the beach with his lovely doe-eyed Tica girlfriend, Angelica. Marcel claimed to be a seasonal lobster fisherman, as were Hugo and several of the others. In the spring, when the spiny lobsters migrate and move up out of the depths by the thousands, fishermen set their traps on the flats, each marked by Clorox-bottle buoys that bob on the surface like albino Portuguese men-of-war. Enough money can be earned in six industrious weeks to pay for the rest of the year. Marcel's problem was that somehow he had lost the boat and motor that Angelica's father had given them.

To supplement his nonexistent income, Marcel served the area as a small-time dope peddler. For a few colons, he seemed always able to scrounge up a joint or two: skinny marijuana cigarettes twisted from the brown wrapping paper used to ship bananas. It was 1971, a watershed year for me; I was about to turn thirty at a time when no one over that age was to be trusted. My personal residue from the sixties contained a conviction that I wrote best when stoned, and in the struggle to start a new work of fiction, Marcel's regular visits seemed almost a necessity.

The problem was, he loved to talk. Something of a braggart, Marcel would perch on the edge of the bed in the loft where I slept and worked and regale me by the hour with exaggerated tales of his amorous exploits or his epic derring-do as a student revolutionary in Quebec. As much as I craved the herbal stimulants he provided, I soon came to dread his long-winded sojourns. To protect my privacy, I hung a cardboard sign, PLEASE DO NOT DISTURB, across the bottom of the stairs leading to the loft. It was intended solely for Marcel, as none of my other beach-bum buddies would have presumed to come by during working hours. The first morning the cardboard was in place, Marcel arrived, stepped promptly over the barrier, and mounted the stairs.

"Didn't you see my sign?" I said in despair.

"Sure," said the ever-ebullient Marcel, smiling. "I didn't think it was meant for me."

Once ensconced, it was impossible to dislodge him and my only defense was to turn the one-sided conversation in directions I found remotely of interest. That day, I steered our talk toward fishing. After a long discourse from Marcel on the perils facing a commercial fisherman, casting himself as a combination of Captain Ahab and Hemingway's old man Santiago doing endless battle with various denizens of the deep, I mentioned that I was a fly fisherman. The mystery of this revelation intrigued Marcel sufficiently to distract him from his

25

diatribe. I soon found myself explaining about trout streams and mayfly hatches, the usual Zen-art balderdash surrounding the mystique of the dry fly. Mentioning friends who had recently moved to Key West and had become avid flats fishermen, I pointed to my neglected, cobweb-draped rod in the corner, confessing that I brought the newly acquired outfit along with me to Costa Rica in hopes of emulating their example.

In truth, although I was perhaps at best only a mediocre trout fisherman, the notion of taking tarpon on a fly seemed the very epitome of the sport. Here the possibilities of angling verged on true adventure. When I mumbled something about the Río Parismina, a famed local tarpon fishery I had only read about, Marcel's black eyes gleamed with uncontained con-man calculation. Suddenly, he was a fountain of enthusiasm, a spontaneous eruption of connivance. Parismina was a fisherman's Eldorado; it was paradise; Nirvana. A man could catch a hundred pounds a day there. Fortunes could be made. Before I knew what was happening, Marcel had fabricated an expedition. If I fronted expenses, he would organize a boat and motor. We'd go for a week. Angelica would move in with my wife. I'd have my shot at tarpon on a fly and Marcel would get rich.

When he left the house, Marcel's normal banty-rooster swagger had exaggerated into a veritable jitterbug of macho over-confidence. I was left in a haze of "happy" smoke, laughing at myself for even momentarily succumbing to such an outlandish pipe dream. Two days later, Marcel burst into the house, a fandango of nervous energy. The trip was on! Not only had he run down an aluminum boat and twenty-five-horsepower motor from a friend who managed the government oil refinery, but with a bit of artful persuasion he'd managed to get a fifty-gallon drum of fuel thrown into the bargain at no cost. All he needed from me was a hundred colons or so for incidental expenses. Among other things, we couldn't take off without something to smoke, could we?

I spent the next few days vacillating between uncertainty and dread. What would it be like, spending a week alone in the jungle with Marcel? Parismina was fifty roadless miles away. Neither of us had ever been there. Between the comforts of the beach house at Playa Bonita and the tarpon hot spot of Parismina lay the unknown, teeming with venomous reptiles and sodden with rot. What if we got lost?

Preparations were quickly made. A doctor friend from the hospital in Limón loaned me a waterproof rubber sack, into which I stuffed several changes of rudimentary attire, my tackle vest, and a blanket. Marcel came by and added his own contributions to the sack: old clothes, the stash, carefully wrapped in plastic, and his fishing gear. Compared with my weight-forward Scientific Angler lines and number-three Fin-Nor, Marcel's Band-Aid box full of hooks and the empty Clorox bottle wound with several hundred yards of monofilament seemed like a political statement of minimalist efficiency.

Angelica arrived the next morning, carrying her things over her shoulder in a brightly woven *bolsa*, smiling her sweet smile. She said Marcel would meet me in Moín at noon, that he had to go into town for supplies. I couldn't imagine what was up. How much marijuana do you need on a fishing trip anyway?

The bus from Limón was a run-down secondhand school bus from the States. It rattled up the dirt road behind our house as far as Liverpool, a shantytown set on stilts above the stagnant mud. I climbed aboard with my bulging rubber sack and tubed fishing rod and rode up to Moín, where local fishermen pulled their boats under open sheds thatched with palm fronds. The place was saved from the picturesque by the discharges of the oil refinery about a half a mile upstream. Black petroleum sludge stained the banks like the ring around a boardinghouse bathtub, tarring the mangrove roots as high as the tide could reach.

Marcel's bus was twenty minutes late, or right on time, given Costa Rica's utter ambivalence toward schedules. He climbed down with a grin and said he needed a hand getting his stuff off. I followed him to the back of the bus, where a large rectangular bundle wrapped in burlap like a mummy waited. My heart sank as I envisioned smuggling a hefty bale of cannabis into the middle of nowhere.

"What is it?" I asked, already assuming the worst.

"Ice," Marcel answered, his lupine smile worthy of a used-car salesman.

"Ice!?"

But of course, Marcel explained triumphantly. He must have ice to keep fresh the vast quantities of fish he planned to catch and haul back to the market in Limón. A small fortune was to be made. Ice was merely a necessary investment.

Feeling like a fool, I struggled with my end of the bulky package, as we sweated and strained to haul the one-hundred-pound cake of sawdust-packed, burlap-wrapped ice through the heat of a tropic noon to the riverbank. Not even mad dogs and Englishmen would attempt something like this. By way of compensation, the first of my dread expectations proved false. There was indeed a boat waiting. Perhaps this extravagant fantasy would materialize after all.

We loaded the ice aboard a twelve-foot aluminum skiff, and Marcel used the single oar like a gondolier to scull us upstream to the oil-refinery boat landing. It was pleasing to observe his skill as a boatman. Dread and despair gave way to hope. The motor and tank, along with a fifty-gallon drum of fuel, were on the dock as promised. Marcel bolted the outboard into place. Our adventure was real.

Reality of another sort confronted us as Marcel pulled repeatedly on the starter cord, producing only feeble coughing sounds from the motor. I took my turn yanking and tugging, but to no avail. The engine was dead, and the trip began with Marcel sculling us back down to Moín. It was not an auspicious beginning, but fate and miracles were on our side that day. Marcel cajoled a fisherman he knew into having a look, and with the baffling alchemical wizardry common to Third World mechanics he soon had the motor started, without the use of tools or spare parts.

We were on our way, up a lazy river into the dark heart of the unknown. The surface was still, without any current, and the color of pale chocolate pudding. A verdant curtain of foliage screened both banks, heightening the mystery of what might lie waiting ashore. We had no maps, for none were available. Our only directions were to take the right-hand turn whenever the river forked.

There was a monotonous sameness to the landscape as it slipped away behind us, mile after mile without variation. Marcel rummaged in the rubber sack, producing the lunches our wives had prepared. After eating, we settled back for a smoke, and my fears of what might happen if the motor conked out again drifted off on the breeze with each aromatic exhale.

Hours passed with only an occasional sloth hanging somnolently from the limbs of a riverbank tree to provide distraction. From time to time, we dutifully siphoned fuel from the drum into the tank. Whenever the river branched, which was often, we turned right. What did it matter if we were lost? As long as we kept our matches dry, the pleasure domes of Xanadu glittered in our narcotized imaginations. Even Marcel's endless ramblings seemed the soul of wit.

Once, we passed a small homestead: a pair of goats tethered to a mango tree and, beyond, a simple unpainted board shack aswarm with children. Concerned by our continuous and unending dextrality,

Marcel called out to the farmer hoeing his taro patch: "¿A dónde es Parismina?" The farmer looked up at us without expression and extended his arm, pointing straight ahead.

Gradually, the river narrowed. Back at Moín it was broad as a football field, but with each successive right-hand turn, the dread and forbidding green reached closer on either side until it seemed as if the jungle were about to reach out and seize us. Mysterious splashings could be heard in the shadows under the tree roots. Marcel identified them as alligators. For once, I was inclined to believe him.

My worst fears were realized when a swing to the right brought us into a narrow channel straight as a mile-long bowling alley. It was obviously man-made. We passed an abandoned dredge, its rusting decks tilting into the water, and suddenly the outboard's prop churned into the bottom muck and the motor died. There was no longer enough draft to use the engine. We were stuck. Marcel regarded me with Gallic resignation and, without a word, we slid over the side and started pulling the boat along by the painter.

I sank to my knees in the clammy unseen murk underfoot. Visions of Humphrey Bogart tugging the *African Queen* seared across my mind. I recalled with horror the dozens of leeches clinging to Bogie's body. But that was only a movie; the slime I was slogging through was real. And the leeches attaching themselves by the hundreds to my pale innocent legs were no rubber mock-ups from Special Effects, but the genuine, bloodsucking articles. What kind of fishing trip was it when you end up the bait?

After a hundred yards or so, the channel deepened, and we were suddenly up to our necks in the malarial water. We hauled ourselves over the gunwales and wiped the clinging ooze from our legs. The hordes of feasting leeches we anticipated existed only in our drug-besotted imaginations.

It was just dusk when we rounded the final right-hand bend and the tiny settlement of Parismina Bar came into view. No sighting of the promised land could have been more joyous. I restrained an impulse to hug Marcel, but the grins we exchanged were genuine. We had made it. In spite of all doubt and fear, the accomplishment belonged to us.

Parismina Bar wasn't much of a town: a cluster of whitewashed shacks perched on a long sand spit. The arrangement of the buildings was haphazard. There were no streets. They weren't needed, since there also weren't any cars. Set slightly apart from the rest of the town was the fishing camp, a modern bungalow surrounded by screened porches and fronted by a long dock. This was where wealthy sportsmen from the States lodged, flown in on small private planes, which landed on the beach. The Parismina club sported the town's single generator, and thus was the only place within fifty miles in any direction to have electric lights and refrigeration. We gave it a wide berth—as if the very notion of comfort was alien to hardened jungle voyagers like us.

Dr. Arguello, who had loaned me the waterproof sack, also provided a letter of introduction to a local resident, who, he said, would be happy to put us up. Luis Dixon was sitting on his steps when we came trudging from the riverbank, letter in hand. He was a massive man of fifty, with skin the color of the mahogany trees he cut in the surrounding forest. His arms were bigger around than most men's legs. As he read the doctor's note, I remembered what I'd been told about his being the bare-knuckles champion of the area.

Luis Dixon said we were welcome to sleep in his shed out back as long as we didn't burn it down. I said we wouldn't dream of it, mentioning his celebrated prowess as a boxer. He chuckled softly. "They still come, the youngsters, to look me up." His voice was softened by the lilting accent of the Caribbean. "I know what they want. Don't need to ask. And I give it to them." Luis Dixon smiled. "So far, I still be champ. But, nowadays, I always get in the first lick. Ain't young like I used to be."

The shed was used for storage, and we cleared the tools and oilcans out of the way and spread our blankets on the bare wood floor. There was still food left from home, so we had a candlelit snack and a final smoke before blowing out the lights. Sleep came easily, in spite of the hobo accommodations. I nestled into a pillow formed from my bundled clothes and soon was dreaming of the tarpon marathon awaiting us in the morning. These reveries were rudely shattered in the middle of the night. I was awakened by something huge and multilegged running across my face. Fear stabbed through me as if I'd swallowed an icicle. Instinctively, I slapped my face, and felt a monstrous squish-crunch against my cheek. What the hell was it: a crab . . . scorpion . . . poison frog? I groped for the matches. With the candle flickering, I scraped the mangled remains of a four-inch-long cockroach off my face. A drowsy Marcel looked on with amusement. I didn't sleep the rest of the night.

Getting up at dawn was no problem; in fact I'd been looking

forward to it. Marcel and I scouted around town, searching out a place that would serve us meals. There were, of course, no restaurants. No streetlights, sewer system, policemen or dentists, either. The most substantial building in Parismina Bar was the school, a modern edifice built of concrete and terrazzo. Costa Rica has no army. The country lacks a military budget and consequently has no sophisticated highway program. (It seems to be a tried-and-true axiom: The quality of a nation's roads rises in direct proportion to the size of its military establishment. Run by generals, neighbor Panama boasts a superb highway system. Costa Rica spends its money on education instead.)

We discussed these political niceties with the woman who gave us breakfast. One or two of the houses in town were also small shops. With the shutters removed, a counter was revealed and behind it were a few shelves housing canned goods, kerosene, and candles. The proprietress, her smile bright with gold, agreed to provide us with eggs, coffee, and bread in the mornings and *gallo pinto* (red beans and rice with a bit of fish or chicken) at night.

Simple fare compared with the double Scotches and rare beefsteak we imagined the boys over at the fishing club to be swilling and gorging. Let them eat cake, Marcel and I conceded, a simple crust of bread was sufficient for jungle rats like us.

The contrast with the rich blokes at the club was more than merely culinary. As we set off from the muddy bank in our dented aluminum skiff with the rusting oil drum standing amidships like a junkyard conning tower and the mysterious burlap-wrapped package in the stern, several sportsmen stood smirking on the dock. They looked like models from a spread in the Orvis catalog, tiny alligators leaping from every pastel breast. Their Tico guides loaded rods, tackle boxes, and Coleman coolers into the club's three trim Boston Whalers. Marcel waved at them, his Clorox bottle clamped under his arm. One of the sports waved back, sunrise glinting on his silver aviators. "Tight lines," he called, without a trace of irony in his voice.

Close to the ocean, the Río Parismina seemed less a river than a bayou marsh. The sky was close and leaden, dense with rolling clouds and threatening rain. The oppressive light made the surrounding jungle positively throb, the intense green so vibrant and lush that it seemed a single menacing organism.

We had no trouble finding the tarpon. They were everywhere, rolling on the surface like porpoises; singly, in pairs, in groups large enough to suggest a mermaid ballet. I stood in the bow, false-casting

31

to work out my line. It was good to feel the flex of a fly rod in my hands again. It didn't take a power cast to make the grade here; often the tarpon would roll less than ten feet from the skiff, close enough to touch them with the tip of my rod. The proximity of so many large fish sent the adrenaline pulsing through me like an electric current. My hands shook, and it is doubtful I could have managed anything more than the short casts required. I expected a take at any moment.

Marcel shared my excitement. He fished from the stern, baiting his hook with a vile accretion of crab guts scooped from a peanut-butter jar. He swung the weighted line round and round his head like a gaucho twirling his bola, releasing it to spin off the Clorox bottle held in his other hand. He achieved admirable distance and accuracy with this method, glancing up at me after each throw, his grin frozen in a rictus of nervous expectation.

In time, our excitement gave way to frustration as we cruised slowly through the various backwater channels. Tarpon abounded. We saw them by the hundreds. But, after hours of concentrated fishing, we failed to get a single strike. By midafternoon we gave up and headed back to town. Tying up, we discussed the situation with a couple of the anglers from the Parismina club, who wandered over for a closer look at the weirdos. Neither of them had done well either. The tarpon were in the river to mate, which explained their large numbers. It was a veritable tarpon orgy. "They're only interested in screwing, not eating," commented one sportsman.

Contemptuous of what struck him as a quixotic effort, to try for tarpon with a fly, a white-haired fisherman sporting madras Bermudas called to one of the local guides: "There's no chance at all. Tell him, Carlos." Carlos was equally emphatic. No way I would ever hook a tarpon on a fly if they weren't interested in plugs or bait. The legendary "Ted Baseball" came here to fish often and he always used lures and light spinning tackle even though he was a dedicated fly fisherman elsewhere. If this giant from the major leagues and the pages of the Sears, Roebuck catalog disdained flies at Parismina, what chance did a mere mortal like me have?

Romantics love impossible odds, and knowing the deck was stacked against me did nothing to dampen my enthusiasm. Our days at Parismina fell into a pattern. Up at dawn after a night on the hard floor of Luis Dixon's shed with a length of mosquito netting wrapped around my head as protection against cockroaches. A quick breakfast at the little *tienda* with the fold-down front. And then, long days out on the river, casting in utter futility at more tarpon than you could literally shake a stick at.

All the while, Marcel's huge block of ice was gradually melting. The burlap wrappings sagged around it like the ill-fitting clothes of a fat man on a diet. The inexorably diminishing ice cake seemed in some silent way to be a bitter rebuke. Every day it grew smaller and smaller, a continual reminder that its services were no longer needed. Neither of us had yet to hook, much less catch, a single fish.

One afternoon, toward the end of the week, I'd had enough. It was no longer adrenaline coursing through my veins at the sight of all those tarpon, but despair. The prospect of flailing away, hour after hour, at giant sex-crazed fish was less than enticing. Let someone else shake his stick at them. I told Marcel he could have the skiff and wandered up the beach in search of other possibilities.

I followed the river to where it emptied into a turbulent lagoon formed by a sand bar several hundred yards out. Here, a monstrous surf roared. The area was alive with currents, and the churning surface presented a dramatic alternative to the slack water we had fished all week. Best of all, no horny tarpon dancing about to torment me. I waded out up to my knees, turning so the stiff wind was at my back as I false-cast. The line reached out across the turbulent water, and on the retrieve I had an immediate strike. I set the hook and, after a vigorous fight, slid a ten-pound crevalle up onto the sand. It was no tarpon, but a distinct improvement on getting endlessly skunked.

I unhooked the grizzly streamer from the side of the crevalle's jaw and eased him back into the water, all the tensions and frustration of the past week slipping away as smoothly as the departure of the powerful fork-tailed fish. For the rest of the afternoon, I cast along the shore, catching a couple more jacks and several mysterious fish which resembled long silver mackerel. I gave one to an old man throwing his hand net into schools of bait nearby, and he told me it was called a *perro-perro*. Knowing it to be a dog-dog didn't spoil the fun of catching them.

When I returned to Luis Dixon's shed, I woke Marcel from his nap with aimless humming. "What have you got to be so cheerful about?" he grumped.

I told him of my catch, and he mumbled something about "les mouches" not being completely worthless after all. He had a right to be cynical. A week of dragging crab guts aimlessly through the water will do that to you. I appealed to him with undeniable existential logic:

33

Catching fish was better than not catching fish. Marcel agreed. Our last day, we would fish the lagoon at the mouth of the river.

Dawn found us out in the skiff, shivering in a light rain. It was surprising how cold you could get in the tropics when the weather conspired against you. We killed the motor and let the skiff drift. At least here we wouldn't have to endure the smart set from the Parismina club cruising about in their Boston Whalers. Abruptly, the rain stopped and a shaft of sunlight stabbed through a rent in the clouds. It seemed a good omen. Marcel grinned as I started to cast. Ten minutes later, I felt a strike so powerful that the shock of it nearly toppled me overboard. What sort of fish hit as hard as that? Instantly, my line went slack. I reeled in and found my leader broken above the shock-tippet. "I think we're in big trouble," I said.

"I certainly hope so," Marcel replied.

While I carefully tied on another tippet, using a knot called a "Bimini Twist," which I had learned from a friend's handwritten instructions on a postcard, Marcel hurled his load of crab guts far out into the churning water. I watched him for a moment, hauling his hand line in and wrapping it around the plastic bottle, then returned to the intricacies of my Bimini Twist.

"Merde!" Marcel shouted. I looked up in time to see him drop his line and thrust a bleeding hand into his mouth. The fifty-pound-test monofilament was unwinding with such speed that the Clorox bottle bounced up and down against the hull like a basketball dribbled by an invisible player. We both stared, stunned into inaction, as the last of the line disappeared into the water. "That was some fish," Marcel muttered, regarding his Clorox bottle, reduced now from fishing tackle to common trash, with the same rueful indifference that a sea captain might bestow on some trinket rescued from his sunken ship.

I had a new streamer on in no time and was working the line out in a wide loop. The cast straightened, and I gave it a little time for the fly to sink beneath the surface. Marcel watched me, nursing the nasty cut on his hand, as I stripped in line with short, hard tugs. It happened as suddenly as snagging a submerged log. The rod bent nearly double. There was no strike, no setting of the hook, just an instant surge and the line was whistling through the guides. I did a little barefoot dance to avoid stepping on the coils around my feet as I cleared the remaining line in the boat. "Your turn to pray," Marcel said.

The tarpon broke the surface about twenty yards from the skiff, shimmying up on his tail in a bright silver explosion. It was as if some hot-water heater had suddenly emerged from the depths. He fell back in a geyser of spray, and I guessed him to be at least five feet long. I'd never seen a live fish that big before.

The tarpon made his run, the line slicing through the water. I noticed how far into the backing he'd gone in such a short time and tightened the drag down as far as I dared. I was afraid the rod would break. Sixty yards out, he jumped again; a magnificent aerial somersault. Remarkably, he was still on and continued the run with undiminished power. Marcel listened to my reel shriek in disbelief. I had no idea what to do. At a hundred and fifty yards, he jumped for the third and last time. He was in the surf line now, his splendor diminished somewhat by the eight-foot waves. The backing reached the core of the reel and broke free with a musical *ping*.

I felt like I'd just been mugged. My heart continued to race even as I heard Marcel's laughter. The whole situation seemed so impossible that I experienced none of the letdown that usually accompanies losing a fish. I might as well have tied my fly line to the back of a Greyhound bus and waved it good-bye. Although I now know that flats fishermen chase a running tarpon in their boats, at the time I had no idea how on earth my Key West friends could possibly catch such monsters. It seemed an absurd impossibility. If we'd gone after this fish, we'd have swamped in the surf.

I smiled at Marcel. "Well, at least we hooked one. . . ."

"Yeah, man." He shook his head. "We surely did."

I felt good. My line was gone but it was worth it. After a futile week, it seemed like success. A tarpon took my homemade fly in spite of dire *pronunciamientos* of *el grande* Ted Baseball. It was something to remember, if not write home about.

The next morning, we packed up our gear, said our thanks to Luis Dixon, and started back down the river. Marcel unwrapped a fish-sized chunk of ice from the sodden burlap and set it up on the bow like an honorary figurehead. Inside of an hour, it was gone. By the time we reached Moín, our stash was gone as well.

The Dead Man on Wendigo Brook

Robert F. Jones

PERHAPS IT was only a trick of the water, a trompe l'oeil of the late summer light, or maybe just one of those hallucinatory visions provoked by hours on end of upstream nymphing. You know the feeling: cast, lift, reach, lift, cast again—over and over, always staring, until the world fades away, sun and bird song and roar of water, until all that's left is the endless downstream dance of the strike indicator. But in that moment, I saw the dead angler clear, down there in the depths beneath the floating red leaves.

I mean crystal clear, in detail. His waxen face with the hair floating vaguely in the current, pale eyes fixed upward on mine, the grizzled mustache trailing like eelgrass over a rueful smile, the blue collar points waving limply above the fishing vest. I could see it all in that mirror-light of underwater. A shattered black rod gripped in the stiff hand, forceps twisting silver from a retractor pin, the bulge of fly boxes in the buttoned pockets. A black-finished leader snips dangling from a D ring. Even the flies hooked into a fleece drying patch—dry flies—a Ginger Quill, an Adams, a Blue Dun, and a fourth I didn't recognize, the brightest of the lot. All clear, all seen clearly in an instant.

As I looked, horrified, he rose a bit from the bottom—lifted, it seemed, by the hackles of those flies on his chest, by some heavenly Mucilin or mystical Gink that urged him free of the rolling current's downward grip. I grabbed for him, got hold of the slippery vest, arm-wrestled the current for a moment, felt the fabric slipping from my fingers, then a sharp stab of pain in my palm. I clenched. He broke away and down again. One hand rose, limply, as if in farewell, and he rolled back into the depths.

I staggered off into the shallows, stunned and disbelieving. Odd things happen to the mind on trout streams. Illusions and delusions are the bedrock of our sport. Maybe I'd imagined the whole thing. Maybe it wasn't a man but merely a waterlogged tree stump, or the carcass of a drowned deer. But I'd seen it so clearly. Then I remember the pain in my hand as I grappled with the body. Sure enough, there was a fly stuck in my palm, dead center. It was the fourth of the flies I'd seen on his vest, the odd one. Buried to the shank. I pulled at it tentatively, and it came right out—barbless, thank God. Absently, I stuck it in my own drying patch, then sat back on the bank, in the sun, to watch the pool for the body's reemergence, but mainly to think.

What I decided, when the body failed to show again, may seem heartless and inhuman, but remember that I am a fly fisherman and the season was winding down. I decided to fish on. What else could I do? The truck was a good five miles downstream, and it was another ten from there by jeep trail to the nearest highway. By the time I got out, it would be midnight—no time to organize a search party with grappling hooks for a man already dead and beyond help. I was fishing my way up Wendigo Brook, a little-known feeder of the Nulhegan River in the so-called Northeast Kingdom of Vermont. The region itself received little pressure from anglers—the locals are mainly "worm-flangers" who fish near the bridges, and then only when the rivers are discolored from heavy rain—and this section was virtually trackless except for logging roads used seasonally and sporadically by the paper company that owns most of the land. I was packing in, light, with only a tarp for cover, and figured to be on the water for at least three days. There was a highway to the north where I could hitch a ride back to the trail, where my truck was parked. So far, the weather had been splendid—high, crisp, sunny September days; frosty nights full of owl hoot and coyote song and, toward midnight, a dazzling display of the aurora. The trout were fat brookies and cagey browns, bright and savage in their spawning colors. Why give that up for a dead man?

A fellow I know told me how he'd been fishing for spring steelhead up in British Columbia once when he came upon his partner, dead of a heart attack on the gravel. "I reeled in the fish that had killed him, released it, then laid him out with a stone for a pillow and his rod alongside him like a knight's lance," he told me. "Then I went back to the river. What the hell, the run was still on."

So I, too, fished on.

It was getting toward evening, time to look for a campsite and kill a couple of trout for supper. Ahead, the stream wound down through a grassy meadow, one of those dried-out beaver ponds that stud the country up there, with plenty of standing, sun-cured drowned trees to provide firewood. I unslung my day pack and spread the tarp under a big white pine, built a ring from a fractured granite ledge, gathered enough wood for the night, and laid a fire, then went down to the brook to catch supper.

Nothing rising yet, just the brown water coiling smooth and deep under the high banks. I pulled the dead man's dry fly from my patch and examined it. A strange fly, this one. It was hair-bodied, kind of like a deerhair Adams a friend of mine ties with a big, fat body resembling an Irresistible or a Rat-Faced McDougall. But this clipped hair was of a color I'd never seen before—all colors, it seemed, the more I looked at it. In that late-afternoon light, it almost glowed, refulgent and refractive at once. Blue and burgundy and mahogany, with glints of fiery green, as if copper wire were burning; a deep midnight luster in toward the hook shank, like the underfur of a fisher cat. It couldn't have been dyed, not with all those ever-changing colors, and I tried to puzzle out what sort of animal that hair could have come from. Not badger or moose or wolverine or skunk, certainly not squirrel or bear—not even cinnamon bear. Marten or sable, perhaps, but I doubted it. Hackle, wings, and tail were clearly from the same animal, and equally deceptive as to their true colors. The hook, too, was of a type I'd never seen. It was a size 12, I'd judge, sort of Limerick-bent with a turn-up eye, japanned in black lacquer like a salmon hook, but of course far too small for that purpose. There was something archaic about it that called up images of Hewitt or Gordon tying late at night by lamplight, with a Catskill blizzard howling beyond the windowpanes, or perhaps Dame Juliana herself in some echoing abbey chamber with rush torches guttering on dank gray walls. Could it have been tied before stainless steel came on the market? Unlikely—the fly was not a bit tattered. Or maybe it just didn't catch fish—that would account for its pristine state. But then why did the dead angler have it on his drying patch? What the hell, I'd give it a try.

I knelt in the bankside grass and worked the fly out toward the far bank with a few false casts. I still had a short leader on, the same I'd been using while nymphing, since this was just a trial run anyway and the tippet was heavy enough to turn over the big fly. The fly was traveling overhead in the higher light, and I could see it from the corner of my eye—glowing. A red-gold firefly, it seemed, above the oncoming dusk. I aimed to drop it on the deep run against the far bank, where a nice fat brookie ought to be lying, hungry and unselective as to his dinner menu. He would fill mine. But before the fly even reached the water, I saw a wake streak toward it. From my side of the water. Then another, from downstream. And another from far upstream . . . A huge dark golden-bellied shape leaped clear of the water and nailed the fly solid, a full foot above the surface. A big brown, by the look of him. He'd won the race. The other wakes turned sharply on themselves and chased after the brown, who hit the water like an anvil dropped into a lake.

Thank God for the heavy tippet. I was so stunned by the ferocity of the onslaught that I failed to drop the rod tip as the hooked fish jumped, then jumped again. The lesser trout jumped with him—half a dozen, it seemed, all in the same instant. All aimed at his mouth, where I could see the dead angler's fly glowing in the brown's hooked jaw. It was as if . . . It was as if they were trying to take the fly away from him.

I snubbed the brown around, took him on the reel, and horsed him in, panic gripping my heart. I hadn't felt like this since I was a kid, fast to my first big fish and frantic that it might get away before I could land it and go running home to show my friends. But when I netted him and lifted him to the bank, he was too big to kill—a good twenty inches long, deep and thick and heavily kyped for the spawning run, far too big a fish for my supper, far too handsome to die. I slipped the hook and sent him back. The other trout were still there, in the bankside water, waiting as if for his return. As he swam off, they followed, darting at his mouth in puzzlement—where was that good bug?

What the hell was this? My heart slowed down and I moved upstream toward the head of the run. Once again I laid the fly out, once again the wakes appeared from all directions. Once again a big trout leaped clear of the water to glom the fly before it hit. Once again the other trout chased it.

Once again he was too big to kill. This was getting upsetting.

I took five more fish on five more casts as the light failed, each the same as the last. Now we've all had similar, or roughly similar, experiences at times, particularly at dusk, when almost any big bushy fly splatted on the water will take trout one after the other. I recall an evening on the South Platte, in the Cheesman Canyon, when I took eight nice Colorado browns on successive casts during a caddis hatch, without shifting a step from my position in midstream. But this night there was no hatch, not that I could see. And each fish took the fly before it hit the water.

I'd often seen brook trout chase one of their number after it was hooked, but brookies are notoriously naïve—some might say suicidal—in the face of danger. These trout, as best I could see, were browns—the Einsteins of entomological discrimination. And not little ones, still learning their Adams from their Baetis from their Coachman, but fifteen- and sixteen-inchers from the graduate school of Selective Sipping.

It was nearly dark by the time I wised up, cut off the dead angler's fly and tied on a mothlike Grizzly Wulff. It took me well into full dark, float following fruitless float on the now-still, apparently troutless water before a lone, ten-inch brookie foolishly gobbled the fly and sacrificed himself for my supper. I knocked him on the head and whipped his guts out, shamefacedly, then stumbled back through wet grass to light my fire. The dinner—fried trout, baked beans, cold cling peaches from the can—leaves no memory of taste behind it, but I must have eaten it, because I remember walking back down to the river to wash the pan. The water was strong and black as ice-cold coffee, but I needed whisky. I lay against the pine trunk in my sleeping bag, sipping Scotch from the peach tin, my mind dancing like a skyful of mayfly spinners.

You've probably wondered, as I do, why certain flies that bear absolutely no resemblance to anything in nature not only catch fish but, at certain times and places, are the only flies a trout will look at. The Royal Coachman, with its white wings, rusty hackle, bristly barred tail, and three-segment body, is perhaps the best example. I've heard it argued that the segmented body makes the trout think "flying ant," while the white wings are there only to help the angler keep track of the fly in fast water. I've got another theory, and it came back to me that night as I lowered my Scotch supply and pondered the strange fly I'd found—a fly I'd started thinking of as *Ephemerella incognita*.

Trout have been around for millions of years on this planet, making a living largely off aquatic bugs, and during that time many insect species have come and gone, whereas the trout in its various forms has remained pretty much the same. Could it be that deep in the trout's racial memory, taped on its genes as vividly as its spots and fin rays and mating instincts, are images of insects long since extinct? Images that, when presented in a certain light or temperature of water, by a certain curl of current over a specific type of stream bed—sand or boulder or pea gravel—trigger a strike as inevitable as a salmon's fruitless leap at a newly erected dam on its preordained spawning river? Maybe trout still feed on a long-dead past, just as men do on books long out of print but nonetheless still compelling. And perhaps this odd killer fly I'd come by, this *E. incognita*, by sheerest chance happened to imitate some splendid bug of prehistory, some trouty equivalent of braised sweetbreads or oysters on the half shell in an age of sawdust hamburgers. . . .

By the time I sloped off to sleep, the Scotch bottle was down by a good three inches.

Fog on the water at daybreak—a pearly pea souper through which the spires of black spruce and the cracked, bone-white fingernails of snags poked, silent and dripping. Heading down to the stream for coffee water, I heard something splash away through the shallows. Moose, I thought. Their big, cloven tracks scarred the shore the full length of Wendigo Brook from where I'd entered it. After filling the pot, I went down to look for sign. I wish I'd never looked. There at the bottom of the run where I'd caught the big trout the previous evening were the carcasses of seven big browns. Clearly, they were the fish I'd hooked and released. But how could that be? I hadn't played any of them to the point of exhaustion. I'd hardly touched them in removing the barbless hook, and none of them had swayed even slightly onto its side before swimming off strong and swift to cover. Now, though, they were just heads and tails connected with bare bones. Whatever ate them had some appetite. The skeletons looked like cobs of sweet corn gnawed from end to end, machine-gun style. Big paw prints surrounded the spot, not the long, plantigrade prints of a bear or a bootless man, but round ones a good hand span in diameter, with sharp, deep indentations, as if from claw tips at the end of the toes. A catamount? If so, it was the size of a Siberian tiger—my hand span is nine and a half inches. Thank God the thing had finished eating before I came up on it. . . .

I hurried back to the fire and stoked it with my remaining wood. When the water came to a boil, I spiked my coffee with another inch of whisky, then waited for the fog to burn off. I dug the .22 Colt Woodsman out of my pack, checked the magazine, and jacked a Long Rifle round up the spout. Not that it would do much good against a creature the size of that one, but it made me feel better with the holster slapping against my thigh as I packed and headed upstream as soon as I could see a hundred yards ahead. I resolved not to joint the rod until I was at least a mile away from that place, no matter how good the water looked.

But as the day brightened and the sun shone down strong and jolly, my worry burned off like the fog. I felt a fool with the pistol on my hip and put it back in the pack. There were trout rising everywhere—in the pocket water, the riffles, along the undercut banks, in the long, slick, stillwater runs and the deep blue-green bottomless pools. Would *E. incognita* work its wonders under conditions like this, where every trout in the river was already glutting itself on the tiny blue-wing olives I now saw emerging? The naturals were no bigger than eighteens or twenties—a fraction the size of the *incognita*. Even if I cast with the utmost delicacy, as fine and far off as I could manage, its impact on the water would probably put everything down.

I strung up, tied on, and cast. At first nothing happened. The feeding trout continued to etch their endless, interwoven circles on the water, and I was about to breathe a sigh of relief—last night's events had just been another of those rare lucky moments in a fly fisherman's diary of strange happenings. But then another huge brown appeared out of nowhere and took the fly at the end of its float. In fact, the fly had been dragging abominably for half a minute while I stood there, falsely relieved that the mystery was explained. I played the fish fast but carefully, took great pains to insure that I didn't so much as touch it while pushing the hook with a fingertip out of the corner of its mouth. Again, it swam off in full strength, even splashing me with a faceful of water as it tailed away. Thus began, ironically, the most frightening, frustrating day of my angling life.

I tried the *incognita* in the most unlikely trout lies—in dead back eddies, in boiling currents too strong even for a tarpon, dapped it directly at my feet in seemingly fishless pools, even bounced it down a shallow gravelly riffle no more than ankle deep. Wherever I dropped it, trout appeared, often as if from the stream bed itself, out of ancient redds long buried under glacial till, springing in seconds from alevin to parr to smolt to full-grown, hook-jawed, bloody-eyed lunker hellbent on suicide. One such—a broad-shouldered five-pounder at least—actually zipped up through water only half its own depth from dorsal to ventral, scooting along the gravel on its pectoral fins like some giant wind-up toy. I'd seen king salmon do that on the Salmon River near Pulaski, New York, when the water was down and the fish themselves pursued by a horde of two-legged snaggers, splashing and falling down in their lust for a kill. But never the dignified brown trout. It was sickening—ignoble, repellent, downright hoggish.

And behind me, as I fished and tried not to look back, I saw fish after fish—all carefully released as tenderly as possible—go belly up in my wake. Every one that the *incognita* bit died. Yet I couldn't stop fishing. Even as my mind shrank from what I was doing, as I cursed myself aloud, I kept casting, hooking, releasing, but inevitably killing trout—trout of such a size and beauty that if I'd seen some worm-flanger catching and killing just one, a day ago, I'd have seriously considered shooting the bastard and leaving him for the ravens.

Poison, I began thinking. Poison on the hook. What I took for black lacquer is actually some kind of deadly venom—like that black tar the Wandorobo hunters use in Africa, boiled down from the sap of the Acocanthera, and smeared on their hand-forged arrows and spear-heads, to kill even rhinos and elephants with the stuff. But I, too, had been stuck with the hook point. Maybe I, too, was dying—going mad first, unable to stop what I hated doing, yet compelled by the poison to continue. Maybe in an hour, maybe not until tonight, I would gasp hopelessly for breath like those spendid fish dying behind me. Maybe I would roll belly up in my sleeping bag, eyes going white with death, and . . .

And what? Provide a midnight snack for that big, round-pawed carrion eater I'd surprised this morning by the riverbank?

That snapped me out of it. I looked at the palm of my hand where the hook had bitten me yesterday afternoon—less than twenty-four hours ago—but the wound was healed. As perfectly as if it had never been there. Nor was the flesh tender when I probed it. Oh, I felt a little woozy, but that might just be a touch of hangover from last night's Scotch, plus the belt I'd had instead of breakfast. And I hadn't eaten a bite of lunch. It was already late afternoon. No wonder I was giddy—

too much fresh air, too much sun, too much adrenaline, too much imagination. When I looked back downstream, I couldn't for the life of me see a single dead fish, yet just moments ago it had seemed there were dozens. Maybe I'd imagined the whole thing.

But the *incognita* was still clinched fast to my tippet. And with a pang of horror I saw that, for all the big fish it had taken today, all the spiky vomerine teeth that had raked it, not a wing was tattered, not a hackle point bent, not a tail whisk frazzled or a strand of dubbing trailing loose. With a shudder, I cut the fly loose and threw it into the current.

Before it could hit the water, a huge brown surged head and shoulders up and onto it—snap, like a giant mousetrap, and he was gone.

At that same moment, a wind kicked up and, under its sudden roar, I heard a low, throaty growl from downstream. I turned and ran. . . .

I slept that night on a rocky islet in midstream, wading out to it through currents that lapped over the top of my chest waders. There was ample driftwood jammed at the head of the island to build a huge, roaring bonfire. I kept the unholstered Woodsman beside me while I ate a frugal supper of beans, Spam, and Bing cherries—no trout for me tonight. I'd killed enough in the hours just past to last a lifetime. I also reduced the Scotch level another few inches, trying to quiet my raging imagination. To keep my mind off the day's events, I dug out a book I'd brought along, as I always do on such trips, to read myself to sleep. Usually it takes half a page or less, after a hard, fine day on the water, but tonight I feared it would take longer. *Keys to the Kingdom*, it was titled, by Zadok Mosher. *Being a Compendium of Myths & Legends Peculiar to Northeast Vermont*. I'd picked it up in a fine little bookstore in Lyndonville that specialized in used books. No date of publication was given, nor was the name of the publisher, but clearly it was an ancient tome—glossy paper, antique typeface, faded leather binding, excellent drypoint illustrations, the sort of book no one makes anymore. I settled down into my sleeping bag, took a stiff wallop of Scotch and brook water, and opened the volume at random.

"The Monster of Wendigo Brook." Uh-oh. But I read on.

> The Wendigo is thought to be a myth of the Cree Indians of the western boreal forests [Mosher wrote]. A murderous creature, half cat, half man, that stalks its human prey through the treetops. When it catches an unwary Indian, alone and deep in the forest, it swoops down

and grabs him, lifting its hapless victim high into the air. Then ensues a pell-mell dash through the night sky, conducted at such speeds that when the Wendigo—dragged groundward by the weight and frantic struggles of its still-living captive—allows the victim's feet to touch the earth, the sheer friction sets his moccasins afire. The Wendigo, like a house cat, likes to show off its prey, frequently carrying it at chain-lightning speed around the camp from which the poor captive strayed. His kinsmen, huddled in their teepees, can hear him screaming all through the night: "Oh, my burning feet! Oh, my feet of fire!" In the morning, nothing is found of the victim but his scorched clothing and picked bones, usually under a tall tree at the top of which the Wendigo, like an owl, has made his meal.

Such, then, is the Wendigo of the Cree. But the Abnakis of northern New England have their own legend—that of the Water Wendigo. Like its western congener, this creature too is a man-eater, though it much prefers fish. It haunts the virgin trout streams of that luckless country, hoping to find a dupe to catch fish for it. To that end, it ties a lure on whatever old hook it can find, using swatches of its own fur to disguise the fatal implement. This fur, the Abnakis say, is irresistible to trout and salmon, some of which have been known to crawl on their fins from lake to lake in pursuit of a lure of such devising. No sooner do they taste of it, than they die. Whereupon the Wendigo dines on their corpses. But since the Wendigo cannot cast a fishing pole by itself, it needs a human intermediary to do its fatal business in its stead. This it handily finds, the Abnakis say, since what man would pass up the chance to catch a fish with every cast of his lure? Should the fisherman object to sharing his catch with the Water Wendigo, the Wendigo kills him along with the fish, then passes the lure on to another victim. No man has lived to tell how. Nonsense, of course. But when you hear a withered old Abnaki tell the tale, in a skin lodge of a still winter evening with the Aurora guttering overhead . . .

That was enough for me. I poured another Scotch and resolved, then and there, to fish no more on Wendigo Brook—tomorrow or ever. Total nonsense, of course, as Mosher said, but I would not press my luck. I was lucky to get rid of the fatal fly when I did. I unjointed my fly rod and slipped it into its case, finished my drink, stoked up the fire, and went to sleep.

The sun was already up when I woke, so sound and dreamless had been my rest. It was a beautiful day, clear and warm with just an apple-bright bite of frost in the shadows, the brook tinkling and purling along its merry way over the timeworn rocks. I looked at my map and saw a quick way over the hills to the northwest which would take me to the highway in a matter of a few hours. I'd have to bushwhack, and there might be a few bogs and beaver ponds along the way, but any amount of hard slogging was a cheap price to pay to get away from this cursed river. Still, I'd better get myself around a good breakfast first—a couple of chunky little brookies, caught on a human-tied, unmystical fly for a change. I went over to where I'd left my rod case leaning against a rock the night before.

The rod case was open. The rod stood assembled. The line threaded bright yellow through the guides to the tip-top. The leader led down to the keeper ring. Cinched in it, snug and bright, was *Ephemerella incognita*.

Again I fled, to the limits of the island. I may well have been gibbering to myself as I ran. I skidded, half fell down through the sharp granite rubble to the water's edge. My reflection shone, unwavering, on the still, cold water. I looked down, dreading what I would see.

The face of the dead angler stared up at me from the mirror of Wendigo Brook. The grizzled gunfighter's mustache wavered, shimmered in the current, the pale eyes stared up into mine—dead at first, then with growing recognition. The face I saw was my own. . . .

The River

Raymond Carver

 waded, deepening, into the dark water.
Evening, and the push
and swirl of the river as it closed
around my legs and held on.
Young grilse broke water.
Parr darted one way, smolt another.
Gravel turned under my boots as I edged out.
Watched by the furious eyes of king salmon.
Their immense heads turned slowly,
eyes burning with fury, as they hung
in the deep current.
They were there. I felt them there,
and my skin prickled. But
there was something else.
I braced with the wind on my neck.
Felt the hair rise
as something touched my boot.
Grew afraid at what I couldn't see.
Then of everything that filled my eyes—
that other shore heavy with branches,
the dark lip of the mountain range behind.
And this river that had suddenly
grown black and swift.
I drew breath and cast anyway.
Prayed nothing would strike.

The Native

Ernest Hebert

WE HAVE plenty of water in Darby, New Hampshire, water of every kind but ocean water. We have a deep, clear glacial lake, shallow tea-colored ponds, fetid swamps, beaver-dam impoundments, fast-running brooks, and a wide, slow-flowing river, the Connecticut. If you listen carefully, you can hear our waters whisper into the wind, "I hold a great bounty; cast your lines." But the waters exaggerate. The fishing here is not bad, but it's not great, either. These are not nutrient-rich limestone waters. This is the Granite State, and these are granite waters, too poor for abundance, too pure for fecundity. Our waters please the eye, stimulate the mind, and disappoint the stomach. Our most prestigious gamefish, the stocked trouts of the state Fish and Game Department, like our Upper Darby aristocrats, don't behave like natives, even though they've been here through several generations; the common smallmouth bass, like our Center Darby commoners, put up a good fight but for no purpose other than the thrill of exercise. But let us begin this survey at the bottom.

In the muck of New Hampshire water bodies, there lives a tough, ugly little fish we call the "hornpout." Other places it's called a "bullhead." The hornpout is a member of the catfish family. It feeds at night, and is caught on a worm. It is black and slippery in the hand. It is easy to catch but hard to kill, and prickly spines near its head (the horns) can stick you when you are removing the hook. It is very tasty fried in butter.

Darby Depot folk fish for hornpout. Around dark, when the trout fishers are sliding in to shore in their canoes and the bass fishers

51

backing their motorized, fiberglass platforms onto boat trailers, the hornpout fishers are launching their flat-bottom johnboats. They prefer aluminum for no better reason than that it's cheap. Sometimes they scrounge leaky wooden rowboats. Wooden oarlocks crick and creak in the delicate night air over water; aluminum oarlocks clunk and clank.

Hornpout fishing is almost never done alone; it is a social activity. You might find two men (drinking), or a man and a boy (the man bossing the boy around), or two men and two boys (the men drinking, the boys heehawing), or a guy and his girl (likely fishing from shore, he bragging about his car, which might not start when they leave, she complaining about the bugs), or a man and wife (abstaining from quarreling during these hours), or an old codger and his old woman (silent), or an entire family (loud).

The men bring six-packs of beer—beer is their salvation—and, standing, half-drunk in johnboats, they pee over the side.

Equipment for hornpout fishing is modest, consisting of a hook, a worm, a sinker, pliers to pull the hook out of the fish's throat, a flashlight to see by, a can to hold the worms, a bucket to hold the catch, and any old rod and reel—usually picked up used in a yard sale or new from the Jupiter discount store in downtown Tuckerman.

Hornpout fishing, aside from being sociable and easy, is also productive. An average haul for a boat might be fifty fish a night, the fish from four to ten inches in length.

For cleaning, a hornpout is staked with its kind on a nail on a board. The skin around the head can be cut and pulled off with fingers or pliers. That's all there is to it. The guts that don't spill out can be whisked away with a thumbnail. Some men can perform the cleaning task with their bare hands alone. They break the head off, ripping downward; this decapitates, skins, and guts the fish, although I can't say how exactly. The men don't tell you how they do it, and you can't tell by watching their hands, for it is all done faster than the eye can follow. A man about to clean a hornpout with his hands gets the same look of concentration as a karate expert who's about to chop a concrete block. A Center Darby or an Upper Darby man might dip into his reservoir of spiritual energy to help him catch a fish, but only a Darby Depot fellow would make the same investment in the interest of cleaning a fish.

The people of Darby Depot know the hornpout intimately and speak of it as if it were a flawed but important relative—say, a drunken uncle who has outlived his soberer brothers.

It is whispered among those who know better that the horns are poisonous, and so the hornpout is also feared, feared out of all proportion to the danger it poses. It's as if a quarry is not worthy of pursuit or consumption unless it can hurt you.

The hornpout is at once revered and despised. The people of Darby Depot understand in a felt, if not figured, way that they have found a creature even lower in the order of things than themselves, and they arrogantly rejoice in the knowledge.

While the hornpout inhabits the Darby Depot psyche at the bottom level of myth, it is of little or no concern to the general public. The state does not regulate the fishing of hornpout. There is neither need nor desire among the populace, because, unlike gamefish, the hornpout invites no symbolism. The hornpout is not "wary" or "moody" or "discriminating," nor is it a great "fighter"—words ascribed to fish such as trout and bass, fish commanding respect. Why should a trout or bass command respect, and a hornpout not? This is my answer: If I were a foreign agent, I would write in my report, "The American thinks of himself as wary, moody, discriminating—a fighter."

The Center Darby man is what happens when the Darby Depot man gets out from under family, clan, and habit, and strikes out for the middle class.

Often, the origin of the Center Darby man is another place, far from Tuckerman County, perhaps even a foreign country. He has, so to speak, put the Darby Depot of his past behind him. He schools himself a bit, lands a decent job, and marries an ambitious woman. Or, he is transformed by war or religion or Dame Fortune—shit luck, in the idiom of Darby Depot.

A common man, to achieve a feeling of distinction, searches for a distinguished fish to pursue. Any distinguished fish will suffice, but a distinguished fish with which the man can identify is preferred. Thus the common man seeks a common fish which itself has achieved distinction. It's not surprising, then, that the preferred gamefish of Center Darby is the bass, a distinguished member of the undistinguished sunfish family. Following the twisted streets of human reasoning, it makes sense, too, that the Center Darby man holds in contempt the common sunfish because it reminds him who, underneath, he is.

A Center Darby man will not eat the fish he catches. A Center Darby man fishes to catch his own self. It is in keeping with his character that, having caught that self, he will kill or even consume it ritualistically (our Center Darby man will eat fish in camp), but not consume it merely for food. He despises "meat fishermen" as any person calling himself civilized despises cannibals. (Darby Depot people are disposed in favor of cannibalism, and that is one reason they enjoy eating the hornpout they catch.) A Center Darby fisherman occasionally will eat ocean fish, but his preferred protein is on the hoof.

The wife of the Center Darby fisherman is jealous of the pleasure her husband takes from his moments on the water. She's discontented, and she scores his contentment as an insult. She understands, in a felt if not known way, that it is his very happiness, brief and private in his boat with a buddy, that prevents him from understanding her desperation and, further, that camouflages his own desperation from her, perhaps even from himself. She'll try to communicate this feeling. She'll say to her husband, "It's raining again. Why does it have to rain?" He'll answer, "How should I know?"

She's acutely female, this wife—beautiful and fashionable and desirable and passionate—but she has interred her femininity. She despises femininity; she regards femininity as the turn of mind that shackled her mother. And of course she is right, and of course she is wrong. In our society, the only feminine adults are drag queens.

The women of Center Darby do not fish for real fish. Society has rigged it so they fish in the brine of men for status, prestige, money, and they are thus burdened by men's work and men's worry in addition to women's work and women's worry. If women fished for real fish, they would fish with spears. They would don masks and snorkels and rubber webbed feet and they would weigh themselves down with lead bars and they would dive into the deepest lakes, and when the waters were dark and cold, they would stand immobile as statues (beautiful and oddly out of proportion, yet perfect, classically Grecian), and when a fish went by, they would spear it. Breaking through water and into air and white light, they would hold fish before their men and shout furiously, "There . . . there . . . understand now?"

It's interesting that the women of Center Darby used to fish. When I was a kid, the gender roles were more clearly defined than today, and yet many folks from Center Darby—not only managers and teachers, but tradesmen and factory workers—pursued fish with their wives. No more. The nature of the pursuit has changed. In those days, one fished for the pleasure of the outdoors, for the chilly joy of the stalk, for the bounty of the catch. The symbolism involved was near the surface, and clear. If you caught a big fish, you had it stuffed and mounted on a wall; trophy fish became furniture. Today the symbolism is deep and murky. The outdoors is said to be "the environment," as if the indoors is a nonenvironment. Men fish "to get away from it all," that is, to escape the nonenvironment of work and worry, the nonenvironment of family and duty. Fish are part of the environment, which is not supposed to be disturbed, but which is, of course, by the very presence of the fisherman. Furthermore, most fish deemed worthy of pursuit are stocked by the state, and hence not part of the environment, but not apart from it, either. The environment itself has been so altered by man's presence that it isn't the real environment. But of course the environment is the environment, whether or not it resembles the Platonic ideal. This is to say that Darby is a stocked pond, managed to some degree by the fish that swim in it.

Fish represent something to Center Darby men, but they aren't sure what; they don't even think about the matter. But the symbolism is there, like the white scar of an injury whose origin has been forgotten, like the echo of a shouted question that has not yet come round. All Center Darby men know is their apprehension that something big and important can be found in the depths, that and the memory of a tug experienced as pleasure in the hands alone. The fish that have been stocked in the pond remove themselves from it and fish for their greater selves. Such a fisherman, having landed a trophy specimen, is not likely to mount it, but, rather, to photograph and release it, or merely to kill it and start the process over again. The more these men fish, the less they get away from it all.

The bass is a school fish but with an independent streak; that is, it can be daring and impulsive and sullen, on occasion brave, but not contemplative or philosophical, even as fish go. If a bass were a man, it would be one of the bar patrons in a television beer commercial.

The bass will chase a plug, sweep live bait off the bottom, even rise to a fly. It can be taken on just about anything, especially when it's breeding. But it's fickle. Sometimes it likes red, sometimes blue. Sometimes it sulks and cannot be roused for its dinner. During these moments, it sits on the bottom, still as stone, from all appearances a deep thinker. Actually, it's like a guy who hates his job, who on a Saturday night in his living room, after the wife and kids have gone to bed, sits drunk and inert in front of the TV watching his perfected self in the beer commercials.

The bass likes structure; it camps in the shadows of rocks, in the camouflage of weeds, in the tangles of roots. It's not hiding, but lying in ambush. Without an enemy, it's unhappy. It's not enmity that excites it, but the thought of an enemy. It may or may not attack. It's not battle that stirs it, but anticipation of battle.

The fellows who pursue bass like to fish it with spin-casting outfits. They like to throw plugs (crank baits, as they are called today), preferably from a chair on the platform deck of a bass boat.

The first boat the Center Darby man buys is, more than likely, a Sears aluminum runabout with an outboard engine of five to nine horsepower. Or it's a secondhand boat, slightly bigger than the new boat he can afford, but run-down and probably with a fiberglass hull, advertised in the classifieds of the *Tuckerman Crier*. The seller bought a bigger boat, or had a heart attack and died, or got cancer and plans to die, or woke old, or his wife browbeat him into selling it. Whatever the reason, there are always fishing boats for sale, and there are always sad tales to go with them. But the anguish of the seller doesn't matter to a guy buying his first boat. What matters is the boat. He'll no longer have to depend on a friend to get on the water. Alone (and sometimes a man has to be alone, if only to allow emotion to surface on his face), he'll no longer have to cast his lures from shore.

This first boat is usually the best boat for Darby waters. The helmsman can troll, anchor in deep or shallow water, row into weeds, paddle into stream inlets, float and drift. It's a small craft but safe and dry, unlike a canoe (sometimes a Center Darby man dreams of canoes, but he rarely acquires one), and easy to trailer or toss in the bed of a pickup truck. The upkeep is modest. And yet from the moment he launches his new boat, the Center Darby man is dissatisfied. He's like a boy stepping into a shower stall of men: it's too small.

He frets. The sight of bigger, grander boats angers him. He has no words to explain his frustration.

"Everything's screwy," he tells his wife.

"So?" She doesn't look at him.

Why can't she understand? Why is she so stupid? Why are women so stupid? He turns his anger upon her.

"You're so smart!" He spits the words at her.

"I didn't do anything. Who do you think you are?"

He doubles his fist and holds it before her. "Gaw-damn, gaw-damn you," he shouts at the fist.

At first she is cowed by the inscrutability of his anger, and then something tells her he will not hurt her, not this time.

They collapse into the ritual of domestic argument. Before they are even aware it has started, it's over. He's miserable; she's miserable. Finally, it dawns on him: It's not her fault; it's his damn boat. It's a sniggling little boat that ridicules him.

"Aw, shit," he says, and because of the tone of his voice, she understands he is apologizing. She forgives him, but silently, so he does not understand he has been forgiven.

That night, alone, outdoors under the stars, taking a leak (because it's *his* land, gaw-dammit), he realizes what he must do. Next day, he gets a loan and buys a bigger boat. The boat is beautiful. It makes him feel tender. He tells his wife he loves her.

The next year, the drama repeats itself. With every fishing season the boat is bigger, faster, more elaborate. Eventually, he finds himself with a boat that has a horsepower rating equal to his car's, an electric trolling motor, water wells to store the catch that he will not eat, a steering wheel, a winch for the anchor, a cooler to hold the ever-increasing amounts of beer he consumes, rod holders so that he will not have to fish while he fishes, an electronic fish finder. The boat builders struggle to keep up with his demands. Someday, perhaps, they will build a bass boat that will not require a fisherman, and then . . . and then the Center Darby fisherman will be content.

Meanwhile, he finds Darby waters too meager for his boat. He ventures out, seeking greater waters—Lake Sunapee, Lake Winnipesaukee, Lake Champlain, Great Bay, the Atlantic Ocean. Eventually (and this passes through his mind in dreams), he is lost at sea and ripped to pieces by sharks. With that image, it strikes him: He's fifty years old. Fear rolls over him like sea fog.

"What is this? What's going on?" He speaks to his folded hands at the dinner table.

His wife looks over. "What's with you, Bunky?" she asks.

The fog clears and he can see. Beyond, there is nothing, just more of what was back there: years.

"Listen," he says, not aware of what he will say next but confident his words will shake a world, "I'm going to sell the boat. I don't care anymore. We'll take a vacation. We'll go to Florida. Or Atlantic City."

His wife looks at him now, really looks at him. He can tell she is reading his age in his skin; he can tell because he is reading hers.

"When it's over, it's over," he says.

She bursts into tears. She does not know why she weeps, nor does he.

★ ★ ★

The native Darby brook trout survives in, of all places, Upper Darby, right under the noses of those aristocratic fly fishermen. It resides in tiny, rocky streams shrouded by forest and pucker brush. It is deep-bodied and colorful as concentrated sunsets, but small. If you can catch one six inches long, you have a lunker. It remains in proportion to the water bodies that hold it, a case where, finally, aesthetics and fitness become one.

These waters are too brush-strewn and tree-darkened, the fish too small and reclusive, to tempt most fishermen. But there is a breed of man who is interested. He's a small, hard worm fisherman, an outcast even by Darby Depot standards. He fishes alone, and he doesn't say much. He's not shy exactly, nor reticent in the New England Yankee sense. He is misanthropic; his only virtue is patience. He likes the darkness of the woods only because nobody bothers him there; he fishes these little fish only because they are available.

Six- and seven-pound brook trout used to populate our ponds, or so the stories go. No one knows for sure, because no one alive has seen a native trout that big. The ponds are not what they were. People busy themselves around ponds and try to improve them, as they try to improve anything that is perfectly agreeable just as it is.

The ponds were dammed early on by the white settlers looking for water power, so today the ponds are greater in area and depth than ever before. You would think the brook trout, like the waters, would be bigger and lovelier than ever. This is not the case. The native variety of brook trout has lost out in the ponds. The reasons for this situation lie in the nature of the people who settled this region and the nature of the brook trout.

As fly fishermen are wont to say, especially when holding forth before non-fly fishermen, the brook trout is not a true trout, but a char, a northern-clime fish, primitive, narrow-minded, vulnerable to change. The only thing that saves it from being just another boring conservative is its beauty and fighting spirit. Unfortunately, it's not so smart. It responds to a worm like a liberal to a new idea. So there you have it: The Darby native brook trout is a mixed metaphor.

The most beautiful thing in its environment, it is touchy about environment. Warm water, dirty water can kill it. When the white folk came to these hills and created Darby, they built factories and sawmills and tanneries around the ponds. They polluted the water, and they killed the native brook trout. They built cottages along the water, and watched the trout-colored sunsets, and let their toilet effluent seep into the water. And they killed the native. The government came along, serious and mannered, and its agents "managed" the ponds, poisoning the water (for the ponds' own good), and introduced a government version of the brook trout—a pretty enough fish, just as stupid as the wild variety, but short-lived, so it never gets big.

It's this nonnative, the put-and-take foot-long-at-best brook trout, that is the local fly fisherman's sole pursuit. The fly fisherman lives in Upper Darby and he owns lots of land and a big house and he's proud to say his woman is his equal and he has a good job—he's a lawyer, for heaven's sake, or a doctor, or an insurance man, or a drug rehab counselor, or a businessman—but pity this poor fellow. He has a lot, but he doesn't have as much as his father, and *his* father before him, not as much land or money or prestige. He can't get over the feeling he's living the American dream in reverse, and yet despite all this he can't help but think his brand of human is better than any other, and he also knows he musn't be a snob—grandfather was a snob—and so he cultivates some generalized guilt, and that more or less takes care of the problem.

He dreams about a place and time that was, and he's scared of his kids, and periodically his wife goes crazy, and he suspects she's having an affair with her therapist, unless he's a therapist himself, in which case he finds his own feelings thinned by the dreary rain of his patients' tales, unless he's a patient himself, in which case he understands finally and completely that what he wants never was and never will be: He's nowhere.

"I'm restless," he says to his wife.

"It's your age," she says, and several days later presents him with a book—*How to Turn Fifty and Like It*.

So he fishes, or perhaps he only thinks about fishing; if he's of a type, that's enough. He dies happy.

He assumes that fly fishing is the only kind of fishing. And he's right. Fly fishing is the cocaine of angling—instantly addictive, its effects permanent in the psyche. The euphoria of casting a fly is everything anybody can feel, and yet it is not enough.

"More," he says.

"What on earth are you talking about?" his wife says.

"Bamboo," he says.

"Oriental brushwork?" She is curious now.

"Orvis," he says.

"Ohhh." Now she understands. He's going to buy a new fishing pole.

He becomes an equipment fanatic. He studies books about insects, so that he can match the hatch. But these stocked trout can't read. Soon, he figures this out, so he goes to Vermont, where there are some real trout. Vermont is not enough, though. And then Canada is not enough. Neither is Oregon.

His friends say he's quite the traveler.

"He's restless; it's his age," his wife says.

Somewhere—say, camping—it dawns on him. Like the stocked brookies of Darby ponds, he doesn't belong in Darby, and yet he was born there, he's a native. At that moment of realization, he understands why he fishes: to reach through a surface and come away with something alive. Home at last, he says, "There's something I have to say."

"Yes?" His wife is on guard.

He can't speak the words; they are too painful. He buries his knowledge.

"I think I'll go to Argentina," he says. "I hear they have brookies there, ten-pounders."

As for me, I am the son of common folk from Center Darby. I fish with a fly rod for the perch. It's small, aggressive in the water but passive on the line. It's the best-tasting fish in Darby. Nobody fishes it but me.

I bring my catch to the daughter of the Upper Darby fly fisherman who forgot his philosophy of life and subsequently died. I cut off the heads of the fish and open up the insides and show them to her. She remarks on the awful smell. She watches as I roll the fish in a batter of beer and egg and flour, and cook them in hot oil. The meat steams as I lift it off the bone. It is tender and sweet.

Rivers That Got Away

Verlyn Klinkenborg

TO ME it has always seemed natural that Prohibition and the Dust
Bowl should have blown in together. But then, I was used to the idea
of moral plagues, even though I missed those storms of temperance
and topsoil by twenty years and more. It was my fortune to spend a
good part of my childhood in northern Iowa, where the gravel-seamed
fields resembled the patchwork of alcoholic opinion. Corn on this
acre, soybeans on that; bourbon here, root beer there; no dust, and
only legislated drought. We lived on one of the dry squares, where the
price of liquor by the drink was carfare to the county line. With the
plain self-righteousness of a well-raised boy, I assumed that this was a
species of divine judgment; if the Biblical floods flowed again, our lot
on higher moral ground would save our skins. It took a long time to
learn that being wet, liquor-wise, did not mean waking up in a slough
every morning.

The water in Iowa tends to be flat most of the time, so we fished on
quiet lakes. But we knew what to listen for. Each spring at town's
edge, warm rain thawed the snow, and by April the railroad right-of-
way near our house had filled with water the color of the fields. Where
the runoff washed out railroad ties or sluiced into a ditch, we heard the
sound of rapids and pretended to be high in the Rockies with a trout on
the line. The sound was right. What was wrong were the federal

corncribs in rows beyond the tracks, and beyond them the slow downward curve of corn stubble out to the most distant silos and winter-dark groves.

When I was fourteen, we moved away from Iowa, and I stopped fishing. The spates went underground in me, like the river Alph. I became, you might say, deaf and dry. But in a dream one night many years later it came to me that the earth is divided into two regions, wet and dry, yet not of the wetness and dryness of drought or drink. I saw that the world has only two places: where you can fish and where you can't. Geography is that simple. After years of stillness to my ears, the earth came alive again with the music of falls and torrents, freshets and eddies, rills, riffles, and estuaries. And beneath their surfaces, fish sang aloud once more, like their feathered brothers in the sky above. Like all true revelations, this one brought the stab of regret. Irrigating my past were streams I should have fished. The one that got away is the oldest story in angling, and what had gotten away from me were rivers.

The first ones I missed were beyond volition anyway, because those years my parents lived in a log house in western Colorado, on the outskirts of a mining town that was all outskirt, and I was only newborn. From Trappers Lake, the White River spilled west to a mile or so from our home. The Gunnison ran eighty miles south. To the east were the Frying Pan and the Roaring Fork and a hundred other waters. While I waded naked in a galvanized washtub, my dad worked riffles and poked around in beaver ponds with Gray-Hackle-Yellows and Rio Grande Kings that in winter lay snelled in a cowhide wallet. In fall, there were mule deer and elk for the freezer; in spring, the gift of a rancher's lamb. Then, when I was two, my parents moved to Iowa, land of corn-fed beef, and took me and my brother with them. Some part of my tissues recalls that transition. There is an annual ring that, when I am felled, will say: Here the beef eating began.

Once, in the June I turned six, we went back to Colorado. From the Black Canyon of the Gunnison came smells unlike any in the farm towns of Wright County: powdery dust and sage, and pine over all when the wind blew down the canyon. If I brought my hands to my face before my mother got hold of me, there was also the smell of trout, seminal and feminine, stale and wildly fresh.

The rivers I rightfully regret belong to a later period, one that began when the family, now six of us, moved again, this time to California. Among the things I abandoned in the move was a set of memories I only lately went back for. If, after puberty, I ever thought of fishing,

63

I thought of dead bullheads, a gas slick near the outboard, or a bird's nest in an old casting reel: flatwater stuff. What I had forgotten were details: a foggy morning in Minnesota, sun just barely over the pines; slipping down to the dock; slapping Hula Poppers and Jitterbugs onto the weed beds near shore until the adults were up and we could go out to big water for pike. Fourteen years old, packing for Sacramento, I was sure that fishing was just a form of retirement suited to small-town types, a metaphor for life in a one-light town with a grain elevator and a John Deere dealer on the county road.

From Iowa, we shipped a few things by rail, held an auction, and headed out, our remaining belongings stowed in a camping trailer. At Yellowstone, I should have noticed that I was becoming deaf to water. Of four days in the park, I recall just two Jaguars, a Ferrari, one moose, and a girl I fell in love with when she smiled at me through the window of her father's car—a Porsche. I see the slides from that trip today, and there I am, looking sideways out of the frame, fists balled in my pockets. Like ghosts in the background slide the Firehole, Gibbon, Gallatin, Nez Perce, Madison, and Yellowstone. They call me now with a voice I couldn't hear then. I was too busy listening for tuned exhausts.

Going west permanently meant crossing a lot of new ground that quickly went old. One day, the alkali basins of Nevada lay in prospect; the next, they were part of a former existence. Out the windshield stretched the future. We had driven through an old migratory myth, and the myth had worked me over the way it did the coast's early settlers. They called California a new Eden. I was more millennial still: I called it rock-and-roll heaven. The radio had prepared me, alone, I thought, of all my family, for the Promised Land. My mojo was already up and working.

As the rivers slipped by and we got closer to the border, my illusions started to command some attention. It was like undressing a girl for the first time: I expected gravity to subside, nature to cease, and nothing to resemble what we had left. Dismay set in at Lake Tahoe. This was beautiful, but those people out there on the lake were fishing, dammit, and from boats. Nebraskans, no doubt. As we banked down Highway 50 following the American River, my amazement grew. Here were families living in small towns. What law, I wondered, had banished them from cities? As we towed our possessions through the sedated streets of Sacramento, I fretted. Where were the promised snakeskin shoes? Whom should I see about requisitioning a surfboard, a girlfriend, and a little deuce coupe?

Like a lot of other things I only half knew about the Golden State, I suppose I understood that Rio Americano, my new high school, was named for the river we followed down the mountain. But we had moved to a suburb of Spanish ubiquity: streets like El Nido, Las Pasas, Bodega, not one of which had a meaning that could be corroborated by anything but a street sign. Who could have guessed that behind Rio Americano an American River would flow? It defied the logic of the flood plain on which the school had been built.

The American is a tailwater river, Middle, North, and South Fork by thirds, detained at Folsom and released by law. It runs down the foothills, flattens, and meets the Sacramento River on a corner downtown. Then they flow to the bay akimbo. They are very different rivers. Though it settles in suburbia, the American River belongs to the mountains, to Lotus, Coloma, Chili Bar. Its bed has been dredged for gold, and it is dragged for bodies routinely, bodies lost in the turbulence of a shifting bottom. The Sacramento is a seaport river, shipper of rice. Below its levees lie orchards and pastel estates, river decks with hanging lights and dance bands, guests who arrive by ski boat. One bartends on the Sacramento: down the American one rafts with a six-pack in tow. Over both swims the valley sun.

Like the Sacramento, a levee cordons off the American River. Once, that dirt-and-gravel embankment, set fifty yards back from the river, kept floods from reaching the hops fields. But everything had changed by the time we arrived in the mid-sixties. Developers laid sewer lines where irrigation had run, and shake-roofed houses rose in place of hop poles. Thanks to Folsom and Nimbus Dams, the levee was no longer needed to restrain the river's excesses, just those of the children who lived near it. Once, police cars had cruised its long slender line for breaches that might wash out the hops. Now, the only breaches anyone worried about were those of conduct. Beyond the metal shop, the track, and the incinerators of Rio, the levee marked the limits of propriety, the edge of out-of-bounds. Even to teenagers, the ironies of that situation could be peeled away like layers of phyllo dough. To mention only one, there was the river's name. Once safely over the levee and into the realm of outlawry, we sported on American territory, and all the noble vagrancies the river inspired were Americanized. No class taught as much about the nation as crossing the levee to the American did. The broad, flat stones of the beach, the tangled trees off the path, the cover of the river's rushing sound meant that all the options were open: It was a land of concealment, exposure, and opportunity.

65

The only thing we did not think of doing near the river was fish. Perhaps we missed our best camouflage. Instead of going over the levee, heads down, with a grocery bag full of beer in our arms, we might have walked erect, our tackle plainly in sight. To be truant with a fly rod has a Tom Sawyer innocence that might have charmed the principal into unwariness.

Each year it must have stunned the shad, for whom the American was boudoir and maternity ward, to see at their return a host of rutting Visigoths on the shore, anadromous adolescents who went to the river to spawn. The shad had ascended the Sacramento and American through a beaded curtain of lines until they reached the river behind Rio. There the atmosphere was felicitous for breeding. Unlicensed connubiality was in the air.

I expect no reader to believe that even now, after my sea change, I would prefer fishing the American to going beyond the levee in the sense I mean. Some moments are eternal, especially those in which Nature has her will of you. But into the most stimulated lives some boredom may crawl, and for those times I should have known about shad, salmon, and trout. I should have remembered. When the tule fogs, flanked by leaf smoke, clung to the ground for warmth, and I was in the melancholy only love can breed, I should have struck out for the American, waded deep enough to bathe my nether parts, and stayed lost between river and fog, casting away rhythmically. Or on those days, hideous to parentkind, when ennui has infected a kid and he loiters malingering like a tubercle, I should have biked to the levee with some of the guys and gone fishing. Sometimes the simple answers are best.

God knows my dad thought so. He has always tried to keep the answers simple with a code he learned on the farm: work hard, pay cash, don't force it. And when the code breaks down, go fishing. Something else the farm taught him was that things are pretty much what they appear to be, if your head is screwed on straight. So while I tried to unearth new moral hieroglyphs from the scree at the foot of the levee, he went fishing, always leaving open the possibility of my coming along. What kept me from it was not just knowing that a fourteen-foot Boston Whaler is a damn small arena for generational conflict. It was blight.

In August of each of my high-school and college summers, I came to the same fork in the road. The pickup stood packed, pointed north in the driveway, ready for the trip to Crescent City or Klamath, where the salmon stacked up offshore. There was room in the cab, an implicit invitation. My brothers went. But the night the truck pulled out, I rearranged the stereo, tethered myself to it with a long headphone cord, and lay on the grass, staring at the stars and listening to Miles Davis. A week later, the truck would roll back in, and my dad and brothers, tanned and laughing, would start to unload. Musty clothes, an ice chest with lettuce stuck to its sides, raw-cut redwood one-by-tens from an old mill on the coast, and then a half-dozen, dozen, fifteen cohos and chinook—sleek, ocean-bright, live-orange. "Nice fish," I would say, and regret the return to everyday order. The "fish" did not translate into the heart attack of coho on the line.

That is the jawbone of the matter. To know the life of a salmon, you need to be there when it first feels threatened by the hook. No good looking at the bodies on the lawn and trying to read their pulses back into them. All those years I thought fishing was a witless analogy for something else: a metaphor for the Midwest, a simile for strife between fathers and sons, a suburban elision of intelligence. If anything, my refusal to fish was a challenge: a doubting, metaphorical mind circling round on itself against the simple answers. What I didn't see then is that metaphors belong only to language and that no image of fishing is as good as the thing itself. Ask me now and here's what I say: Things are what they appear to be if your head is screwed on straight.

That, I learned on another coast. After ten years in California, everything I owned fit into a Plymouth Valiant, and I drove all the way east, reworking the myth as I went. Over the Sierra Nevada, across the Rockies—a kind of continental levee—through the high plains of Wyoming, past Iowa, deep into the folds of the opposite coast. And the thing I discovered about American myths is that they're reversible. I didn't see the rivers this trip either. But I saw how dry the gullies in Manhattan were and how quickly its streets flooded. No place is less likely to recall the accents of a Midwestern boyhood than New York; yet one spring there it was: a heavy rain late at night awash down Third Avenue, and the very sound of the runoff in Iowa, the sound of white water at camp on the Gunnison. After that night, no river ever looked the same again.

Especially the rivers that got away. Those rivers hold the whole thing in promise, full of the smell of trout. Coming to them with my new fisher's mind is like finding another angle on iridescence: What I thought I knew is swamped by a reluctant palette of colors. This is why nowadays I fish like a madman. Every river I wade reminds me of the ones I didn't. And when there's room across the country in the pickup cab, I go. One of these days, my dad, who started above me, will fish downstream, and I, who started below him, will fish up. We're going to meet in a wet, wet county and look back over that dust bowl in our past.

The World's Greatest Trout Stream

Russell Chatham

SOME OF you may be wondering how it is I have the brass to follow the title of this story with the story itself. Everything I tell you will be the absolute truth. Hard as you may search, however, you will find no clues as to the locale of this extraordinary water. The reason, which is simple enough, is that this may be the only place left on Earth to be so pristine and untouched. Only a very small handful of people have ever seen it during recorded history. It is as fragile as a sheet of gold leaf in a windstorm.

Assuming a certain degree of guile and efficiency, two common traits abundant in the character of successful poachers, one unscrupulous meat packer could kill most of the trout in the waterway in one day. So I will not divulge the county, state, country, continent, or even hemisphere of this perfect river. The names of my companions will obviously be fictitious, and you will find neither flora nor fauna correctly named.

Up on the north slope of Mount Tamalpais, flowing into Alpine Lake, in Marin County, California, is a beautiful stream called Cascade Creek. My friend Kelly Dunnigan located it on his map, and we rode our bikes up to the dam one Saturday, and then walked up to the creek.

It is mostly waterfalls, too steep for fish to negotiate up or down, so

obviously someone must have planted a few little trout in it once. It is not good fishing. But then, you have to remember that there is really no trout fishing per se on the California coast.

The native fish are seagoing rainbow trout, known as steelhead. Young steelhead from seven to twelve inches can be caught in all the creeks and rivers; usually they are released so that they can go to the ocean and come back as seven- to twelve-pounders. In Cascade Creek, however, these little fish were going nowhere, unless they wanted to swim over a few fifty-foot falls and down into Alpine Lake. So Kelly and I decided we were trout fishing.

We had walked along the steep, fern-lined trail for some distance, then climbed up a steep, rocky face. At the top we peered over the lip and were looking across an almost magical pool right at eye level. It was round and deep, and flowing into it was a twenty-foot waterfall, not much more than a trickle really. While I was staring in amazement, Kelly whipped a tiny Bear Valley spinner across the hole and immediately caught an eight-inch trout. We let it go, and it was the only fish we ever caught in Cascade Creek.

Not long thereafter, I decided to write a story about trout fishing. I made up an ideal stream based roughly on that beautiful pool. I flattened Cascade Creek out and made it into a succession of remarkable riffles, falls, and holes embroidered around huge rocks, cool forests, and ferns. The sky was clear, the temperature a sublime seventy-five degrees, the water as clean as the spring air after a rain.

Even though I didn't even know how to use a fly rod then, it didn't matter; I saw myself moving along this mythic creek, casting a fly in my childish story. The fish were ten-inchers—even at that, an exaggeration of the reality I knew. I had no idea that thirty-five years later I would actually find this fictional river, and that it would have real ten-pounders in it.

The reason this stream remains protected is that it lies in a largely unpopulated region, and even after going to the trouble of reaching this region, it's a long walk getting to it. You can't fly in, because of the forest and rough terrain. A hard day's walk takes you to the start of the fishing, which lies at the head of a violent two-mile series of holes, rapids, and waterfalls.

I saw the first pool in deep shadow early one morning from a vantage point somewhat elevated and back from the river. It was just starting to become autumn. I stared at it while standing by the fire with my friends Larry, Moe, and Curly. At the time, I didn't know we were seeing the world's greatest trout stream.

Larry, the titular head of our do-it-yourself crowd, was the first to point out the trout. They weren't that hard to see really; it's just that they were so big you could easily mistake them for rocks or sticks or moss. There were two: the small one would be six or seven pounds; the larger one, a couple of pounds heavier.

This piece of visual information took a few moments to process. I felt the way you do when you come down the outside of a fast Ferris wheel. I rubbed my eyes idiotically, like one of the dwarfs in *Snow White*. Then the lenses focused, and I was burning a hole in the water, watching the slow deliberations of these enormous trout.

Sometimes they lay motionless in the crystal-clear water, which was as emerald green as a crown jewel in the early-morning light. Then they would describe a long oval, perhaps defining their territory, or searching for a bit of food. Their world was perhaps a hundred feet long, fifty wide, and eight deep at its deepest point, which is not a very large area to support two creatures such as these. Perhaps there were others, too, up in the fast water where we couldn't see them.

Taking charge, Larry directed Moe to be the first angler. I was envious, but oddly relieved, because I didn't have to worry about blowing what was clearly going to be one bitch of a cast. Luckily, Moe was pretty handy with a fly rod.

Moving into position fifty feet behind the lower fish, the larger one, Moe whipped out a beauty, placing his dry fly half a dozen feet beyond the trout.

On the flat, slow surface, his fly looked like a perky little sailboat. It sailed over the fish evidently unnoticed.

Larry, who was watching along with us from a respectable distance, called out to advise Moe that he might have to change to a nymph. Moe agreed.

The weighted nymph made the cast harder, but Moe punched it out there and the ugly stonefly landed with a plop. The big rainbow nailed it with the speed and violence of a bitchy actress slapping a busboy who tries to reach for her tinkler.

Terrorized, Moe struck, the fly pulled out, and the fish sped to a hiding place. Moe was furious.

"Never mind," called Larry. "Move up and cast to the other one."

This time the fly had time to sink a little, before the second trout took with a force equal to that of its poolmate. And in spite of Moe's every caution, the fly didn't stick this time, either.

After a stern debate over hook styles, timing, and the fish's heritage, we started upstream. Our route took us some distance above the stream, through many different kinds of cactus and sinewy hanging vines, which could entrap and strangle you to death if you weren't careful. The others were far ahead of me. For purposes of this tale, think of me as Oliver Hardy.

Within a fairly brutal half hour, I caught up with the boys, who were peering over a boulder about the size of an elephant.

"You're up, Ollie," said Moe. "Where the hell you been?"

"My feet were writing a check my heart had trouble cashing."

Below the rock I could see the fish. Larry said it was a six-pounder. From down on the stream, I could no longer see beneath the water because of glare, so Larry yelled directions.

I had a handsome little caddis fly tied on, but this fish refused to rise to it, so I replaced it with a Trueblood Otter nymph. I heard the yells before feeling the fish.

My line slackened, and I realized the fish was coming downstream toward me. I hand-stripped line, and the fish glided past, every detail sharp through the aqualine water. I noticed in particular the huge square tail. The trout easily took a hundred feet of line before the hook pulled out. We had another discussion.

There was no discernible trail along the river, and again Larry led us up into the thorns. When I caught up this time, the boys were looking down a hundred feet or so into a cauldron of white-and-light-green foamy water. Back where it cleared and darkened, two trout were lying deep down near the bottom. The small one was perhaps a five-pounder, the other at least a couple of pounds more. It was Curly's turn to fish, and we knew he was going to have some trouble with this for several reasons. First of all, he was pretty new at fly fishing. Second, there was only one place to stand to fish the hole, and he would have no visibility. Third, the noise of the nearby falls was approximately like that of a jet taking off, so he would not be able to hear any directions. Larry briefed him and sent him in with a pat on the butt.

It was a painful display. After countless false casts, he managed to lob one up ahead of the fish. One of them seized his fly, but because of slack line being pushed at him by the current, he couldn't see or feel the take. And because of the thundering falls, he couldn't hear us screaming ourselves hoarse.

With all diligence, he kept flinging his fly back into the pool. We could see the angst on his face even from far away. Presently, the other fish struck and spit out the fly, just as the first had done.

73

We gestured to Curly to come up, so we could explain what had happened. He looked like a cross between a man who had sat on a whoopee cushion and someone whose wife had just confessed her infidelities with an entire sports team.

We walked on and soon arrived at a clearing that was truly a part of the dream I had had three and a half decades earlier. The valley opened up to let in more sunlight. The air was now a sublime seventy-five degrees, and the water so clear at times that you were almost convinced there wasn't any. The pool was relatively shallow, with a riffle coming into it on a slow gradient. We could see there were at least four fish in the pool, all more than four pounds.

Larry, as mentor and counsel, was refusing to take the rod, so once again it was Moe's turn to be the entertainment.

Two of the fish were holding high in the water toward the tail of the pool. Moe waded to within forty feet of them and laid out an excellent cast. One of the fish took with a slow, deliberate turn to the side. Moe struck, and we all simultaneously cheered as the trout ran forward into the hole at great speed. The hook pulled out, and Moe's rod stood lifeless.

A certain purplish tone invaded his face, and subsequently his speech, as he came ashore. We didn't say much. After all, how much more was there to say about hook design?

We decided to sit back from the pool and have a little lunch. The soft tundra made a good picnic spot. As we munched and chatted, we could see four or five trout huddled deep in the center of the hole, just below a big rock that deflected the current.

Half an hour later, Larry said to me, "I believe it's your cast, Ollie. Throw a few flies at this spooked group, just in case one of them is feeling better."

I drilled many fine casts here and there, but nothing moved. I think those trout were digging some sort of hole with their fins, in order to have a better place to hide.

"Let's get along," said Larry. "If I'm not mistaken, there are mucho truchas grandes still ahead of us."

As we trudged upstream, Larry froze—much like a heron about to stab a frog. Something was up. He turned slowly to us and addressed me.

"Have a look at this, Ollie. It's still your turn."

It was not really a pool, but, rather, a peculiar run strewn with rocks. In one of the troughs was a magnificent rainbow of about seven pounds, hovering high in the current. Its demeanor was all nerves and bestial alertness as it quivered in the full current. It came up and took an insect with almost military deliberation.

This is it, I thought. Nothing can stop this keen, voracious feeder from sipping in my dry fly. Everyone sensed it was a sure thing.

I moved into position, assessed the distance, appreciated the vagaries of the flow, pulled just the correct length of line from the reel, and commenced false-casting. I was precise and confident until, about three strokes into it, I came forward against solid resistance. My fly was hooked onto an immovable bristlecone pine.

Ever alert, Moe rushed in and freed the line. Cursing, and more careful now, I started to false-cast again but could no longer see the trout.

"Please," I whined to Larry, "tell me where to cast. I can't see the fish."

"He's gone. He saw the movement of you boys playing in the forest back here."

Somewhat soberly, we moved along through a dark avenue of ferns and tall redwoods. What a soft, damp peace there was on this side of the river. Clearly a thousand years meant nothing here, although, when I looked up and saw a vapor trail high overhead, I could feel the twenty-first century breathing hotly down our necks.

We had scanned a mile or so of the river, without seeing anything, when we arrived at an enormous and rather eccentric pool lying between two rocky cliffs.

Larry screamed, "It's a bloody ripper! My God! Careful, boys. Here, look through these palm fronds." We were plainly seeing a ten-pound trout and its slightly smaller mate nestled into their living room.

Technically, it was Curly's turn to fish. Unfortunately, a vicious wind had arisen and was gusting downriver, and these trout were in a terribly tough lie. It would take a long cast into the wind over slow-moving water, and we all knew, Curly most clearly of all, that he simply would never be able to make it.

Moe climbed down into position and waited for a lull in the wind. There wasn't any. It took repeated casts before Moe finally slipped one under the air. We had trouble seeing through the crinkled surface, but these fish were so big there were still their long, black forms, one of which turned and rushed downstream.

"Strike," screamed Larry, but it was too late. The fish had spit the fly out already. To boot, the one fish spooked the other, and both of them made a hasty trip in among the jumble of rocks ten yards upstream.

"Bastards," I heard Larry say as he pulled up his parka hood and started on his way. "We've got to break this streak."

"Well, how about you taking a turn then," I insisted. "We've never seen fish like these. You're not as nervous as we are. I'm not real sure anymore if we're operating with too much hair trigger or in Mexican overdrive."

Not surprisingly, the next pool had a good fish in the tail of it. Larry addressed the situation in no-nonsense fashion. A very competent fly caster, he wasted no time in placing a small black nymph right in front of his target's nose. The target lunged and took. In the confusion that followed, the target elected to go over the riffle back downstream.

"I believe we'll get this one," Larry called out just a moment or two before the hook pulled out. There wasn't much else to do but laugh out loud together.

At this point we heard a yell from upstream. It was Curly, trying to tell us he'd found a real lunker feeding furiously right under his nose. We ran up the side of the river we were on, which was the opposite one from Curly. As we came abreast of him, we saw the fish immediately, a beautiful six-pounder literally slashing flies off the surface.

Curly knew enough to get cracking, and it was a piece of cake for him to cover the fish, which immediately grabbed his fly. Moe had sidled up to offer a little advice at his elbow.

It was a good pool in which to play a fish—not too deep, long, and uncomplicated by any obvious snags. And here was Curly, who had us worrying that he wasn't having a very pleasant day, firmly attached to the biggest trout of his life, a trout that looked as though it would be the first one landed by any of us.

Curly handled the job very well. He kept the pressure on while the rainbow ran first to the head of the pool, then clear to the tail. Moe, to his credit, did not badger Curly, but stood off behind him ready to help if needed. We were very pleased, because the weather was worsening and another such opportunity simply might not present itself. This fish would mean a lot to Curly, and I already had several good photos of him playing it.

Then the rainbow did a remarkable thing. It ran over to our side of the river, and rather calmly, we thought, circled a rock and broke

Curly's leader. I would like to say we all felt worse than Curly did, but that was not the case.

"This is becoming damned serious," murmured Larry. "There are only three or four more pools before the falls. We mustn't be shut out."

The next pool was quite flat and shallow. Larry told me with all certainty that if we spotted a fish there, it would take a dry fly.

"A good, honest dry fly will change our luck," Larry stated.

Sure enough, a fish was there and rising. We agreed that Curly should be the one to fish. This trout looked like another beauty of five or six pounds.

Larry was right beside Curly, trying to forge the event to a successful conclusion. After several failed tries, Curly landed his fly ahead of the fish, but too far to the right. The trout left its position anyway and executed a bizarre rolling, slow-motion take. In a moment of uncontrolled excitement, Curly whipped his fly rod back to strike and made one of the most depressing backcasts of his life.

Larry was losing his sense of humor. Perhaps he thought we were blaming him somehow for this ongoing comedy of errors. Maybe he thought Moe would punch him in the nose, or I might allow a grand piano to land somehow on his car, or Curly would slap him and twist his ear, making odd noises emanate therefrom.

There followed, then, five minutes of reassuring gibberish, about how fine it was just to have seen all this, how privileged we all felt to have been led to this most heavenly of rivers.

I stepped up to the next pool with a sense of weariness and resignation, two attitudes I secretly hoped would allow me to catch a fish by accident.

It didn't work. The trout we were fishing for was impossible for me to see, so I cast where Larry told me. He yelled, "Strike," and I did. Need I go on?

Larry gathered us around in a huddle. "Gentlemen, the last pool lies just ahead of us. Moe, you're in the gun seat. I have already seen a couple of rises up there. Put on this dry fly and try to think like a professional athlete."

The situation looked promising. The pool was simple and open, the current perfect, without any obvious treachery, and two trout were feeding aggressively. There was no need for Moe to be the least bit nervous just because this was our last chance and these trout were eight-pounders.

I must say that Moe delivered the goods. We all envied and admired

77

his cast. The fly turned over perfectly even in the gale-force wind and started its jaunty ride on the current. It seemed like an hour before the fly rode over the fish's tail and left it like a tiny shuttle leaving a spacecraft. An odd thing happened then, still in excruciating slow motion.

The huge rainbow did a perfect about-face, raised its dorsal fin and part of its considerable back above the surface, and began cruising straight toward the little fly and, of course, toward the stunned Moe as well.

One seldom sees an eight-pound trout with a mouth the size of a boxer's right hand glower at you as he gulps in a glassful of water along with a Dan Bailey Royal Coachman. I'm convinced that anyone would have done what Moe did under the circumstances, which was to pull the fly directly out of the fish's mouth.

So, there you have it, the horse collar on the world's greatest trout stream. And even though at the outset we had all agreed to kill no fish in this river, even if we caught one the size of an Electrolux vacuum cleaner, we had thirteen opportunities and muffed them all.

Sheridan Anderson, my dear departed friend for whom I frequently mourn, had this to say in his wonderful comic book *The Curtis Creek Manifesto*: "Is there really a Curtis Creek? Possibly, my darlings, quite possibly; but I will say no more because that is your final lesson: to go forth and seek your own Curtis Creek—a delightful, unspoiled stretch of water that you will cherish above all others. . . . There are few Curtis Creeks in this life so when you find it, keep its secret well. . . ."

The Fisherman Who Got Away

Thomas Williams

RICHARD ADGATE was at Romeo LaVigne's fishing camp on Baie Felicité, Lake Chibougamau, with two friends. They were three Americans of middle age, husbands away from their wives and families.

His wife had been unhappy about his coming on this trip, but he'd been working hard, and how often had he ever done anything like go off fishing for a week? He'd asked her this with a defensive stridency she'd of course detected, she, the woman he'd lived with for a quarter of a century. He could feel what she felt. She couldn't understand why on earth he'd ever want to escape her, she who considered herself fair-minded and good to him. That he wanted to go away with two friends—pretty good friends—why? The children were grown and gone now, and she could easily have come, but she hadn't been asked. How would he like not being asked?

And so it was like that, not something he thought about every minute, but there was an edge, an incompleteness that made him a little too surprised when on the broad lake a series of ponderous golden

boulders as big as houses suddenly appeared beneath his keel when he thought he was in deep water. He didn't want to look down, to have the other world rise up like that to within an arm's reach.

He'd gone out by himself this afternoon in one of Romeo LaVigne's rental boats, a seventeen-foot aluminum square-ended canoe with a rock in the bow for ballast and a four-horse Evinrude motor. Pete Wallner's boat was a little crowded with three in it, and Joe Porter was getting a divorce and needed conversation, reassurance, or whatever; that was no good with three, either. It seemed unfishermanlike, Joe's constant preoccupation with his problem. Or perhaps it was that a real getting-away, a forever getting-away, was antithetical to the furlough of a fishing trip. "She" was the word constantly on Joe's lips. "She." Her name was Lois, but it was always "she," and in spite of the immediate unpleasantness, Joe was about to be free of her after all the years. There was a perverse sort of envy in his listeners, too, and Richard could only wonder what it would be like if there were no "she" to make him return, no tether of loyalty and pity and partner-ship.

In any case, here he was, Richard Adgate, a man no better and no worse in his frailties than other men, he thought, forty-nine years old and quite alone in the suffering of his wife's disapprobation. Her name, empowered by the years, was Nora.

He'd been trolling around a small island a mile or two from Romeo LaVigne's rather shabby log cabins, the only man-caused things in sight except for the Indian camp a couple of hundred yards farther on—log frames with bright red and blue plastic tarps over them. Pete, who had a Lowrance sonar, had told him that the depth dropped to forty feet about fifty yards out from the island, and then to ninety feet ten to twenty yards farther out, so he trolled a silver Mooselook Wobbler on lead-core line, with about six colors out, hoping to find that small plateau and not get hung up too often.

The July day was blue, clouds forming always to the southwest, growing, looking dark, but not amounting to a rainstorm. The little island was covered by the narrow spruce, virgin spruce less than a foot in diameter, so thick you couldn't push your way through them. So far he'd seen a scruffy-looking red fox, a beaver, a sharp-tailed grouse with five or six chicks (the first he'd ever seen), a vole, ravens, uniden-tified ducks, a killdeer. This was the boreal forest, chilled and stunted most of the year by the polar winds. But in July the air was mild. The lake was warm on the surface, but a foot down it was forty degrees, and the lake trout (*grise*, to the French) were not very deep.

After a while, with no fish taking the silver Wobbler, he reeled in, shut off the idling motor, and let the mild wind and little waves tilt him and move him slowly to the northeast, toward a distant, spruce-black shore.

He got his map from his pack and opened it along its folds to where he was, feeling the familiar small shock caused by a map's ideal, formulated authority, its precision reflecting the wide, moving actuality of the lake and the distant, oddly shaped hills. Magnetic north was nearly twenty degrees west of true north here, a knife-sharpening angle. He balanced on his spine in the canoe, above the depths of another inhabited world.

To the east, according to his map, was a narrow northward extension of the lake, a passage five or six miles long that opened into a large bay with many islands, where a good-sized river entered, with the symbol for rapids. Lake trout were fine, beautiful fish, but most of his life he'd been a brook trout fisherman, and only occasionally a troller. For him, the fish most familiar to his hand, least alien to touch, was the squaretail, the brookie, here called "speckled trout" or *moucheté*.

There were supposed to be large brook trout in the rivers hereabouts, especially in rapids. But up that long passage, into a place where no one else would be, miles away from anyone—did he really want to go there? Wouldn't those islands loom strangely, and the bottom rise up to startle him? The far bay had a name: Baie Borne; and the river: Rivière Tâche—he didn't know what they meant in French.

Along with his rods and tackle box, he had, in his pack, a sandwich, some chocolate, two bottles of Laurentide Ale, and all of the usual outdoors stuff: a compass, Band-Aids, nylon line, aspirin, binoculars, safety pins, toilet paper, bug repellent—things gathered over the years. He didn't consider himself fussy or overcautious in these matters. When he went out in a boat, he wore a life vest, and when it might rain he wore a broad-brimmed felt hat and took along raingear. It was stupid to suffer the lack of any little thing. On his belt he wore his sheath knife and a pair of Sargent wire-cutter pliers.

He was drifting toward the entrance to the northern passage. He had a full three-gallon tank of gas. Why not go there? Because he was here in northern Quebec in some ridiculous way without permission, and because, for all his years and his knowledge of the water and the woods, there was still within him a small child afraid of the deep and the dark.

In his life he'd never jumped into new things, dangerous things.

He'd always crept in, somehow, slowly and cautiously, and gotten to the danger all the same. Not that there could be real danger here, unless a storm came up, and even then it would be nothing serious. He could always run to shore and wait it out, no matter how long the storm lasted. Even if his motor conked out, broken beyond his ability to fix it, he had a paddle. It would be only time that he could lose. So his friends might worry about him—so what? But it did worry him that they might worry—a small threat of anxiety, a small twinge of that psychic nausea. It all seemed so demeaning that he decided he would have to go to the strange bay and the river. He liked to be alone. He did. He was always saying that he did. He started the motor and swung northeast, looking for the passage. Of course he might go in, and he might not.

The entrance to the passage toward Baie Borne was narrow, full of boulders, and had a definite current. He could see that the passage beyond widened and deepened quickly, however, so he throttled down and just made headway as he left the broad lake. He thought of those who explored caves—spelunkers (where did that word come from?)— who sometimes crawled into holes so narrow they'd have to bet upon a larger space ahead because they couldn't crawl out backward. A cowardly thought on a bluebird day. But he got through without touching and went on, at least for now, with dark hills rising on each side.

He didn't know how deep the water might be, but since he edged into this passage at trolling speed, he let out the silver lure, its long leader, and a couple of colors of line. One swath on the western hills had been logged, and the greener brush was a wash of light. On top, some birches had been left, their tall trunks against the sky like African trees—a view of Kenya that slowly passed. A small bay opened on his left and, yes, the map was disconcertingly true again. As he passed the bay's entrance, it silently let him by, its farther regions secret, not caring, set for eternity. A heavy cloud to the north, moving away, made his pathway dark.

His rod quivered—a snag or a hit. A fish, he knew as he picked it up, because it moved a little to the side, undulant, like a heartbeat, a small spasm of opinion. He shut off the motor and checked the star drag as he reeled, feeling the caught thing, the line alive between them. A pull from below answered the question of size; it was small, probably a lake trout. It came up against all of its will, no match for his eight-pound leader, the silver three-pronged hook in its flesh somewhere. He would see it soon.

Thomas Williams

The fish was dark and narrow—a small pike about fourteen inches, hardly a keeper. The brown eyes in the slanted skull saw him. The way to grab a large pike, he'd been told, was to put your thumb and middle finger into its eye sockets, squashing the eyes into the skull; this was supposed to stop their thrashing. He reached down and grabbed this one behind its head, the smooth body a muscle, and forced the tines of the hook down and out, a fragment of white cartilage, broken by a barb, flowing half-loose. His too-strong hands let the small pike go back down. As he let it go he felt a little magnanimous, slightly closer to the vision all fishermen would like to have of themselves someday—a distinguished older man with well-patched waders and a split bamboo rod, Yeats's wise and simple man, the paragon of dignified age who is usually observed in the middle distance as he performs each ceremonial fishing rite with understated skill. He always catches a fine brown trout and of course releases it, his sparse gray hackle glowing in the falling light, a tiny hatch, like reversed snow, haloing his old felt hat. Oh, yes, the classic fisherman, his aesthetics honed to the finest moral patina. With age was supposed to come wisdom that was not detachment, mastery that was not boredom, experience that never bred despair.

His canoe moved steadily north through the dark water. He hoped the northern cloud would soon pass and the water would turn a less forbidding blue again. Was he really going to go all the way to the river and its indicated rapids, or not? Looking back, the entrance from the lake had disappeared behind God knew how many hills. That the larger bay and its many islands would come up, inevitably, on map and in real distance, had some of the quality of the sudden boulders that had appeared beneath him in the broad lake.

The motor plugged on smoothly; the long bow moved ahead exactly where he had it go. He might troll, but decided not to because of apprehension about what he might catch. No, not apprehension, but because to catch something here might delay him too much. He would catch a Silkie, a monster half fish, half woman, both natures writhing with hatred as they died. He could see in the deep the golden scales on the thighs, the fish-belly-pale shoulders, the inward-turning teeth of a pike. If he trolled he would be mixing exploration, which was perhaps neutral with the gods, with the intent to do harm.

He leaned forward and hefted the gas tank; of course it was still heavy. He could go ten times the map distance with that much gas, and he knew it. If he were at home, he would be safe, though deprived of

84

the opportunity to make this lovely, lonely choice. Of course his wife was home right now, her unhappiness a distant and unsettling power.

Rivière Tâche must be a mile or so farther, with rapids at its mouth, and in some wonderment at his deliberate progress he steered on toward it. Rocks here and there caused tan blushes near the surface of the water, between deep places where to look down was to see, hopefully, nothing but the dark water-gray of depth.

Across the wide blue of Baie Borne he moved, now over sand with patches of weeds here and there, and then into the positive current from the river. The spruce came nearer on each side, and ahead were rocks and some white water. The southeast wind was at his back, so he shut off the motor, the wind holding him against the current, and got his fly rod out of its tube. In his reel was a sinking line, an old leader, and a tippet he was too lazy or impatient to change. He was always nervous as he strung the leader through the eyelets, but he got the line correctly strung and chose for a fly a medium-sized Gray Ghost. His fingers trembled as he tied his knot and clipped off the tag end. The water was five or six feet deep, the rocks below darker, denser-looking than the boulders out in the bay. His canoe turned in the wind and current, and he tilted the motor up before casting. He would begin here and then go up toward the frothings of white water.

After the first cast, which was only a half-decent cast, in fact a lousy cast, with the leader dropping in a messy coil not ten yards away, he began to strip in his line, worrying only about getting a knot in his leader and not at all about a fish. But the line jerked out straight, and his supple rod bent. "My God!" he said. "It's a fish!" He wasn't ready at all; there was a sense of bad timing, as though he'd rather not have a strong fish on just yet, after such a stupid mess of a cast. But the fish was there, whatever it was. He should have changed the tippet; surely more than three pounds had already stretched it out. His nerves went down to the invisible tippet as he let out line, let it out and recovered it. Careful, now! The fish ran upcurrent, then held for a moment before running down along the far bank, not quite to a snag angled into the water—a complicated dead spruce. He just managed to decrease by tender force the radius of the fish's run down that bank. Then it stopped, and he kept what he hoped was a permissible pressure on it, and then just a little bit more, but he couldn't move it. He was afraid of the sudden emptiness of no connection. "Don't happen," he said. "Don't happen."

He didn't know what kind of fish it was, only that it was big and strong. If it was a brook trout, it would be the biggest one he'd ever seen, he was sure of it, a salmon-sized brook trout. It might be a pike, or a large walleye, or a lake whitefish—what else was here? With one hand, he freed his boat net from the paddle: presumptuous to think of netting a fish he couldn't even move. But then the fish came in a little, maybe just a foot or so; the canoe was moving, so it was impossible to tell. But the fish didn't like that, and pulled so hard, so suddenly, he knew the tippet had to break, and for a moment thought it had, a hollow moment, but the fish had come toward him, and now it veered away upstream, the line cutting the surface. He must keep the fish from winding the leader around a rock—just to the limit of what he could do with a three-pound tippet, which was probably good for at least five pounds, except that it was old, so God knew what strength it had. He mustn't get used to its holding.

He had to see this fish. He wanted to own it, to have it. What a will it had, what strength! But the long minutes with his rod quivering, line in and out in desperation, might be too worrying for him. He'd deliberately put himself into a situation in which he felt anxiety. Why had he done that?

Beneath the water, the cold muscles fought for life against this fragile extension of his touch. How sickening it must be to be pulled by the invisible—like having a fit, epilepsy, a brain spasm. What did the fish think pulled him so hard, and what part of him said no? He must know the fly itself was too small to have such power; everything he'd ever hunted and eaten told him that, but some force wanted to haul him away from the dark rocks to the ceiling of his world and out of it. Everything smaller than he that moved in his world was food, yet now this small thing he'd tried to eat was overpowering him, little by little, with a constant pressure that felt like death. What else must he know in his neurons, in his lateral canals, and in all the circuits of his perfect body, when he'd lived a life of caution, too, hunter and hunted both?

The wild thing deep in the current was so tenuously bound to him by his skill and desire. . . . By what skill? He was a nervous wreck, trembling and sighing. His line looped at his feet, a coil of it encircling the shank of the paddle. If the fish ran now, it would be all over, so he held the rod high and reached down to free the line. The bunched collar of his jacket pushed his hat forward, and because he hadn't thought to fasten the chin strap, a gust blew the hat overboard. He reached for it and nearly shipped water, came upright again and noticed that his tackle box, weighted by the open tray, had dumped lures and eyelets and split shot and all kinds of necessary little objects into the bilge. His hat floated away; the coil of line was still around the paddle. He saw, but didn't feel on his line, the fish as it came to the surface of the water in a quick, in-turning swirl. It was black on its back, deep in the body, spotted, with a flash of orange at the fins; every memory, every known subtlety of shape and behavior said trout, said eight to ten pounds, the fish of his life that would make this moment, for better or for worse, forever a brilliant window.

He did clear the line from the paddle, and miraculously the fish was still on. He hauled in line as the fish came straight at him. He'd meant to get a multiplying reel and make it left-handed, so he could reel all this line in—why hadn't he done that? Why hadn't he done that long ago, as Ray Bergman had suggested in his book, *Trout*? The stripped line slopped half in and half out of the boat, some of it among his spilled lures, so that he'd probably have a bloody Christmas tree of ornaments on it when it came up again.

Something shoved him hard in the back—a mean, hurtful sort of shove; the canoe had drifted into the bank, and it was a dead spruce stub that wanted to push him onto his face. The fish moved upstream again, well out from the bank, thank God. If he could just get hold of the paddle, or even that nasty stub, and push himself away from the bank. He couldn't see why the fish was still on. It could just run away if it wanted—take out his line and all his backing and easily snap the tippet. Of course the next thing the wise and skillful fisherman would do would be to capsize the boat.

Where was his hat? Over by a sand bar, beached by the wind. He could get it later, if there was going to be a later. His arms seemed to be pushing as well as pulling—pushing against his tendency to pull too hard—and were getting tired. He must keep the fish working against the pitifully small pressure he dared use. He knew he was never going to possess this fish, because it was too good, too beautiful for the incompetent likes of Richard Adgate.

For a long time the fish hung into the current. He managed to reach the paddle and to push away from the hostile bank—at least for the moment, though the canoe turned perversely in the current and wind, as if it, too, had an opinion about the outcome.

He had time to think that he was not enjoying any of this. His hopes were ridiculous; whatever gods of luck there were had chosen him for their sport.

Yet the fish fought for its life, and did Richard Adgate want to kill to have it? He *had* to kill in order to have it—a soft hesitation immediately gone, banished as too stupid to consider. If only he hadn't been so impatient, and had put on a new leader, maybe six to eight pounds; this was no little midsummer trout brook in New Hampshire. What all this showed was a major flaw in his character, the story of his life. *Unprepared* was his motto.

But the fish stayed on. The wind had been coming up, blowing the canoe up into the current, but at least near the center of the river. Though he'd been turning and turning, he began to see a pattern in the fish's runs; it liked a certain oval area of water and never went to either bank or to the dead spruce. Maybe bigger monsters lurked there and kept it away, although what of its own element might frighten a fish this large he didn't want to think about. Maybe the fish was as stupid as he was, but you didn't get that large by being stupid.

Time passed, and passed, his arms aching, his nervousness institutionalized, solidified. He had a vaguely hopeful theory that the longer he kept the fish from its fish-business, the weaker it would have to become. Sure, just think of salmonoids as weaklings.

He found himself guiding, turning the living fish but thinking of other things. He wondered if he would ever be brave enough to camp out alone here, say on one of the small islands in this bay, alone in the dark night. Could he endure the blackness of that night, the silence of it, when even in broad daylight he was unnerved by the strange coves of a small bay seen in passing?

A rose-white slab glinted over there on the surface—a large fish rolled, and it was his fish, on its side for a moment, its tail giving a tired-looking scull or two before it sank down again. Then there were a few pulls, weaker shakes of the head, weak though irritated: What *is* this thing pulling on me all the time? And he thought all at once that he might actually bring the fish to the side of the canoe. Maybe. It had been on more than half an hour now.

The fish came, slowly. When it first saw the canoe, it ran, but not far, and he gently snubbed its run and turned it again. If he startled it too much, it would simply run away from him, because it was not really as weak as it seemed. Nothing was as it seemed. With the rod in his left hand, the line snubbed with his fingers, he sneakily got the big boat net handy, then went back to his gentle urging, turning, and soon the fish was next to the canoe. With desperate strength he took the net and scooped it up and into the canoe amidst all the spilled and tangled gear and line and who cared what. He was on his knees, his hands over the net and his fish. What teeth it had! It was a brook trout, all right, but changed by size into something oceanic, jaws like forearms, gill-covers like saucers.

The Gray Ghost was deep in its tongue, the tippet not even in existence any longer. His metal stringer was in the mess in the bottom of the boat, and he clipped one hanger through the trout's lower jaw and another around a thwart into the chain—of course he would never trust it in the water. As if it understood, the trout thrashed itself out of his grasp, into the air, then came down thrashing on the mess of lures, eyelets, spoons, net, line, sinkers, flies, reel-grease tubes, spinners, hooks, split rings—all the picky little toys and trinkets a fisherman collects.

And it was all right. He could sit back, drift where he would, and look at the sky, which he did for a while. Then he paddled over to the sand bar and retrieved his hat, his good old felt Digger hat that had protected him from so many storms. Good old hat!

He took his De-liar from his fly-fishing vest and measured the fish: twenty-eight inches, eight and a half pounds. The beautiful great fish trembled, dying as it must, as it must. And with that flicker of sadness the world changed for him. It was seven o'clock on this subarctic afternoon, a crisp southeast wind raising a few whitecaps on Baie Borne, the bluest of waters. He pulled the canoe up on the sand and carefully cleaned everything up, put everything away, sponged out all water and slime, made everything shipshape and Bristol fashion.

On his way back through the long passage, he headed into the wind, his bow pounding across the larger waves, a Laurentide Ale in his hand. There lay the trout, monstrous, outsized, beyond dreaming of. It didn't matter that it was nothing he deserved, that because of his clownish errors he should have lost it six times. The knowledge of his fear and awkwardness would only heighten memory. All the rest of his life he would see the pure and desolate bay and the pulse of incoming river, its turbulence meeting the blue water. The black density of the spruce, on island and hill, grew vividly into the past.

But what if he'd lost this fish? Would the shadows fall across these hills in tones of lead? Maybe that alternate fate was past and gone, as were so many alternatives, large and small, to the course of a life. No matter now; he was brought back, for better or worse, along a line as sure and fragile as his own.

Cold Water

Donald Hall

step around a gate of bushes
in the mess
and trickle of a dammed stream
and my shoe fills with cold water. I
enter the shade
of a thicket, a black pool,
a small circle of stunned drowsing air,

vaulted with birch which meets overhead
as if smoke
rose up and turned into leaves.
I stand on the roots of a maple
and imagine
dropping a line. My wrist jumps
with the pain of a live mouth hooked deep,

and I stare, and watch where the lithe stripe
tears water.
Then it heaves on my hand; cold,
squaretailed, flecked, revenant flesh
of a Brook Trout.
The pine forests I walked through
darken and cool a dead farmer's brook.

I look up and see the Iroquois
coming back
standing among the birches
on the other side of the black pool.

The five elders
have come for me, I am young,
my naked body whitens with cold

in the snow, blisters in the bare sun,
the ice cuts
me, the thorns of blackberries:
I am ready for the mystery.
I follow them
over the speechless needles
of pines which are dead or born again.

Doing It for Money

Ron Rau

I WAS always nuts about fishing. Don't ask me why—I don't know. I don't even want to know.

My earliest memory is of catching a fish, a Michigan bluegill. I caught it on a hot summer afternoon in the shade beneath a farmer's homemade wooden boat dock. I used a casting rod, a size 6 snelled hook, and a redworm. I couldn't pull it through the dock slats, though, and my father had to help. This is my earliest memory. I can't remember anything important happening before I caught that bluegill.

My major interests in high school were fishing, hunting, baseball, and football. When I had to choose among them, however, hunting and fishing won out. Hands down. On prom night, four of us went bass fishing instead of promenading. We were more interested in what we could lure with the gyrations of a Fred Arbogast Jitterbug than with Elvis Presley contortions.

After high school, I chose Central Michigan University, partly because of nearby trout streams, partly because of duck marshes and grouse cover. I remember one fall when I rented a shack seven miles from town. The shack was on a dirt road and in ideal hunting and fishing country. When I got tired of studying, which was often, I just picked up the appropriate gear and walked out the door to trout, ruffed grouse, wildfowl, deer, pheasant, and cottontails. Owing to these, I stayed around long enough to graduate.

I have spent the last nine years of my life fishing for a living in Southeast Alaska. And I still fish with a hook and line. Before then, I had never been on an ocean. Now, I can't get off it. I have an ocean-going boat, a thirty-thousand-dollar fishing permit, and an insurance salesman to support.

Some days I wish I were back at that shack in Michigan, studying and trout fishing. Mostly, though, I love fishing for money. The more fish you catch, the more money you earn. The simplicity of this has brought tears to my eyes. Second axiom: The longer you stay in business, the more you learn, the more fish you catch. Imagine having a job that pays you exactly for what you know?

Every year you learn enough to make a whole new set of mistakes. You also repeat, at least once, most of the old ones, which is another thing I have learned about this business.

Here's still another: Pacific salmon are not color-blind. I've spent a good ten grand learning it. All trollers have large inventories and color combinations of lures, most of which are the same basic shape and size. We are convinced that salmon can somehow distinguish a minute change or mixture of color, though it might be the only thing trollers agree on. Metal spoons, plastic plugs, and rubber-skirted hula-dress hoochies of various colors are what we spend our money on. If what they really want is a size 228 plug, it can pay you well to have at least a dozen on board.

King salmon. They have driven me through these nine years as snow through fire. Nine summers in a row gone, entirely consumed by a singular activity—the pursuit of Pacific salmon. And particularly for a single species of Pacific salmon—the king, or chinook, or, as the Canadian Indians call it, *tyee*. A live forty-pound king, shiny and gasping on the deck, and dripping wet and brilliant with color, is what keeps me going. It's the *possession* of this creature that keeps me going and has held me to the ocean these nine years.

King salmon are simply that beautiful. They are what a brook trout would look like if one ever got that big. They never cease to make you stop in wonderment as you go about boatly chores, stop whatever you're doing to stare at a trout so big. I know I shouldn't call them trout, but that's how I see them sometimes. Ocean trout.

There are approximately a thousand of us in Southeast Alaska who make a living trolling for salmon. And since we do so in an area that is so sparsely populated, we actually have some political clout. We have just enough to keep our salmon stocks healthy and on the rise, just enough to keep our fishery alive and make us believe that we'll be able to troll and earn a living into the year 2000.

We sometimes refer to ourselves as the last of the buffalo hunters. Maybe that explains why there are so many trollers from Montana. The old roundup reflex took them all the way to the Pacific shelf.

Of the hundred or so Alaskan trollers I know, five are from Montana. But I also know people trolling in Alaska from Ohio, Kentucky, Vermont, South Dakota, New York (*City*, even), New Jersey, Idaho, Louisiana, and Wisconsin. I know of five women who own their own trollers, three goofy New Zealanders who used to hunt deer commercially, and two Mexican trollers. There's a Swiss who has been trolling for twenty years and who spends his winters in Mexico, where he fishes for sharks and pesos. There's an ex-professional Italian basketball player and the brother of an NFL linebacker in our fleet. There's a black man who's married to a gypsy, and there are entire villages of Norwegians—all excellent fishermen.

The commercial trolling season in the Southeast opens October 1 and lasts until April 15. In October, there are only a few hundred boats working full time. In the summer, there are a thousand or so, meaning that in October, like anywhere else, the crowd is gone and you can sometimes have the "stream" all to yourself.

In October, you leave town and head immediately for a reef that you haven't fished for nearly a year. If there are no kings there, which is possible but highly unlikely, you just make the "pothole circuit." You can fish two or three potholes every day, which is not unlike trying two or three streams. In nine years, I've discovered a lot of little streams in the ocean and among the islands. Now I've got just about enough to keep me busy and I've nearly quit looking for new ones.

What freedom to be iced, fueled, and groceried for two weeks and running toward a reef you truly love (as much as you can love an underwater pile of rocks), a reef where you once had a two-grand day in November for just thirty-three fish. It's a reef that you considered leaving the ocean for many times last summer, and a reef that you really should give a try sometime in late July. But it's also a reef where you have planted a few hundreds pounds of lead trolling "cannonballs" and put in a hundred hours or so watching the fathometer and landmarks, meaning you've more than paid your dues to know and understand the reef. Now, though, you know it as a trouter knows a favorite stream.

The reef I'm fishing is the underwater extension of a prominent point halfway down this side of the island. The reef sticks out a mile or so into the strait, where a red navigational buoy marks its end. The buoy is an important key to fishing this reef, and so is a mountain ten miles away, on another island. When the distant mountain lines up with the little evergreen that grows by itself on top of the big rock at the very end of the prominence, it's my signal to turn out.

Mostly, however, I follow my "trout stream," one hundred and twenty feet below, with the fathometer. It's roughly four miles long, and I work its nooks and crannies, pillars, holes, shelves, plateaus, and tide-rips with my hand on the wheel and my eyes on an electronic blip.

The first hour of fishing pretty much tells you what you're in for. Either you're catching or you're not. If you are catching, you are continuously back and forth between cockpit and cabin (unless you have a deck hand), landing fish while the boat is in a long gentle turn that will take you over the same spot again. If you are not catching, you merely stay at the wheel and steer the boat and power the cannonballs over shallow water—wondering the whole time why the hell you aren't catching. As the boat nears the end of the drag without a bump, you get more and more depressed. You were, of course, hoping for another two-grand day. What you got, though, was nothing. Zero.

A fact emerges: If you're not a manic-depressive prior to becoming a professional fisherman, you will be after a few years. It's an occupational malady. Fish are manic-depressive, as are the ocean and the weather. Since these are your elements, you can't help but get caught up.

Fall and winter king fishing is for the enthusiast who owns a very dependable boat and A-one anchor gear. It's also for "low-liners" with shaky boats who fish out in front of town all day. The post-equinox storms charge down off the Canadian Rockies all of October and November like the cavalry of a drug-crazed and bloodthirsty general, and the only defense is to hide!

The winter troller has a large collection of anchorages that are protected from sou'easters. These storms last from a day to a week, and you fish between them. Any fish you catch in winter are a bonus, windfall money you cannot really count on, and therefore consider pure profit.

Most "high-liners," though, try to tie up for the winter as early as possible. It's a matter of pride and common sense. Tying a boat up as early as possible—sometimes as early as late August—is also the closest thing in the business that describes success.

Summer is when the troller makes his money, and the "money fish" is the silver salmon. We call them cohos and, fondly, locos. Some cohos will fight the troll gear with such fervor that they separate their throat latches, bleed to death, and come up trailing behind the boat like limp dishrags.

Cohos are also the most unpredictable of the five Pacific species. Some years, they hang twelve miles offshore all of July, and then, on a single tide, rush the beach and plug the inside waters all the way to the spawning streams. Other summers, they come to the beaches right away, and it's worthless to fish very far offshore. They might come all at once, or in waves, or maybe they'll just trickle in all summer long. When the other species are late, cohos tend to show up early. The only constant that I have noticed about cohos these last nine years is that on the Fourth of July they will bite like the firecrackers they are. The Fourth is usually the first really good day.

During the peak of the run, an ocean-going troller is looking for at least a hundred cohos a day. And the thing that haunts every single one of us is that somewhere along the three-hundred-mile Southeast shoreline, on any day in July, someone is catching that many . . . or more. The highest score last summer was five hundred and eighty fish. That, I hasten to add, is the highest score anyone has heard of in quite some time.

Trollers favor one of two basic strategies. The first is called the "Homesteader" strategy. These trollers concentrate on about ten miles of shoreline that they know very well. They take whatever comes along, and usually catch enough to make expenses. But even Homesteaders will leave if they go two or three days without covering costs.

The second strategy is called "Smokeholing." Smokeholers are radio fishermen. They outnumber the Homesteaders and provide most of the summer's entertainment. A guy I know, who owns a boat called the *Patsy*, once got word (via sideband radio) of a big bite at Cape Muzon, the southernmost cape in the Southeast. It was noon, and he was fishing off Cape Fairweather, roughly two hundred miles north. He raised his gear, dropped the throttle into the "smokehole," and arrived at Muzon at noon the next day, just in time to kill the bite. That evening, a partner who had stayed at Fairweather coded two hundred, meaning fish had suddenly showed up. The *Patsy* went into the smokehole again and arrived back at Fairweather in time for the evening bite the next day. The absolute worst thing a Smokeholer can see coming toward him on a smooth horizon is another Smokeholer.

Even when a troller is having his best day of the season, he's still haunted by the thought of what's going on at the next cape, forty miles away. Or maybe he's coded with someone fishing there and knows what is going on and it "seems" to be better. Another axiom of the business: No matter how well you're doing, someone is always doing better.

During the summer, the VHF channels are dominated by trollers calling each other for information. This information is passed along subtly, in code. Year after year, elaborate coding systems are created between partners, or groups of partners. Possibly a "secret" channel is used at a specific time each day. The code tells where you are and how many you're catching. If someone has a red apple at the Fourth of July place, it could pay you well to know what a red apple is and where the Fourth of July place is. Two of the best radio fishermen I know are independents, who don't habitually code with anybody. After years of listening in on radio conversations, though, they have learned the habits of the fleet and know where certain boats like to fish. They have listened to enough coding conversations between the partner groups to crack the code sometimes simply by the way it's delivered. All's fair in love and war . . . and commercial fishing.

The steadily increasing competition for king salmon, the steadily decreasing fishing season, which was drastically reduced in the early 1980s, and the growing efficiency of the fleet make it harder and harder every year to earn a living by trolling. Beginning on the first day in July, you can't afford to miss a single fishable day for six weeks running. Which means I can't afford to take a day off and go fishing.

There is a scene repeated every summer that reminds me of this. I'm leaving a harbor early on a July morning, the weather is gorgeous, the water glasslike, and the swell only that of the breathing ocean. Coming out of the harbor and rounding a bend, I see the ocean horizon and notice hundreds of birds feeding a mile or so up the beach. I know I should ignore them and run a course straight offshore, where everyone knows most of the cohos are hanging. I should finish breakfast, drop the lines six miles out, and grind away until sunset, which is sixteen hours away. If I do, I'll have a hundred fish. After all, it's been that way for the past three days.

But nooo, oh, nooo. I have to check out the feeding birds, which invariably are diving on needlefish that the cohos have pushed to the surface. All around the boat, the glassy water is alive with the raindrops of thousands of needlefish. When I look into the water, I suspect there may be millions of them and not merely thousands. Beneath the surface and as far down as I can see is a biological mass that leaves me speechless.

And the cohos. Oh, the cohos! Big and hungry and slashing through the surface as if they're on a take-no-prisoners mission are feeding cohos. I stand on the deck and watch this. Something cosmic is happening before my very eyes. God whispers to me and says: "Thus have they always done . . . forever and ever."

The sky is full of activity as all kinds of sea birds are in on this bite—gulls, sea pigeons, murres, and other diving ducks. Birds are arcing in midair, diving headfirst into the ocean, squawking, flapping, hovering, fighting each other, tossing their heads back to gulp down a wiggling silver sliver and then jumping back into flight to go after another. The racket of the birds creates a screaming melee that actually drowns out the diesel. The bite is on.

What I can't hear is the slashing water as cohos break the surface. I can only imagine what is going on below, which I assume mirrors the frantic activity of the birds above. And not being able to hear the coho boils is maddening, for it's the sound that excites a fisherman the most.

Sometimes I'll shut the engine down and just listen. I yearn to be in a wooden skiff bobbing silently inside this show, this circus. I yearn to be in it with a fly rod and Silver-and-Yellow Bucktail. Instead of being three feet above the ocean, let me be into it, as far as my weight sinks the skiff. Let me be there among these *millions* of needlefish and have a coho slash into the mass. And as these little bait fish comically jump ki-yi-ing out of the water ahead of a charging salmon, let a dozen or so jump into my skiff, which will leak just enough to keep them alive and squirming.

And also, King Neptune, sir, let me hook just one coho of at least ten pounds. Let me fight it a great long while, so I can finally feel its desire and power. Let it take all my fly line and then all the backing as it races and charges through the ocean. Let it dance and run and dive and tail-walk. Let it do all these things and prove why cohos are truly the fighters of all the Pacific salmon.

But no. I have all those bills to pay. Hell, I have to pay for simply *being* here. So I restart the engine and usually decide to fish right there, even though I know it won't last long and the coho school probably isn't all that large. I put on lighter leads, raise the lines to ten fathoms, and troll up and down through the melee.

At nine o'clock the sun is high, the cohos have gone off the bite, the needlefish have sunk to the bottom, and only a few birds still hover over what once was and is no longer. I've lost another cannonball and have only twenty fish aboard. The boats offshore have forty or fifty by now, and all I can think is: I knew it, I knew it . . . I knew it.

Confessions of a Catfish Heretic

Stephen J. Bodio

I WANT to sing the praises of a fish whose pursuit will never be chic. In an era when stockbrokers and Manhattan models dress themselves from the pages of the L. L. Bean catalog, when blue jeans cost more if they're partly worn out, some forms of outdoor recreation are more equal than others. The trout, for instance, has progressed from an already high establishment status to being *the* yuppie fish. Whereas the catfish, whether a hornpout the size of a bullfrog tadpole or a blue cat with the heft and docility of a Harley Davidson, is not going to make the cover of *Field & Stream*, let alone the columns of *Esquire*.

You can still talk about fly fishing in New York. It enjoys all kinds of comfortable associations—literary, gentlemanly, nostalgic. Successful writers fish for trout. I'm told that Mikhail Baryshnikov does. Even fashion magazines run four-color spreads on Hardy reels. Meanwhile, subliterate entrepreneurs use catfish to sell stinkbaits in the classified section of *Fur-Fish-Game*.

Catfish are socially unacceptable. Your basic trout angler stands in a glossy-magazine river idyll, sporting a military mustache, clothes by Ralph Lauren, vest by Orvis. His cat-fishing counterpart is a gap-toothed yokel in stained coveralls with a cheek full of Red Man and a tractor cap, hoisting a slimy monster with all the presence of a feed sack full of bowling balls. If his picture appears at all, it's a grainy

photo in the back pages of a Kansas weekly. As one salmonoid snob said to me, "Ugly water, ugly fish, and not very beautiful people."

Don't get me wrong. I'm not here to apologize for mudcats. Nor do I wish to elevate cat fishing by using fancy tools. It's just that, to me, the dark corners of sport are where essence and art still lurk.

I was raised right, as they say out here. I grew up near Boston doing all the correct things. I cast dry flies to rising fish, crawled up tunnel-like mountain streams after tiny native trout, waded shifty winter sand bars near the mouths of tidal rivers searching for "salters." I can (or could) lean an angled roll cast in under the overhanging lip of cedar in a black-water swamp while simultaneously brushing away black flies with my left hand, knowing that if I did everything *just so*, the bright line against the darkness would disclose a perfect brookie.

And then I moved to New Mexico. In the pools and ditches of the Rio Grande, I discovered the catfish.

Some of my friends, especially Easterners, say it's a case of "love the one you're with." You know, down there in the desert and all that, so far from the water, the poor bastard's gotta *make do*. But it's more complicated than that. Far more complicated. For one thing, New Mexico probably has more miles of blue-ribbon trout water than Massachusetts, full of bigger trout. Also, the catfish lurk forty miles away and two thousand feet below, steaming in the summer's heat.

I think it has more to do with the fact that, over the last ten years, fly fishing has begun to make me nervous. It has become high tech and pseudo scientific, full of "significant innovations" that are immediately surpassed by even *more* significant innovations. Streamside chatter is heavy on entomological Latin; people who didn't know a mayfly from a mosquito ten years ago discourse on *Hexagenia* and *Baetis* in a cloud of pipe smoke. In fact, I fear that my old pastime has become the blood sport of urbanites and vegetarians, so refined that somebody who actually eats fish is considered to be as spooky and recidivist as a cannibal. Theirs is a sport that has no place for a piscivorous man with one old cane rod, an ancient Pflueger reel, and a firm attitude of "fish the Adams, ignore the hatch."

Bass fishing is even worse. Maybe it's still pursued by "good old boys"—but what kind of sport, for the poor romantic, is one that involves ten-thousand-dollar fishing machines and reels that look, at best, like someone sat on them and, at worst, like ray guns? No, if we're going to get down to the essence of fishing, we're going to have to get down to bait—the truly organic lure—and catfish, whose only bard compared them to animated mud. Preferably big catfish.

I have to admit that I love to cast big live animals after big ugly predatory fish, to probe murky water with a necessarily stout rod on a slow river at night. And, unlike neighbors who prefer the rather bland white flesh of the catfish to anything else—personally, I was raised on blues—it's the fishing itself, bound up inextricably with its unique environment, that excites me. I still love fly fishing: the arc and curve and line and flex of it, its tools, finer than anything used in sport except possibly fine double shotguns. But there's something biological and smelly and wholly real about sitting down here in this beautiful, nightmarish swampscape dangling a four-footed animal into another world, searching for something that scares divers.

Of course, you work up to this kind of thing by stages. In my case, I started by going out with neighbors. My recollection of that initiation is warm, and as vivid, I think, as the impressions of any trout fisherman when he is first introduced to a gurgling New England brook.

We're sitting on a sandbank on the west side of the Rio Grande, maybe a quarter-mile south of the San Acacia diversion dam. On the bridge over the dam, you stand in a roar, with water cascading through the spillways in a standing wave that would smash you like a fly if you fell off the narrow catwalk. The air is full of swallows and oxygen, and the wet smell of life and decay. Upstream the river swings through flat-water bends and sand bars, with a promise of waterfowl in the fall. Downstream is a maze of riffles and waves, sand bars and drowned willows. You know that these holes and backwaters contain fish, thriving on the oxygen-rich water and the bounty of the stunned river creatures created by the dam.

This is theory. My friend Chubby Torres embodies practice and empirical knowledge, demonstrated by his laden stringer containing two fat little yellow bullheads and four channel cats ranging in size up to one that might go seven pounds. As we arrive, his partner, Shirley, is skidding in another fish. It glows brilliant yellow as it turns belly-up in the liquid silt. "Just a bullhead," says Chubby. "Throw it back. They taste muddy." Although I have eaten and enjoyed its relative, the black bullhead or hornpout, back east, I say nothing. I'm here to learn.

"Here's how you do it," coaches Chubby. "We use crappie rigs—room for two hooks and a little sinker at the end. Hook your worms through the collar so they oscillate in the current." Chubby is even more given to trisyllables than I am.

"Now cast upstream, reel in twice, and let the current take it." He suits the action to his words. The line comes tight at about ninety degrees from the bank and swings downstream at a startling rate. "I let it go down until it fishes the hole right by that big rock. The fish get tired of fighting the strength of the current and look for slow places. I put my rod down, right here"—he leans the rod on a fallen cotton-wood snag—"and wait. If it's a bullhead, it gives a hard tug. If it's a channel cat, it'll just give a nibble. I wait a minute and then hit it hard," says Chubby, striking an imaginary catfish so hard that his spin-casting rig bends double.

He seems to be right. Five minutes haven't passed when he takes the line up with his index finger, tests it for a moment, then makes another dramatic strike. This time the rod tip stays bent, vibrates, pulls down nearly to the water, and then up again. "These fish fight," Chubby explains, still in his teaching mode. In a couple of minutes, he works it in close to the bank, a shining, popeyed creature with a spike dorsal and a Gorgon's snaky beard, wiggling in the mud like an amphibian. This one is eighteen inches long—no mere bullhead, but a real channel cat. "And they *are* good to eat."

Yes, they are. I can testify to that. I've caught two of the river's species of catfish so far—the scorned yellow bullhead and the channel cat, *Ictalurus punctatus*. The bullhead is an ungraceful, toadlike, rotund little creature, though with a brilliant canary-yellow belly; I suspect its unpopularity has more to do with its ugliness and small size—usually about a foot long—than with its gustatory quality, though the books agree with Chubby that if not iced soon after capture, its flesh will be "mushy."

The channel cat, though just as likely a consumer of worms and stinkbaits and rotten chicken necks as its little cousin, will also take baitfish and lures and even—though I maintain that using them is a little pretentious—flies. It has obviously evolved to fight stronger currents than the bullhead, currents that have carved it into a classic gamefish profile. Channel cats are the number-one catfish of big rivers, commercial ponds, and southern fish fries. They are stream-lined and graceful, with deeply forked tails and pointed heads. Even their olive or steel-gray-and-white color seems classier than the bull-heads' mud brown and frog-throat yellow. And perhaps because stronger muscles are needed to fight the current, their flesh is firmer and finer than that of their peasant relatives. In fact, to an unbiased eye, a channel cat is more graceful than any bass that ever lived, and, in shape, except for its broad mouth and rolling eyes, not dissimilar to (I have to say it) a trout.

You can fish for channel cats in much the same manner as for trout. If you follow certain iron-hard dirt roads off Highway 180 in the Gila until you reach the upright bars that mark the edge of the de jure wilderness, you can hike down into a landscape that, from above, looks about as hospitable as the moon. The climb down will make your joints creak, your knees ache, and your calves vibrate like plucked guitar strings. In the summer, it's also hot enough so that you should probably start at dawn, or at that precise point in the afternoon when the sun is low but not so low that you will have to hike past rattlers in the dark.

At the bottom, though, despite the heat reflected from rock to rock, it's a different world. The Gila sings over head-sized rocks and seethes through pebbly runs. Clusters of walnut trees blossom in the angle between the wall and the river, a tropical green so vivid that they look almost poisonous. Some trail veils of wild grape. Their shade is precise and almost cold. Golden Scott's orioles and luminous tanagers flash on and off like Christmas lights in the branches, and dozens of small unidentifiable flycatchers make short flights over the river and return, again and again, repetitious as skipping records.

Here is a good place to ease your transition from the Northeast to the tropics. The setting is alien, but the water itself is almost familiar. If you go far enough upstream, you can even find trout: first, stocked browns, then stocked rainbows, finally, if you are persistent enough to backpack in, native goldens. This stretch, however, has no trout, but contains a healthy population of smallmouth bass. Cast your spinner or a streamer fly, and that flash in the riffle is likely to be the same fish that attacks the same pattern on the Saco in Maine. Except when it has *whiskers*.

There is at least one more species of catfish in the rivers: the huge, ugly, voracious flathead, *Pylodictis olivaris*. It is narrow-tailed and broad-headed, mottled brown in color, and can weigh a hundred pounds. I have never caught one.

The flathead bears a close resemblance to the legendary European catfish or wels, *Silurus glanis*, which grows to fifteen feet. English writer and scientist Stephen Downes says of the wels, "There are various popular European stories, too, of the wels' feats: of the Hungarian angler who ran for three miles upstream by the treeless banks of the Danube with a giant wels in play; of the German wildfowlers who, instead of claiming to have seen waterfowl snatched under by giant pike, report the loss of their retrievers; Slavonic claims of child-eaters, man-eaters, horse-eaters . . . I repeat, they grow to fifteen feet."

Both the flathead and wels are predators. You don't just dump any old inanimate bait in the river to catch them—they like their meals to be alive. You can use worms, but a fish of a size you wouldn't necessarily throw back is better. Best of all is the waterdog, a colloquial name for the neotenic or permanently larval stage of the tiger salamander.

You get these things out of stock tanks, and catching them is a minor hunt in itself. I recommend taking along an eager child like my friend Floyd's thirteen-year-old son, Brandon—their reflexes are quicker and they don't mind getting soaked. I finally managed to grab one myself as it lazed above the weeds near the tank's surface. It was about ten inches long, soft and slimy and vibrating with cold life. Its face looked a lot like the face of a catfish, and its color was a mottled olive. It had hands and feet. I do not mention this lightly. Even though it evinces little pain when hooked through its gristly lips or membranous tail, a waterdog is just a little too much an "animal" for me to be entirely comfortable using it for bait.

Yet I did want to go monster fishing, and I wanted very much to do it right, to suspend a large, active, living creature above the bottom as the dark came on and the great nocturnal predators began to stir. . . .

I have done just that. I have gone down in search of river monsters a half-dozen times now, down in the flooded no man's land south of the Bosque del Apache and north of Elephant Butte reservoir. This is a strange place, flat and low, overrun with the feathery alien growth of tamarisk. The desert looms up above. The only solid ground is ditchbanks. They run with geometrical precision along acequias that vanish ahead in perspective points like railroad tracks and that provide the only clear lines of view. Little groups of black, semiwild cattle appear and disappear in the salt-cedar thickets. It is hot and sticky and smells like water and dead fish and perfumed blossoms all mixed together. When a fitful breeze passes, it rattles the leaves on the immense cottonwoods that still dominate the ditchbanks. The birds are primitive—black cormorants, coots and gallinules, a tropical profusion of herons and snowy egrets. As dusk closes down, they begin to tune up, and the river sounds like every grade-B adventure movie you ever saw when you were a kid. The only thing missing is crocodiles.

107

★ ★ ★

I'm down at the very end of the ditchbank road, where it runs out into the narrow north end of the reservoir. The sun is down, although the high desert ridges across the river still glow. Mosquitoes are whining by often enough to make me glad I reek of repellent. There is a night heron squawking across the ditch and something moaning in the weeds. I sit beside a seven-foot bait-casting rod, rather like the popping rods they used to favor for tarpon off the Texas coast, a rod I picked up in an Albuquerque store after rejecting dozens of too-short bass rods. It is equipped with a one-pound yellow Australian Alvey reel and two hundred-odd yards of twenty-five-pound-test monofilament over a bedding of braided line. The rod juts up from a nest of rocks. Occasionally, its tip bends a little from the exertions of the foot-long salamander that swims in tethered circles thirty feet out. I watch it like a hawk, waiting.

I have been coming down here for weeks. I have caught silver and olive channel cats in the river by day and big-scaled reticulated carp in the ditches and backwaters at dusk. I haven't yet found a flathead. But I know he's out there.

My Friend, My Friend

Robert Traver

SOME OF the loveliest places I know to fish are also some of the toughest, and for many years Frenchman's Pond was one of them—that is, until Jim the Indian came along.

The pond is fed by a narrow stream that begins in a sprawling cedar swamp lying several miles north of it, as well as by the many underwater springs that line its entire length. These springs keep spouting ice water all year round and doubtless account for the joyous fact that only wild brook trout dare live in it. Their presence also explains why my fishing pals and I are so drawn to it, despite the many hazards of fishing the place.

The pond's swamp-fed feeder stream joins it about half a mile above our fishing shack. There, it suddenly swells into a wide and mostly shallow body of crystal-clear ice water, hazard enough in itself—as all chronic pursuers of the elusive brook trout well know or must soon learn. There were still more hazards to face, though.

The entire camp side of the pond is lined, up to the water's edge, by a dense growth of tall trees, mostly spruces and tamaracks, extending clear down to the old beaver dam. And each one of these many trees seems to take a special delight in parting fishermen from their favorite flies.

Consequently, we learned early to fish from the open bog on the other side, where there was plenty of room to cast, and to which we soon built a wooden footbridge at a narrow spot just below the camp. But the boggy side, though easier to reach, presented plenty of problems of its own. For the entire bog was covered with a tenacious

growth of swampy bushes that extended clear back to the low glacier-honed granite bluffs that run a serpentine course along both sides of the pond. This growth was not only a hazard in itself but also served to cover the many hidden water holes that lurked beneath its course.

This treacherous growth grew right up to the water's edge and down into the pond itself, causing a constant danger of snarling lines and leaders, not to mention lost tippets and flies, as well as trout. For a time we tried trimming these bushes, especially along the water's edge, but this only seemed to stimulate their growth; so we sighed and put down our shears and took up our rods again. We also tried wading or floating in rubber tubes to avoid the bogs, but soon gave that up because of the treacherous bottom, an incredible snarl of silt and slippery rocks and sharp-edged ancient beaver cuttings that had evidently been accumulating ever since the last glacier passed that way. A further reason, in fact the main one, is that we soon discovered that any fisherman who dared to expose or suspend himself in all that ice water for more than a few minutes risked freezing his (here the appropriate idiom is optional), leaving him in a semicomatose state that doctors more elegantly call "hypothermia." We also soon discovered that ice-water fishing gravely depleted our bourbon budget in our efforts to revive each other.

For a spell we tried boating, but soon abandoned that for both practical and aesthetic reasons. Practical because the minute one stepped in a boat and started clanking one's way among all those wily trout in all that clear water seemed only to scare the hell out of them. Aesthetic because sitting in a rocking boat attempting to cast a decent fly possessed all the charm and grace of trying to court a reluctant mermaid in a slippery bathtub. So back to the bogs we went, teetering and floundering, once again stoically losing leaders and flies, along with trout and our tempers—that is, until that lucky day when Jim the Indian came along and saved us.

I'd been fishing alone for hours, teetering and balancing my way from one boggy spot to another, lurching and stumbling along like a drunk on a trampoline. Thus far I'd only snarled my leader three times and lost two flies. The trout were occasionally rising, mostly out of range off the opposite shore, and I was having trouble finding the magic fly. Just then, a nice trout rose right off the boggy bank where I stood, so I swiftly changed to that season's favorite fly, called—my, my, I plumb forget; our favorite flies change so often.

First, I deftly fed out enough line to reach the trout, all in accordance with the latest dope in the casting manuals; then I made a quick double-haul and went into my business cast. Out, out sailed the line, the leader and fly following because they had to, the latter two finally folding forward with the grace of a ballerina's arm, the fly coming to rest upon the water's surface with the elfin lightness of a windblown wisp of thistle.

The trout rose; I struck; *ping* went my flyless leader as it raced back toward my ear. I stepped back to avoid it, and found one leg bogged down in an unseen water hole up to my thigh.

"Hi!" I heard a voice calling as I wallowed to extricate myself. I paused to look, and standing on the old boat dock across the pond was a smiling bear of a man carrying a loaded packsack, holding a rod case in one hand, and saluting me with the other.

"Hi!" I managed to croak.

"I'm Jim Washinawatok, from Wisconsin," he called across to me. "I live on the Menomonee Indian reservation down there."

"Oh," I called back, still trying to extricate myself. "Give me a minute—or maybe an hour—and I'll be right over."

I finally made it and wallowed my way down to the bridge, where a smiling Jim met me, and we shook hands. He was a powerfully built man with sloping shoulders and straight black hair framing a handsome, carved-looking face, much like that of the man who once modeled for the old Buffalo nickel.

"How'd you ever find your way, way back here?" I asked when at last I'd caught my breath.

Jim explained that he'd read some of my past yarns about Frenchman's and had long wanted to visit both it and me. But he didn't quite know where to write me, so he finally decided to come.

"But how did you track me down?" I repeated.

"Got hold of a county plat book with all the township maps showing land ownership, and finally tracked you down."

"My, my. I feel like a dismounted John Wayne. First time I've ever been tracked down by a real Indian," I said. "Welcome to Frenchman's Pond."

Just then, there was a whoosh of wings as a pair of ducks flew over us, upstream bound, veering upward and then down once again, barely skimming the water, like a pair of practicing jets. As if by signal, a nice trout rose in their wake, and at the same time we heard the haunting cry of an unseen loon. I glanced at Jim, whose lips seemed to be moving as if in silent prayer.

"Like the place, Jim?" I asked.

Jim nodded before he spoke. "Being in this place at this hour is like coming home after a long absence," he said. "Not only do I like the place, but I've already fallen in love with it."

Another good trout rose off the boggy shore to our left, and as we watched its outgoing ripples, still another trout rose just above where we sat.

"Better get rigged up, Jim," I said, getting up and grabbing for my rod. "Those rises seem to have revived me, so let's go give it a try."

After Jim had rigged up, I took him on a quick tour of the place: the camp, with its long folding bed that was a couch during the day; the crowded toolhouse; the winding trail to the outhouse. Then we hiked down to the dam along the wooded granite bluffs on the camp-side trail. We found the trout rising and fished for an hour or so, returning all the fish except two, which I insisted Jim keep for his breakfast. (I, still a slave to indoor plumbing, preferred to sleep at home.)

We crossed over on the arc of the dam, gathering a batch of wild watercress on the way, and then hiked back toward the bridge on an old needle-carpeted game trail, picking a mess of chanterelle mushrooms to go with Jim's trout and watercress breakfast. We had almost reached the bridge when Jim, who was behind me, touched my arm.

"Look," he whispered, pointing to where a lovely buck deer, its horns still in velvet, was standing under a giant lone white pine tree in an open patch of granite. The deer stood facing us with large unblinking eyes, looking as still and frozen as a statue on a lawn.

"*Whew!*" Jim blew, sounding like a deer himself, and the deer wheeled and leapt and suddenly was gone, leaving only a lone pine tree growing out of an open patch of granite.

"Great place to put a tepee," Jim said, staring at the scene.

"Great idea," I absently said, my mind more on a certain six-pack that awaited me back in the bush car.

Once across the bridge, Jim cleaned out his trout while I raided the six-pack and turned on my battery-run tape player. Then we sat outside batting mosquitoes and watched the sun go down and the trout begin to rise, all to the piano music of Claude Debussy.

It was then that Jim, almost shyly, broached the subject, asking me if I'd ever thought of building a few rustic wooden platforms out from the water's edge on the boggy side. "Might make casting easier and also save some leaders and flies and possibly even a few trout," he smilingly explained.

113

"Never really thought of it," I confessed. "Maybe someday I'll give it a try."

"Mind if I try making a model," Jim said. "Saw a lot of old rough boards and two-by-fours piled behind the toolhouse."

"Fine, Jim," I said, finishing my beer and reprieving Mr. Debussy and heading for my bush car to take off for home. "See you tomorrow. Can I bring you anything?"

"Maybe two or three pounds of mixed spikes," Jim called after me as I left.

The next day I arrived at camp around noon, bristling with spikes. As I rolled down the hill, there stood Jim across the pond, calmly fly-casting off a brand-new platform that he'd already built and anchored in place since we'd parted the evening before.

"Great idea, Jim," I hollered across to him, walking down to the dock.

"You ain't seen nothing yet," Jim hollered back. "There's two more new ones just below the bridge. Rig up and come give 'em a try."

"But you should have waited for me to give you a hand, Jim. How'd you ever get them across the narrow bridge?"

"Boated 'em across."

"But the old boat leaks like a sieve," I hollered, coining a phrase.

"Not any more. Caulked it last night with some of the bags of unused cement I found when I cleaned out the toolhouse."

"Well, I'll be damned," I said, hurrying back to camp to grab my already rigged-up rod. Once there, I found a spotless camp, even to freshly baited and re-set mousetraps. "Place hasn't been this clean since it was built," I murmured to myself as I grabbed my rod.

Jim's love affair with Frenchman's Pond began the time he built those first casting platforms on his first trip there nearly twenty years ago. Since then, he's come back every chance he's had, which is at least once a season, and usually more. During that time, he has transformed the place from a bog-teetering sanatorium for frustrated fishermen into a kind of sylvan anglers' paradise. All this he has somehow managed to do without much changing the wild and unkempt look the place must have had from the time of the last glacier.

I could probably write a fairly hefty book about all the things that Jim has done to improve the fishing at the old pond. He still prefers to work alone; one of the reasons, I suspect, is so that he can continue to surprise me. There are now over a score of casting platforms along both sides of the pond, all joined together by boardwalks of rough planks. All he seems to want or expect from me is to keep him well supplied with spikes and planks and two-by-fours.

One morning when I arrived at camp, I found him toting an entire tree down to the narrows, just above the bridge, as the starting "anchor" of still another protective brush pile for the trout, of which he had already built several.

The tree was a "leaner," Jim explained, that is, one already uprooted by age or the wind, and he had sawed off the uprooted bottom and trimmed the branches and lugged it at least a half-mile, a feat roughly akin to carrying an upright piano across a freshly plowed field.

He has also built a series of anchored rafts at strategic spots, not to fish from, but as protection and cover for the trout, many if not most of whose enemies seem to come from above, ravenous creatures like ospreys, eagles, kingfishers, and loons—as well as us loony fishermen. He has also built several extra-long casting platforms from the tree-lined side to allow for guarded backcasts at persistent rises that could not be reached from the boggy side.

Then came the summer when I arrived at camp and found still another big surprise: Jim had brought his wife, Gwen. I had known he was married and had two daughters, but he had neglected to tell me that he had wedded a woman who looked like an Indian princess. With her gleaming black hair framing her large dark eyes and comely face, she also conjured up boyhood pictures that I still carried in my mind of the beautiful Pocahontas.

Gwen did not fish, but preferred to sit outside and watch our antics while she sketched or sewed or worked on the studies she had brought along from the state university. She had already graduated in nursing but was continuing to take courses in medical and related subjects, so that she might one day permanently return to the reservation and both teach and spread her knowledge among her own tribespeople, particularly in the world-afflicted area of alcohol and drug abuse.

The first evening, after fishing, all three of us sat outside and watched the sun go down behind the ancient granite bluffs across the pond, a scene broken only by the rising trout and the evening flight of birds and the call of the frogs. The sight was so primitively beautiful that I overstayed my leave and, instead, sneaked up to my bush car and brought back my tape player and a favorite cassette.

It was well I did, because as the sun finally sank and darkness began to take over, the sky slowly began to brighten and glitter, suddenly becoming aflame with a series of eerie lights: the first northern lights of the season. I reached for my tape player and sat and watched the strange lights shifting and melting across the sky in great dripping organ pipes of silent melody.

Listening to Anna Moffo singing the haunting "Vocalise" by Rachmaninoff on the tape player was moving enough in itself, but doing so while beholding such a rare heavenly spectacle left us frozen in the grip of ecstatic chill. Even after the music had ceased and the lights in the sky had faded, we sat there in silence. Finally, I heard someone speaking, or half murmuring, in an awed, feminine voice: "I love this place."

After that, Gwen accompanied Jim on his annual trip to the pond as frequently as she could. Often, instead of fishing, the three of us would go exploring the back roads in the bush car, pausing to pick whatever wild berries or cherries or mushrooms might be out, sometimes winding up dining at some obscure rural café on such neglected "gourmet" delights as genuine Cornish pasties or Italian polenta— rarely found anymore in even the fanciest franchised restaurants.

Then came the recent summer when, for family reasons, I had to be away during the last few days of Jim's annual visit. When I returned home, I quickly mounted the bush car and headed for the pond, rarin' to go, hoping that Jim hadn't left yet. But he and his car were gone, and instead I found a note pinned to the camp door written in Jim's beautiful script.

> *Before entering this castle, sir, please cross the bridge and start down the deer trail, pausing at the lone pine.*
>
> *Jim*

I followed orders, wondering what new surprise was coming this time, pausing at the lone pine, and there, standing next to it on the bare granite rocks, was a beautiful towering Indian tepee, the tall slender trees that supported it reaching witch-fingered out of the top.

Back inside the camp I found a note lying on the table:

> *I did it myself, using only "leaners," and I hope you like it because it's the first one I ever built.*
>
> *Jim*
>
> *P.S. Take a look behind the camp door.*

I looked and found a fresh strip of white birch bark framed in birch twigs hanging from a nail. There was writing on it, so I sat at the camp table overlooking the pond, the better to see, and this is what I read, written by my friend and fellow writer Jim the Indian, out at Frenchman's Pond:

COME BACK, GRANDFATHER

We walked here once, Grandfather.
These trees, ponds, these springs and streams,
And that big flat rock across the water over there.
We used to meet with you over there—
Remember, Grandfather?—and
We would smoke and talk of many things.
We would drum and dance and sing
And after a while make offerings.
Then we would sing the travelling song
And would go our ways
And sometimes we would see your signs
On the way to our lodges.

But something happened, Grandfather.
We have lost our way somewhere and
Everything is going away.
The four-legged, the trees, springs and streams,
Even the big water where the Laughing
Whitefish goes, and the big sky of many eagles
Are saying goodbye.
Come back, Grandfather, come back.

The Way a Woman Thinks

Dan
Gerber

I LOVE to watch Norman work out a fly. It's like a ballet or something, the way the white line loops out against the dark trees. Like rope tricks or a magic show. I don't know how he does it, but I probably catch more fish than he does, with only a worm on. Sometimes I'll put on a Mepps or something and cast, but then maybe the line gets all screwed up on the reel. Norman says it's 'cause girls' elbows are built funny, but I don't think it matters. He says catching fish is nice, but that that's not the point. "Gracie," he'll say, "if all I wanted was fish, I'd use a net."

Norman's my brother, but he could be my father. He's old enough. He'd been living in New York for three years when our parents died. And until he moved back to look after me, he was mostly just someone my mother cried over and my father wouldn't talk about. He was married once, too, to somebody named Kate, but I never met her. They were divorced before he came back to Brainard. He said he wouldn't have come back otherwise, but that now he was glad that he had. He says home's the best place for a writer. And he says that the best thing our mom and dad ever did was make me.

Norman doesn't always keep the fish he catches, either. He takes 'em off the hook and kisses 'em, actually goes smack on their lips and then throws 'em back. He says he does it 'cause they've brought him pleasure, but I think it's because he doesn't want to clean them. Norman always finds a way to get out of cleaning fish. I don't mind, even though it's yucky to pull the guts out. I love a mess of perch or bluegills fried up with butter and flour. Norman's as good a cook as anybody.

I like being alone with Norman, just us on the river or the lake with the sound of the water and the birds. There're always birds to watch. I like kingfishers the best. They look like punkers with greasy hair and they swoop down over the water and chatter away like idiots, like they owned everything. Once I saw an osprey come out of the woods with a snake in its claws and circle the sun three times, like something out of a fairy tale. That was on the Muskegon. Norman says you can see all kinds of things when you're fishing that you can't see otherwise, because when you're fishing you're not really there in the ordinary sense, not just collecting sights, but really a part of things that are happening. He said that the animals don't see you as a person anymore. They see you as a crane or a heron or any other thing like that. He said that once at a place called Hell Roaring Creek, he saw an eagle swoop down and pounce on a rabbit and tear its heart out and eat it while the rabbit still kicked at the eagle's breast feathers, like it was trying to push it away. When he told me about it, his eyes got like there was some important message I was supposed to get out of it, but I just mostly thought it was gross.

Norman says I'm probably his best fishing companion. He says being with me's almost as good as being alone, because I don't have to talk all the time. He gets plenty of talk with Bonita. I lie awake in the dark and listen to them in the kitchen, talking. They fight a lot, and I think it's because Bonita's too smart for her own good. Norman's the smartest person I know, and he's famous. You see his books everywhere. He's been on TV, and they write about him in the magazines. I've been to New York with Norman, three times. We went to the Empire State Building and lots of museums and Radio City, and I got to sit in the studio and watch when he went on the "Today Show." I wish Mom and Dad could've known how famous Norman was gonna be. I remember how Dad used to say Norman was a useless bum and a troublemaker. I think I remember, or maybe Norman told me that. I was only nine when their car went off the bridge.

I asked Norman why he never writes about fishing, and he said that when he writes he's somewhere else, some other time and place, and that fishing is how he gets back into the world. Norman's not like other guys in Brainard, but he tries to be. When we go down to the Co-op to buy feed for the goat, he hangs around and talks about how we need rain and what the price of corn might be in the fall and stuff he thinks will make him sound like a farmer. It makes me laugh. "Why do you do that, Norman?" I ask him. "You don't know beans about farming."

"Ink for the pen," he says. "I have to know how real people talk."

"Real people?"

I wish I was a boy. I know it'd be easier if I was. Then Norman could talk to me about all the things men talk about. When he's drinking, he talks about women like they were skunks or some other kind of animal you wouldn't want around. He says he doesn't mean me, says I'm different, but still . . . I don't want to grow up to be a bitch. Norman says Bonita's a bitch. She's from the Philippines; that's what she says anyway, and she's real dark and beautiful. They argue, and they drink a lot, and they laugh. Sometimes I hear them laughing through the wall of my room. Bonita's laugh is low and husky, like someone with a cold. And then they're quiet, and then I hear the bed squeaking and the headboard banging against the wall and Bonita laughing again.

There is something about Bonita though, something that draws Norman to her, the way insects gather on the screens on summer nights when the lights are on in the house. And maybe it's the same thing that makes him hate her sometimes. Once when Bonita and I were driving home from Bill's Shop and Save, she said, "You're lucky, Gracie. You've got the best part of Norman without his meanness. I wish Norman could be friends with me like he is with you."

"Did you and Norman have a fight?" I asked her.

"We always fight, honey," she said.

I felt funny when she called me that, but I liked it, too. I like Bonita the best of any of the women Norman's had around, better than Beverly or Lois, and I wished I could let her be friends with me. But I know it wouldn't last.

"I'm sorry, Bonita," I said. "That you and Norman fight, I mean." She reached over and squeezed my hand, and I could see that she was about to cry, and we didn't say anything else all the way home.

Sometimes, when Bonita says something funny, Norman claps his hands and kisses her and says she's brilliant, about like the way he carries on when I get all A's on my report card. And sometimes he yells, "You bitch, you stupid slut," and they throw things at each other and pull hair and scream. And in the morning Bonita's gone and Norman's sick from drinking too much Jack Daniel's. I find him asleep

121

in the kitchen when I'm getting ready for school, slumped over the table with his face in a puddle of his own drool. I'm glad we live in the country. I don't know what'd happen if we had neighbors. One time I came home from school and Norman had shot holes in the wall so you could see the sun coming through. He was sitting at the kitchen table with his .22 Remington across his lap, and he said he was trying to see how close he could come to the three on the wall clock without really hitting it.

But don't think Norman's not a good person for me to live with. He helps me with my homework, except for math. He's no good at math and says so like he wouldn't want to be good at it even if he could. And he takes me fishing about any time I want to go. That's one thing he doesn't do with Bonita or any other woman I know of. "You only go fishing with someone you really like," he says.

"Don't you like Bonita?" I ask.

"I love Bonita," he says. He strokes his mustache and sucks on the ends of it where it comes to the corners of his mouth. "Sometimes I need Bonita." He gets up from the table where he's been helping me diagram sentences, and he goes over to the counter and pours some whisky into a juice glass. "But I don't like Bonita. She's not a friend of mine. She's not someone you'd like to go fishing with."

Bonita takes me shopping with her sometimes in Muskegon, and once she took me to a symphony concert in Grand Rapids 'cause she had tickets and Norman didn't want to go. I thought it was nice of her, even if the music was kind of slow and predictable, but Norman said she just did it to make him think she'd be a good mother for me. He says no woman who tries so hard to be a good mother could ever be one. I don't understand that. It seems to me everybody's got to try or they'll never be anything. Sometimes when Norman gets off on one of his screwy ideas about people, I just leave him alone. I figure it's 'cause he's a writer.

Some of the writers who've come to visit have been pretty strange. One of 'em wouldn't eat anything but brown rice and egg whites, and he got up at the crack of dawn every morning and burned incense and chanted a lot of "Om" stuff on the front porch. Then one night he ate some of the roast beef Norman had cooked and drank almost a whole bottle of brandy, all by himself. And when he got sick, he said it was because Norman served him meat, even though Norman knew he was a vegetarian. Norman took him fishing, and said the guy talked all the time about how unfair the critics had been about his last book, and then he got careless climbing out of the river and broke the tip of the Orvis bamboo rod Norman loaned him. And the next time Norman and I went fishing, he took that guy's book and tore it up, page by page, and threw it in the Au Sable River.

"Will we always be friends, Norman?" I ask him. I put down my *Warriner's Grammar* and rest my chin in my hands.

The whisky beads up on his mustache hairs, and he sucks at it with his lower lip. "Sure, Gracie, we'll always be friends." He takes another sip of the whisky and leans across the table and looks me real close in the eye, like he wanted me to be sure he was telling the truth. "And do you know why we'll always be friends?" His voice is real soft and low, so I have to listen very carefully to hear what he's saying.

"Why?" I almost have to keep from laughing, he looks so serious.

"Because we'll never be lovers; that's why. Because you're what I'd be if just one little Y chromosome had got switched around in a fit of passion thirty-five years ago. You remember chromosomes, don't you? You remember when we studied about what makes people men and women?"

"Yes." I almost whispered, 'cause I never know what's gonna happen when he gets that look on his face.

"Well, you are my good and true friend," he says, "and you're too intelligent to argue with, and, most of all, you don't think like a woman."

"How does a woman think?" I asked that 'cause I wanted to know how not to be. I don't want the way a woman thinks to sneak up on me the way menstruation did.

"Don't you worry about how a woman thinks," Norman said, "because you won't think like one, not with me anyway. A woman thinks about what she can get from a man the way a bear thinks about getting honey from a tree. She sees the right kind of man, and all she sees is a big glob of honey, and the little windows in her brain start opening and snapping shut. She may not even know it. It just comes over her the way some butterflies migrate to Mexico without even knowing why."

Norman is always saying things like that, things that sound real vivid but that don't necessarily make any sense unless you push him on it. And if you do, he makes up another story to make you believe the first one was true. I remember one time when I was little and I'd had a bad dream about being chased by huge snakes in the woods, and

Norman came in my room in the middle of the night and picked me up and held me in his arms and told me I was never to be afraid of anything. "Not even if evil sucks the windows out of your house. Don't be afraid," he said.

Evil sucks the windows out of your house? I could just see evil out there in the dark, sucking on the windows. But what did he mean? I asked him. "How could anything suck the windows out of a house?"

"Oh, Jesus, Gracie, believe me. It's like . . . it's like . . ." And then it was like a light bulb went on over his head, like when someone gets an idea in the cartoons, and he says, "But no, I'll tell you. A tornado, that's how." And he laughed like he'd just won at Trivial Pursuit or something. "A tornado comes by and sucks all the pressure out of the air around the house, and then there's so much more pressure left inside that the windows blow out like it was full of dynamite."

But I was still afraid of thinking like a woman. I was afraid that before I knew it, I'd be after what I could get out of Norman, and we wouldn't be friends anymore, and I'd be a lonely conniving bitch, like Bonita or Beverly, or Lois, the one before her.

It was mid-July, and the perch were running. I put a minnow on my hook and let the sinker carry it down till I felt it *tunk* on the bottom. Then I cranked it up about four turns on the reel and imagined it there, just off the sand, where a yellow perch coming in from the big lake would see it just waiting there for him, like a piece of candy or a takeout order from McDonald's, or a big glob of honey. I don't think Norman will ever get married again. There'll be other Bonitas and Beverlies, but he won't really like them for very long. I guess we'll go on sharing the house with Bonita till Norman trades her in on a new one.

We sat there for a long time, maybe half an hour, but the perch weren't biting. We watched boats full of salmon fishermen with down-riggers idling out the channel to Lake Michigan. Some had so many rods sticking up they looked like porcupines. Norman drank a couple of beers, and I skimmed a few dead minnows out of the bucket and tossed 'em to the sea gulls that were hanging around overhead. It was so quiet a big yellow butterfly came and landed on my rod. She sat there for a couple of minutes, and then she took off again. I watched her wobble out over the lake. Maybe she was headed toward Mexico, I thought, and I wondered how she'd ever make it all the way across.

Jim Harrison

 want to die in the saddle. An enemy of civilization,
I want to walk around in the woods, fish and drink.

I'm going to be a child about it and I can't help it, I was
born this way and it makes me very happy to fish and
    drink.

I left when it was still dark and walked on the path to the
river, the Yellow Dog, where I spent the day fishing
    and drinking.

After she left me and I quit my job and wept for a year and
all my poems were born dead, I decided I would only
    fish and drink.

Water will never leave earth and whisky is good for the
    brain.
What else am I supposed to do in these last days but fish
    and drink?

In the river was a trout and I was on the bank, my heart
    in my
chest, clouds above, she was in NY forever and I, fishing
    and drinking.

125

Blunder Brothers: A Memoir

Rip Torn

I HAD met Richard Brautigan in the fall, in a sushi bar in San Francisco. Now I was back in San Francisco, not to see Brautigan, but to meet with the poet Michael McClure and discuss directing his avant-garde play *The Beard*, which was to be produced in New York. I waited for McClure and some of his friends, who wanted to check me out, at Enrico's, the writers' bar across from the City Lights Bookstore. Along with McClure came Don Carpenter, a novelist and playwright; Emmett Grogan, author of *Ringelevio* and a famous outlaw; and Jim Walsh, a producer from New York. Jim had seen my production of Kenneth Brown's *The Happy Bar* at the Actors Studio and was championing me as director of his project.

What I remember of that day at Enrico's is excellent linguini and white clam sauce, and the sight of Shirley Temple Black at a nearby table. I nodded in her direction, and she coolly nodded back. We were of different political persuasions, but belonged to the same fraternity of acting. This cut across the status barrier—she a UN ambassador and me a prolabor, unemployable, troublemaking movie actor.

But Richard wasn't at Enrico's. In fact, it wasn't until after the owner, Banducci, sat with us and treated us to espresso and Courvoisier that Richard's name was even mentioned. McClure, who could tell I would have been just as content to stay at Enrico's all day, started to giggle. "I wish I didn't have to work today," he said to me. "Well, we won't wait up for you tonight. You and Richard are going fishing. Two Aquarians!" And he laughed and shook his head. "Try to get back before the week ends."

Carpenter said, "Are you really a fly fisherman? Richard's one of the best. He's going to take you down to Stinson Beach."

Richard had an apartment on the north side of Geary, where it tunnels under Presidio. Sears was right across the street. The door opened. A woman friend of Richard's said, "I'm on my way out. Richard's in the back brewing some tea." I stepped over the threshold and over the sign of the fisher of men. There was another fish on the floor in the kitchen. When I had first met Richard at the sushi bar, he had hidden from me. This day I got a better look. Richard was a giant, but he stooped; standing up, he would be around six four. His turned-up hat and old-fashioned glasses made him look like Custer or Mark Twain surveying the terrain with a falcon's gaze. He truly was a Confederate general.

We drank tea and talked about McClure's play, about the San Francisco poets, about *Beowulf*, about fishing for half-pounders in Oregon, where Richard grew up, and all the time he was rummaging through tackle looking for some 7X tippet material, which we would need to go after these small nine-inch fish bottled up in a fresh pond behind the sand bar. I was fishing a twelve-dollar Berkley Sweetheart and getting it rigged up. Taking some needle-nosed pliers, Richard bent down the barbs of a few size 18 Royal Coachmen and Mosquitoes. We ran over to Sears to get some fly dope, picked up my rental car from the Sears parking lot, and were on our way to Stinson Beach.

"Everybody says I'm crazy," said Richard, "that these fish are just rainbows planted by the parks department, but I think they're little steelhead waiting for a rain so the creek will cut the sand bar and they can go to sea." Here he handed me a pair of hemostats. "We won't even take them out of the water."

Richard checked out my gear. "Bass fisherman." He grinned. "I think you'd better use a tapered leader," and he took leader spools from his vest. He tied me up a good nine-foot trace with a 7X tippet. I followed suit, biting my tongue to get the blood knot right. I didn't cast badly, but nothing compared with Richard's effortless form. I confessed I didn't know a thing about trout fishing and that all I had ever caught on dry flies were bluegills, and that even then I preferred a Black Gnat fished wet. Richard caught and released three small fish, and I caught one.

"Look," he suddenly confided, "so many times someone will want to go fishing with me, and I end up tying all their knots, taking off all their fish, rebaiting their hook. Hell, if I wanted to be a gillie, I'd get paid. We're all friends of McClure's. We hear you're right to direct his play, but I'm leery of New York and, well, I figured if you checked out as a real fisherman, were telling the truth about that, you were probably straight in the art department, too. Let's leave these little fish to the Rain God, who can get them to sea, and go to Sausalito and have a sundowner at the No Name Bar. We'll plot some real trout fishing."

Sometime after our afternoon in the No Name, Richard called to say he wanted to go fishing on Deer Creek, below Big Sur. I remember his words tumbling over each other and the funny chortling noises he made. "I don't know, Richard," I said. "If I can get a real cheap flight, I will."

I was married to Geraldine Page then, and she was going to L.A. to do a film. She decided to fly out early with me and take the kids. We flew to San Francisco, borrowed a car, picked up Richard, and drove down to Monterey, where we visited Bruce and Price Dunn, friends of Richard's who were going fishing with us.

At the Dunns' home, we sat on cushions at a round table for supper, and the boys had prepared an apple-box table for our daughter, Angelica, and twin boys, Tony and Jon, who were two and in diapers. We planned our fishing trip over linguini and pesto, and Gerry and the kids decided to visit with the Dunn women and not leave for L.A. right away.

The men piled into Bruce's car and rocketed down the Coast Highway toward Big Sur and Deer Creek. Richard said that Deer Creek was supposed to have a lot of trout, maybe some steelhead—but no one really knew.

Sometime near noon, we turned off onto a dirt road that led to the creek. Excitement built as we traded stories about growing up in small towns, about fishing set-hooks, trotlines, and jugs for channel cats, about going "noodling" for big yellows. (As a kid, I wouldn't stick my arm under a riverbank or my hand through willow roots into the den of a sitting mama catfish weighing almost a hundred pounds— past the cottonmouth and past the horny beak of the snapping turtle, a finger to tickle the mama's chin in order to get your hand in her mouth and out past her gills to grab the plate and then try to tear her from her nest. Those big mama catfish could drown a man, and sometimes did.)

We were all more civilized now, using light tackle, but we delighted in describing the terrible outlaw ways poachers used—mashed buck-eyes in a sack thrown in a pool, a field telephone to crank them up, dynamite, so popular in Mexico, the Philippines, and the USA.

We were a mixed bag: Bruce, a spin-caster; Price, a bait-dunker; and Richard and I fly fishermen. Soon we hit a turn, an abandoned farm perched right on the rim of the deep gorge carved by the tiny glint of water far below—Deer Creek. Like military men, like the crackers they were, Richard, Bruce, and Price surveyed the best route to take. Fixed on that glint below, they ignored the old machinery and farm houses, grabbed tackle and beers, and over the edge we plunged, whooping rebel yells.

It took us about forty minutes to hit the creek and about three hours to climb out. But down at the bottom, the creek was nearly dry. "It looks like—" Richard paused— "it looks like an army of hippies has bivouacked here." Sinkers and lines and hooks were draped over every tree, bush, and boulder. What trout we saw were so terrified, they burrowed like gophers between the rocks in the shallow water. I told a trout, "I'm not going to bother you, fish." There was one campfire that had gone out, with the remains of a card game thrown in it. Burnt kings, queens, and deuces.

The Confederate general surveyed the terrain. "Better get out of this canyon before it gives me the willies." For a while, I kept up with Richard and Price. Richard started to chortle. "Rip, do you think Hollywood would be interested in a series called 'The Blunder Brothers'? We've got a fine cast here. We could profit from our blunders, and, looking at this crew, I doubt we'd run out of script, even if we ran as long as 'Gunsmoke.' What do you think? Hell, this bunch could never run out of blunders! There's two cold beers in the truck. First up top gets 'em." Richard and Price poured on coal, and soon I was trailing, climbing now with Bruce. Halfway out I panted, "Hey, you don't have to meet nobody for dinner, do you?" He said, "What do you mean?" "Well," I said, "they've got the beers and done 'em, so there's no reason we shouldn't sit down and have a smoke, take a break." "Oh, Lordy," said Bruce, "I was hoping you meant that."

A little later, we came up out of the canyon. Richard looked at his pocket watch, tapped it, and said, "We've been here, I don't know, thirty-five minutes. Time to have a game of cribbage." I said, "It's more like fifteen." "Here—" he pitched me a cold can— "we saved you laggards a brew to share."

Blunder Brothers, we plotted our way up the coast. Well, what is the most famous fly-fishing river in America? We didn't know. In Montana, the Madison. In the East, the Au Sable or the Yellow Beeches, or maybe the Beaverkill. But in Northern California, we agreed, it was the Feather, the north fork of the Feather River. . . .

About five months later, I got a call from Richard. "I'm getting another Blunder Brothers Act together. Interested in a Feather River adventure?" "Damn right!" I yelled back. And the Blunder Brothers plus two fellows from Boston, whose names I can't recall, got together in another old car and headed toward Sacramento, where Richard was to give a poetry reading at a small college.

Richard was a splendid reader, of his poems and of others', and the crowd was excited. He became interested in a redhead in the audience, a nurse. She looked enraptured with Brautigan, but leaving the party after the reading, Richard said, "I talked too damn much and ruined it. I scared her off. Dammit! They said they were going to feed us, and all they had were dips and cheese balls and cheap wine."

We stayed near the college in Sacramento. It was an upstairs back-of-the-house apartment with a screened-in porch. We had half a bottle of Jim Beam, a few beers, and, on the stove, a vegetable stew that we kept dosing with bonita flakes, lemon, and Tabasco.

Down to his skivvies, Richard headed for the mattress on the porch. He poked his head in the door. "Ah, dammit! No blanket. I hate to ask you, but I'd hate worse to have to get dressed again." I was going to sleep in the car, where the bedding was. "Sure, Richard, I'll get you one." He sighed and scratched. "You see, I talked too much." But as he lamented, there came a shy knock at the door, and in walked the red-headed nurse. By the time I got back up, they were out on the porch and on the mattress.

"You want your blanket? I'll leave it on this chair next to the stove." "Forget the blanket; where's that Jim Beam?" Richard asked. "I'll take a snort and leave it right by the door," I said. "No, bring it here. I'm a poet and she's a nurse. We don't care. You can have a look. She's beautiful. Give old Rip a look. It'll keep him warm." They laughed as I set the bottle of Beam inside the door sill. I went out and down the stairs to sleep in the car. It sure got cold in the night.

When the nurse left in the early morning to go to work, she forgot to cover the bare-assed poet, and he caught a monstrous head and chest cold.

★ ★ ★

We got on the road and hit the north fork of the Feather about sundown. By the time we made camp, it was dark. A blunder of a camp. It was right off the road, and what seemed a nice clearing was studded with root gnarls and outcroppings of stone. And, at about five in the morning, a squad of motorcycles roared up the canyon, about seven in all. The Feather River Commandos. Geronimo! Here come some more! Battle stations!

Around eleven-thirty, I burned out on the Feather and sat on the bank airing out, my waders down at the knees. Richard came down the river and then turned to fish the tail of a great pool. The sun, nearly overhead, shafted down into deep blue holes, intersected by giant stone ridges and caverns. Gorgeous water that should have had some real alligators in it, big old cannibal 'bows or browns. Richard didn't like to false-cast, but he did. He lengthened his line and with effortless grace sent it to the far end of the pool, some sixty feet away. The poet was poetry in performance. The line and leader floated down. "Why aren't you fishing, Rip?" "I don't know, Richard. There's something funny here. I haven't seen any fish except those two little suckers over there. There's also no insect life in the weeds or on any stone that I can find."

He cast again and chortled, "It's like fishing over mausoleums." Reeling in, he said, "Let's go into Oroville for a chicken-fried steak. I'm gonna feed this cold and get some medicine before it kills me." After chow and the drugstore, we hit a grocery and tackle shop, where we bought size 14 egg hooks, spinners, and three jars of Balls O' Fire salmon eggs.

"Want any corn, marshmallows, worms, boys?" asked the owner. "We might use Velveeta, if we stay skunked," said Richard. "Where ya been fishing?" asked the proprietor. "North fork of the Feather, one of the premier fly-fishing rivers," we replied. "Usta be, boys, usta be. Didn't ya know? Couple years ago, PG & E and the Fish and Game Department established a put-and-take policy on the Feather, and at the end of the season they poison the river to check the program. What they've done, though, is poisoned the entire historical life of the Feather, killed everything wild, including the bugs, to promote hatchery trout that eat poultry pellets. Try the north fork of the Yuba, boys."

That afternoon, we fished the Yuba. I was amazed at how a trout could come rocketing up to snatch a bit of bait in the tumbling white water. Throwing spinners and eggs, we all caught fish in the wonderful clear waters that cascade past old gold digs, boulders, and tailings, past rusting machinery that once sluiced the gravel banks and turned the Yuba muddy.

"Here," said Richard, pulling in another one, "we're finally gonna eat fish! I'm tired of chicken-fried steak. We've caught enough with bait. Put this on, Rip." He bit off my egg rig and tied on a tippet and a Royal Coachman. "See right there? That big boulder in the cascade? There's fish behind that boulder. You can't see them because of the bubbles, but then, they can't see you either. Cast right where that rill comes over that crack in the stone."

"Gimme some fly dope, Rich," I said, "some gink to smear on this fly. How am I gonna keep it dry on top in that water?" Richard replied, "If it floats, fish it dry. If it goes under, fish it wet." I placed the Coachman right on top of the boulder. For a second, it spun around in the rill and then washed over. Like an electric spark, a silver-blue-and-pink flash hit the Coachman and was hooked. "That's him, Rip, downriver." The fish jumped, a good two-pounder, and was barreling down the river with me in hot pursuit. My heart was pounding so hard in that thin, cold air that I didn't notice I had skinned my ankle. I slid the 'bow onto a tiny beach of sand, jumped on him, and flung him back into the rocks, where I hollered like an Indian, quickly thumped him with a stone priest, and took out my old yellow Case pocket knife, so I could gut my fish and examine its innards. Sticks and gravel.

"These are caddis houses, or casements, and this little fellow"—Richard pointed to a small, cream-colored worm he had pulled out of its house of sticks and stones— "is the caddis worm. I've caught a lot of fish using these on a fine hook and . . . Come on! We've got enough fish. We're gonna fry 'em up with some bacon and onions. We got ketchup and lemons and parsley and potatoes." And, stumbling, wheezing with his flu and rattling excitement, Richard set off.

Richard loved to cook, and we really rustled up that grub, because nothing compares with fish that are taken right from the water to the flame.

We camped on the river, across the road from a high butte. When the sun went down, it was like opening the door on a freezer. All the cold air in the world flowed down that butte to our little camp. Gorged to the gills with trout, Brautigan was wedged between two boulders. He was asleep, but he was shaking and didn't sound good at all. Bruce Dunn said, "Do you think he'll make it through the night?" I replied,

"He might, but I'm not sure about myself. We need to get some medicine, like a big bottle of Spanish brandy." We counted out change and uncrumpled bills. I talked to the boys from Boston, and they coughed up some. Bruce put another blanket on Richard and woke him to get the rest. "Hurry!" wheezed Richard. "Look at this!" His hand was puffed up and red. Somehow, in spearing fish or bacon or spuds from the skillet, telling a story with a wild comical gesture, Richard had stabbed himself with the tines of the barbecue fork. With a groan, he pulled the lobster claw back under the covers and disappeared between the boulders. "Thanks for the blanket, boys. Why didn't you give it to me sooner? Hurry up!" he croaked.

Legend has it that Richard's mother was a barmaid, a good-hearted woman with lots of boyfriends. She had a baby boy and an older girl and sometimes abandoned them for long periods to run and throw a fling. Richard told me that, at about age four, his mother took his sister and left him in the care of a boyfriend, a fry-cook who lived in a corner room of an old hotel and worked in the kitchen below. The fry-cook, having no funds for a baby-sitter, tied Richard to the bedpost. Richard remembered this man with affection. "He gave me enough slack so I could get to the can and, more important, I could get to the corner and look out the window."

The mystery of Brautigan is: How, out of that tortured childhood, did he manage to find the joy and the cheer and the enthusiasm that shone from his character? In those days, he had a lot of friends, and on that cold night along the Yuba, two of them were hurtling through the dark, following the headlights in search of a roadhouse.

About an hour later, after conversation with the locals at the bar, we wheeled back to the river with the medicine. The brandy we located wasn't Mexican or Spanish, but a California brand, which wasn't good. Richard may have grown up dirt-poor, but he had exquisite tastes, leaning to the likes of Courvoisier and Martell, at least three-star. Since he had contributed a lion's share to the cost, we decided we'd better sample this quarter-star stuff to see if it was worth his while. After all, we had driven all that way and not yet touched a drop.

The hardest part of our journey was from the road, where Bruce parked the car, down to the river to find the patient. The Blunder Brothers had picked a ghostly old gold camp to bed down in. So Bruce and I eased along the spoil bank to locate Richard. Slipping on the rounded stones, we finally stood where we had left our partner. He was nowhere to be found. Did we walk by him in the dark?

Bruce reminded me of my uncle Weldon before he gave up the sauce. "You better grab the bottle if you want a drink." I did. "Hold it, Hoss—save some for me," said Bruce. It was then, while we were sampling the medicine, that we heard a muffled groan and felt the ground shift. We hadn't lost Richard. We were standing on him.

I didn't see Richard for a few years after that. When I did, it was during the time when I had been eighty-sixed from films, television, and Broadway, and was doing a summer-stock tour. It was just before our opening at the summer theater in Westport, Connecticut, that I got a call from California. It was Richard, and he wanted to come east and fish in the Catskills. I warned him that I barely had time to piss, much less fish, and that I'd probably only see him after the show at night. He came anyway, because of a publishing party to be given in his honor in New York.

I finally got some time and called Richard in the city. "I've caught my breath," I said, "so we can talk and maybe fish the Saugatuck, which flows into Long Island Sound at Westport. They say the river's got some sea-run browns in it."

Gerry, the kids, and I were staying at a farmhouse near the salt pond in Westport, and the moment Richard set foot in the place he became itchy and perturbed. He didn't like the family we were living with. And one night after our host had told us stories of the old days in Connecticut, which I thoroughly enjoyed, Richard and I stayed up alone, and I asked him, "Didn't you enjoy those stories, Richard?" He shot back, "Hell, no! They're so goddamned middle-class. I come across a continent to talk with you, and what do you do? You sit around bullshitting with those damn people. I'm going to see your plays, we're going to fish, and I'll ride back to the city with you and your family, because I want you to go to my publishing party."

"Okay, General," was all I could say.

We fished but didn't catch anything more than five small bluegills and one stunted bass. On our way back from fishing, I tried to joke about our not catching any trout and pointed to a sign that suggested why we hadn't. Painted on an old and abandoned factory, it proclaimed, EMBALMING FLUIDS. "Look, Richard, it's *Trout Fishing in America*." He was not amused. I never went to the publishing party.

More than a decade passed before we got together again. In that time I had separated from Gerry and gone to live with Amy Wright in

California. That didn't work out either, so I lived by myself in a place above Malibu and below Paradise Cove.

Gerry called me one day to announce that she could no longer manage the twins. They were sixteen and undisciplined. "They want to go out and live with you. Now we see who they love," she said. I told her I'd give it a try but that it probably wouldn't last long. "Tell 'em it'll be a different ball game living with old Dad."

So my boys came west, and at sixteen they were writers, directors, actors, and poets. They devoured books and movies and television. "Listen, boys," I said, "if you want to be artists, learn from life. And learn some discipline." They had no discipline. They couldn't even keep their shoelaces tied.

What my boys needed was good old-fashioned work. I wanted them to learn what it was like to work all day and sweat your ass off and feel good about it at the end. I called my friend Joe Sedgwick in Montana. Joe owns a ranch on Big Elk Creek, above Two-Dot, and is a champion Montana cowboy. I couldn't think of a better place for my boys to learn about hard work.

Joe said, "Hell, Rip, I ain't got time to entertain 'em." And I said, "I don't want you to entertain 'em. I want you to work the piss out of 'em." There was a pause while Joe considered what I had said. "You mean shoveling shit? Pounding post holes?" I laughed and said, "Sounds just right." His answer came without hesitation. "Send 'em up, Rip. We've got enough of that kind of work for everybody!"

So I put the boys on an airplane and sent them to Montana. When I visited them a month later, they were a lot closer to being men. We fished Big Elk Creek and the Musselshell near Two-Dot and caught some nice browns on spinners.

After our day of fishing, we went down to Chico Hot Springs to have dinner and visit with Mike Art, who owns the place. I asked about Richard. "I've lost touch with him. He's been eighty-sixed out of every bar from here to Bozeman. He's welcome here, but he's mad at me . . . or someone. We're worried about him. I'll call him for you, but he won't come," he said. "Tell him I'm here with my boys. Tell him Jon and Tony are here," I replied. "Okay, but . . ." Mike said as he sauntered out to the office. Mike came back with a big grin. "Son of a bitch! Richard'll be here in about forty-five minutes." And amazing everyone, as if a ghost had appeared, Richard slouched in a while later. He'd never looked better.

He was tickled to see Tony and Jon and asked questions and teased the hell out of them. Richard had on the kind of Norwegian cap with a button on top that Montana ranchers wear instead of Stetsons. At some time in the evening, he wanted to trade hats with me. We wore about the same size. I got his blue one and he got a black bill with the logo "CAT." I had worn that cap in a film called *Jinxed*.

Someone was puking in the men's room, and Richard smiled and said, "I'll try the road—and a little air." He went out for a moment. Mike Art said, "That's the old Richard."

Richard came back in the bar and gave me a hug. "I want you boys and your dad to take a walk with me down the road. Let's drink to Tony and Jon," he said. "I like these boys; I liked them when they were tykes and I like 'em now. They get on their feet, come to you, and shake your hand hard and look you in the eye." And he hooted a rebel yell. "Hey, Jon, can you catch?" Jon, who was famous in the family for his fumbles, said, "Okay, sure." And Brautigan rifled a bottle of brandy across the road. Jon caught it against his chest with one hand, and we cheered that night in Pray, Montana.

The last time I saw Richard was the summer after our reunion. The twins and my daughter, Angelica, were working for Mike Art at Chico. One day I took them to visit Joe Sedgwick and his family. I taught the kids to drive in a little rental car with the stick on the floor. We shifted gears and bumped down the road where Richard's house stood and left him a note asking if he would like to get together with me and the kids.

To everyone's surprise, Richard invited us over. He came out of the top of his barn, waved, and came down his stairs to the ground between his house and barn. He blinked in the light like an owl, yawned, scratched his pot under his union suit, squinted at the sun— Custer, Mark Twain—hooked his thumb, placed his hand on his back. He looked his falcon look at each of us and spoke to my kids. "You see your dad's timing is still good." Then he grinned. "Let's jump in your car and get some groceries. You see, today, just before you came here, I was finishing my novel. It's done. I've turned into a hermit, but I want to celebrate." We rocketed to the store and back to Richard in his extended living room, one of the old cars in his yard, the General with a battle plan. "I don't fish anymore!" He smiled shyly, as if to say he'd given up making love or drinking. "No, I don't fish anymore," he said. "I've given my gear away."

I went out alone and caught two trout, and that evening we had a party. From somewhere appeared a bottle of champagne and some kind of hooch—Daniel's or Dant. Richard's old chortle, his grin and excitement made him a kid again. As for the trout, we discovered a can of mushroom soup, and Richard said, "Let's poach these beauties in this soup. And how about a dash of champagne?" I and my kids and the hermit had a feast. Toward dawn, Richard went to bed and we went back to Chico.

I never saw Richard again. His last book, *Before the Wind Blows It All Away*, was savaged by the East Coast critics, for whose approval Richard greatly hungered. His career was reassessed and found wanting, and Brautigan was dismissed as unimportant. The main damage was not to ego, but to income, and Richard knew he had to lose his place in Montana. He retreated to Bolinas, facing a taste of the poverty that he had escaped for a while.

I was in the basement of the house that Gerry and I shared in New York when my son Tony came downstairs to talk with me.

"I suppose you saw that small notice on Richard in *Time* magazine," said Tony.

"About his book? I heard they killed it," I said.

"Yes, Dad," said Tony. "They killed his book, but I guess you don't know . . ."

"Don't know what?" I said.

"Dad, Richard shot himself. He's dead."

I called Don Carpenter, and he told me what he knew about Richard's last days. Richard had gone to North Beach, in San Francisco, and had run into Akiko, a Japanese woman whom he had broken up with some time before. The story goes that when they met, Richard ran away from her but she followed. He ran into a bookstore and she came up behind him. When she put her hand on his back, Richard fled. He went to a friend's house and borrowed a gun, then returned home to Bolinas to kill himself. Cut up by the critics, his ex-wife counting coup on him, Custer went for his gun. Brautigan was standing when the bullet hit him. That's the story they tell.

Richard, when I was in San Francisco I visited Carpenter in Mill Valley, and there was your picture on the wall looking at me over a bedpost. I said to Don, "Let's go to North Beach to Enrico's and see if Richard's there." We sped across the Golden Gate Bridge. Enrico's has been remodeled. We sat at the new bar under the portrait of Bill Cosby and had a brandy in your honor, Richard. Don doesn't booze anymore and had a soda-and-lemon. We saluted the owner, Banducci, who nodded back. I said to Don, "Richard isn't here," and Don replied, "No, he isn't." We paid the check and left.

I lift a fly rod and get glints of you, Brautigan. I salute you, Blunder Brother. I'm on the road now, Coast Highway. I'm reporting to you, General. Zuma, Paradise Cove, home to Hidden Beach. Black horse up on the hill, fields of mustard. Sky's blue and clear out here on the Pacific shore of America. Brother, I'm praying for your tormented soul. Be at ease. Stand in clear water that rushes to the sea. Keep that humor and enthusiasm you had on earth in the days before you stopped fishing.

In a play by John Arden, a soldier, facing the threat of imminent death, says:

> . . . a man can laugh, because or else
> he might well howl—and howling's
> not for men but for dogs, wolves,
> seagulls—like o' that ent it?

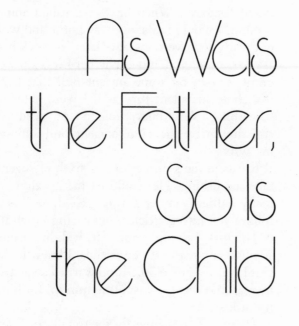

As Was the Father, So Is the Child

Gene Hill

I NOW have no doubt that for most of my earliest days, the only times I was in any real contact with my father were when we fished together.

Now, when I reflect on those times, I know that my father was troubled by my being with him in the woods. He was a young man, less than thirty, when I was old enough to insist on tagging along. Even when I wasn't wanted, which was often, I would follow him from a distance, knowing that he knew I was there. He would never stop and wait for me, never slow his woodsman's pace to accommodate my young legs. He knew that when the distance between us reached a certain point, I would finally turn around, hurt to the point of tears, and go back home.

When my father was running his trap line, I would short-cut through the woods and wait, silently, for him to come along. I would see him appear through the trees and along a brook, watch him crouch to check a set for mink, and know that he knew I was watching him. As often as not, he would ignore my being there and go on about his business of checking a set or running it again if it had been sprung.

Other times, though, he would be angry and march up to me, pulling a switch from a tree along the way. He would yank me to my feet and bring the switch across my legs. The switch would raise red welts that lasted for days. When he was finished and I picked myself off the ground, I would make my way home and wonder why. And when he got ready to leave a few days later to check his trap line again, I would ask to go and often did—whether I was allowed to or not. I was, I now know, drawn by some ancient pull that I could not resist, offering myself to his silent fury as if I were determined to be sacrificed to something I would never understand. And here I am, ten times older, still drawn by the same ancient pull and still without understanding why.

It was in the summer of my sixth or seventh year that he began to take me fishing. He would let me go along, not grudgingly but not really willingly either. It was "just along," as you might let a farm dog follow you into the fields, not caring much if it came or not.

The little I thought about it, it didn't seem to me that a father and son had any reason to be friends. I knew he had to care for me, to see that I was fed and clothed and warned away from harm, but I could see no reason, except my wanting him to, for him to like me or even want me at his side.

There were few boys for me to talk to. Even with them our conversations never drifted to the subject of whether we liked or got along with our fathers. Our society dictated that you keep your own counsel. If you were in the mood to ask "strange" questions, you kept your questions to yourself, or asked them in the dark, silently, as an apologetic footnote to nightly prayers.

Fishing was one of the few pleasures my father allowed himself. But even such a simple pleasure as fishing had to be earned. He couldn't simply go fishing in the evening after a hard day's work. The work had to be finished for that day. If there was something that had to be done in the long twilight, it was done first. The garden, which supplied us with much of our food, was a constant chore; it had to be watered by hand-carried pails from the brook that ran close by and constantly weeded—as much for the fact that weeds indicated a level of sloth as anything else.

An evening's fishing was rarely discussed in advance. After supper he would get up from the table and go outside to the shed that held his tackle (an old bamboo plug-casting rod and a tin box with "baits" in it), hand me the bait box, put the oars over his shoulder, and start walking to the lake.

I knew he didn't mind my going with him, because I'd be perched up on the back seat of the rowboat in spite of the fact that the kitchen woodbox hadn't been filled to the top, or there was still a section of lawn not mowed or trimmed. An entire evening could pass, fish or no fish, with no more than a few words being exchanged. Most of the words spoken were directed to me to keep quiet or to quit fooling around with the flashlight. I never considered this a disappointment, though, since neither of us could be called chatty; he by normal country reticence and me in imitation of him and because no one (mothers, grandmothers, and dogs excepted) listened much to the ditherings of small boys.

I believe I was expected to learn about fishing through osmosis. Although I was taught how to hook several kinds of bait and tie a few knots and, eventually, row a boat, I believe any instruction I received was intended to make me less a bother to him and not necessarily a better fisherman. It was not an unkind act, not really, just a practical one.

It was obvious to everyone that I was willing to do anything to be allowed to go fishing. I was not permitted to go alone, however, until my father knew I could swim. So one morning he told me to get my bathing suit and come along. We went to where we kept the rowboat and where there was a small shingle of sandy beach. My father waded in and called for me to come out to him. I did so, quickly and eagerly. He told me to climb on his back and feel how he did it and that when I felt I could do it on my own to slide off and try it alone. I had been fooling around in the brook enough to have lost any fear of the water, and even had a slight idea of a swimming stroke. It was a good thing I did, too, because we swam across the entire lake that morning. We swam and floated and I rested on his back when I was tired. When we started walking home, he told me that he thought I was a good swimmer but to keep working at it. Then the day was forgotten and neither of us ever mentioned it again.

I was probably eight years old when one morning my father told me we were going to town. He told me to put some good clothes on and wait for him in the Model A. When we got to town, we parked in front of the hardware store. I thought we were there to buy seeds for the garden, the usual supply of nails, wood screws, flashlight batteries, lantern wicks, and, if I was lucky, maybe some popcorn for me.

As usual, once inside I headed for the glass case that held the fishing tackle. Hooks, green and red bobbers with yellow stripes, sinkers, twine, casting line, and a modest assortment of spoons, plugs, spinners, pork rind, and pin-eyed minnows frozen forever in brine were arranged in neat rows on glass shelves. While I gazed into the case, I could hear my father and the clerk discussing a new variety of radish or cucumber off in the distance. Then, while I daydreamed about Pflueger and South Bend reels and True Temper rods, the clerk was suddenly standing next to me and taking a new Akron reel and spool of braided silk casting line from the case. Next he reached up and took down a new steel rod from the rack behind the case. I turned to see who else had come into the store, but discovered that my father and I were still the only customers. My father paid the bill, handed me the bag of seeds, kept the fishing tackle himself, and walked to the car.

All the way home I couldn't speak. I was a bit of a stutterer when I was excited or nervous, and now that I was both, nothing would come out. I knew that the fishing tackle wasn't for me—life wasn't like that. I hadn't *earned* them. I hadn't done my chores when I should, I had sneaked the dog up to my room, and I had forgotten to oil the lawn mower when I put it away. I couldn't think of anything I'd done right or when it should have been done . . . except feed the chickens and take care of the hounds, my two favorite chores, which I didn't even consider work.

The fishing tackle that my father had bought that day in the hardware store *was* for me. I had forgotten it was close to my birthday, and never considered that when we went to town it was good sense to buy as much as we could for as far ahead as we could.

I know now how hard it was for my father to give me those birthday gifts. He was not comfortable when it came to such things as giving presents. He didn't want anyone, especially himself, to know or even think that he might be spoiling me.

I remember that day, though, when I saw him go into the shed where he kept his fishing tackle and come back with the new rod and reel and line. He just handed me the packages and said that he didn't expect to see any weeds in the garden that summer, that he expected to have the lawn mowed without having to remind me a dozen times, and that anything as easily come by could be taken away just as easily. I was almost afraid to accept the gifts. I never wanted them taken away.

It took years for me to understand the complications of a man afraid of love—either giving or receiving it. And it took years for me to realize that among the things I was taught was the same fear—the idea that affection was weak and to be guarded against, and that demonstrating love was fickle and like wishing for something instead of working for it. My father had found a way to love without showing it or perhaps even admitting it to himself. His way was through our fishing together.

When you fish with someone, there's little need for small talk or often any talk at all. There are the small gestures of loving: letting the other cast to a rolling fish, taking the weeds off the other's lure, pointing to a mallard hen with her young, or stopping and listening together while the long call of a loon rolls out across a still cove.

We fished together through the ice of winter and high-running brooks of spring. We fished for spawning perch, bobbed for eels, seined for shiners, waded for helgrammites, and broomed the grass along spring runs for leopard frogs. For Christmas and holidays, we offered brown parcels that rattled with Jersey Wows, Pikie Minnows, Creek Chub Darters, Hawaiian Wigglers, and Pflueger Chums.

My father grew less harsh, less quick to scold when I was old enough to take the bus to school in town. And when summer came, I often fished with new friends, who would ride their bikes out to our house and spend the night. From that time on, it seems, it was only once in a while that we fished together. I had found a new independence, along with a feeling of escape, and a chance to talk and dream out loud.

I should have seen then that he needed me. Perhaps I did and wouldn't accept it, or perhaps I did but refused to let my well-remembered childhood resentment die. I could be the one who called the dance—yet I didn't. It could wait. "As was the father, so is the child."

From the army through college, I hardly fished at all. Nor was I really ever home. There was nothing to draw me there that I hadn't learned to live without. The bonds that were never really that tight were easily loosened. Or so I thought until I realized that here I was, now as old as my father had been when we first fished together.

"Want to go fishing?" I asked him when I returned home after being away for many years. "It's the dark of the moon and a long time since we went out and caught a mess of bass."

He didn't have to think about his answer for very long. He just shook his head and said, "No, I don't think so. I've lost interest in it." I smiled and said, "I'll row the boat." But he only shook his head. "Row one of your friends. I gave most of my stuff away."

Hurt and angry, my childhood resentment welling up inside me, I

145

said, "You never gave anybody anything in your life . . . except a whipping." And I went fishing by myself.

On the lake, I felt an uncomfortable sense of satisfaction. I had gotten to him and I knew it. Then I thought, Why? What was the point after all these years? What was the point in being like the part of him I so feared and hated?

I sat in the rowboat where he had sat so many times. I could see myself in my bib overalls, barefooted, sitting at the stern of the boat. I could remember exactly how I felt, how different from him I would be when I grew up. Then I cried into the dark of the moon. I cried aloud, for myself, for my father, for the first time in over twenty years.

Colors

Thomas McIntyre

IT WAS my plan to drive south through a desert where black vultures turned as gradually as the hands of a clock in a cloudless blue sky. I would pass cattle that appeared to be no more than worn hide stretched over a framework of bone, see them grazing amidst the green leaves of a jungle, and then hear a tropical August rain drumming on the roof of my white Land-Rover. And when I could at last see an ocean, I would hire a boat whose yellow hull needed scraping and repainting, and smell salt air. I would hire the boat for a single purpose—to catch my first great fish, either a sail or a marlin.

My plan was this clearly worked out ahead of time inside my head. And when I arrived in Mazatlán I found the exact boat and a crew to carry me out onto the ocean—just as I had known I would.

The captain was almost eighteen and his mate a year or two younger. They carried their lunches in two enameled pots that were tied up in checkered cloths, and they removed their shoes before climbing aboard the small diesel sportfisher, like Japanese entering their cramped wooden houses. That morning as we headed out, the gulf lay flat and featureless beneath a broken leaden sky, leaping manta rays flashing on the horizon like spinning coins.

As we ran toward the fishing grounds, the mate sewed up flying fish with heavy thread and a rusted needle, affixing them to the hooks and leaders, running them out on the monofilament lines behind our white wake, then hoisting the lines up into the outriggers. After that, the mate climbed up into the flying bridge with the captain, where they looked like boys sitting together in a tree house.

I sat in the rickety fighting chair, watching the planing baits and envisioning how it would be when my first great fish hit, how I would let him take line before I set the hook, how he would sound, and I would fight him back to the surface, where he would leap and leap

again before tiring and coming to the boat. I saw him, as I opened a cold Mexican beer, coming over the transom, huge-eyed and alight, his body pulsing fierce luminescence. All of it was already there for me to see.

It was around noon when one of the fifty-pound lines snapped off the outrigger. Before I could set down my beer bottle, the barefoot mate had left his lunch and jumped down from the flying bridge to lift the rod from its holder and hold it poised. I wanted to say something to him, but it seemed that I had not worked this part out in my mind beforehand—at least not as clearly as I had assumed—because when I looked off the stern and saw two ocean-blue sails tacking through the water toward us, I realized I had no actual idea how to hook a great fish. I watched silently as the mate let the sailfish eat the flyer, his thumb lightly touching the turning spool on the reel. Then he threw the brake and struck once. Then he struck again. Then a third time. Then the mate handed the rod to me.

The line played off the reel against the drag, and the sailfish came out of the calm ocean churning and shaking, flinging arcs and ropes of sea water off itself. The fish's power, far out there where a hook was set in its jaw, was much greater than I could have anticipated. Yet even then, when it ran most desperately, it had a gliding ease. The fish's strength felt like the smooth tidal power of the Pacific, while mine was only convulsive force, the awkward lurchings of someone crudely straining to lift a weight that was beyond him. Now that it was all out of my head and alive, none of it was as I had pictured it. So I tried picturing it another way. The sailfish would soar into the air one time more, high and hard enough to straighten the curve of steel that now restrained it, then free-fall back to the water. That is the way I knew it would be now, but all I did was go on fumbling and struggling against the sailfish.

In time, the captain was able to back the boat up to the fish. He threw the throttles into neutral and came down off the bridge. Both he and the mate leaned over the transom, where the diesel fumes idled up from the exhausts, and the captain had the leader in a gloved hand and the mate the fish's bill, and I wanted to say something now, as well, but I did not know the language. As I watched, the mate, both hands around the bill as the hundred-twenty-pound flat-sided fish shook, held it out of the water while the captain lifted a sawed-off *beisbol* bat from the deck. The sound was wet and hollow when the bat was swung against the sailfish. Then I watched the captain swing it once more, and the fish stopped quivering.

149

The captain and the mate hauled my first great fish over the transom and unfurled its ocean-blue sail for me to admire.

"*Look* at the pretty colors!" the captain sang happily.

I did not look at the colors of the boated sail, but looked instead at the second sailfish, which had followed the first to the boat, as it slowly swam away. When I finally turned my eyes back to the dead sailfish, its colors were darkening swiftly, except for the thin bright thread of blood that ran down its flank from its gill. I was trying to remember how I had imagined it would look.

"Beautiful," I told the captain and the mate. I was nineteen.

The Fat Lady's Thigh

David
Seybold

SITTING ON a boulder at the tail of a wide pool in late afternoon, I find myself exactly where I want to be. That I have arrived well before the evening fishing begins is not so much an accident of timing as an act of self-indulgence. Even though I live only minutes away, I fish here only a few times a year, when conditions are optimum. So I sit atop this granite throne, take in the river and pool and surrounding countryside, and draw deeply on a cheroot. The blue smoke drifts upward, and I am confident and all proprietary as I survey my immediate domain.

Beneath my hands and outstretched legs, and pocking my throne like fossilized pustules, are the abandoned nymphal skins of stone flies. They are the color of old coins and appear prehistoric against the gray stone. I touch them with the tip of my finger and then examine the ashen smudge. I imagine the nymphs' journey from the deep of the pool to the shallows of my mid-river perch. Then I imagine the fate of those that never made it this far. What monster brown trout with viselike jaws crushed and devoured them? Where are those brown trout now?

My name is John Thurlow and I have been on this boulder many times before, ever since Henry, my grandfather, first put a fly rod in my hand twenty-six years ago, when I was a chapped-mouth kid of

ten. Each time I come here, I figure to accomplish what I have never done before, and what Henry did on an annual basis: catch a brown trout the size of "the Fat Lady's thigh," as Henry liked to say.

Though I have caught many large browns here, I've never taken one over three pounds. I've had them on my line, so close I could almost touch them, but something always went wrong and they broke off. When I was younger, it used to infuriate me and I'd swear and kick the ground and want to break my rod into a hundred pieces. Henry always claimed that the reason I lost them was that they knew what I would do once I caught one. What I intended to do was have my first big brown mounted, so that I could hang it on the wall and know for as long as I lived that at least I *had* caught one. Henry, on the other hand, would always release his big fish. It drove me mad. He would catch a magnificent brown and then spend fifteen minutes holding it under water and reviving it so it could swim away. "Why," Henry would say to me as I stared in disbelief, "would I want to kill something that has given me so much pleasure? If I let it go, it will live and grow and maybe come back to me again." Then he'd look at me and I could tell from his expression that it was all right for me to be thinking the way I did. "You're young yet," he'd say. "Someday you'll learn for yourself that the most valuable things you'll ever own are those that you let go."

Twenty years ago, I would have traded my Go-cart to be able to catch one brown trout over three pounds. These days, I just mutter, shake my head, and say, "Next year." Why I've mellowed out doesn't make sense to me. Maybe it's because I'm older; maybe it's because when Henry died nine years ago I no longer had to suffer through watching someone else catch one and then release it. But I still want a big brown on the wall.

It always surprises me that everything is the same as it was when I first was brought to this stretch of the river. The pastures and high meadows, the hardwoods and old pines, even the logging trace that cuts through the pines and follows the river's course, remain unchanged. So much of the countryside has been subdivided, sold off, and developed that I regard this spot as a sanctuary, as divine and holy as any place of worship. But I know that in time even this place will be transformed into something tame and urban, and that to expect otherwise is wistful and unrealistic.

Lately, I've learned a lot about realism and change: As of last month, for instance, I am a divorced man. When the formal letter decreeing the dissolution of my three-year marriage arrived in the mail, I thought I should do something, though I didn't know what. I remember spending an entire morning wondering what to do with the letter—save it? throw it away? have it framed? What does one do with such a proclamation? Put it with one's birth certificate? I ended up placing it on the mantle in the living room, where every day I see it and wonder what to do.

I'm not happy about being divorced, though I confess a certain relief. When my wife left me, nearly a year ago, I felt as hollow and lonely as I think is humanly possible. Knowing for six months before-hand that she was going to leave did not lessen the feeling of sudden abandonment. Though I fought her wanting to leave, I knew I had no choice. She wrote me for the first three months, and then I was notified by a local lawyer that she wanted a divorce. Now I've passed through the worst of it and find I am reasonably intact—as intact as a man can be when his wife, whom he still loves, leaves him. But I've discovered that time really does heal, or at least lessens the pain of, all wounds. So, yes, I'm relieved it's over, glad that she's hundreds of miles away, and thankful that our settlement did not include having to sell my farm, which Henry left me when he died. All she wanted was her Saab 99, Milly, our golden retriever, and her cameras.

It's the first week in July, time for the annual *Hexagenia* hatch, and my best opportunity to try to catch a truly big brown. The pool, now calm and undisturbed in the setting sun, is only an hour or so away from becoming a virtual mayfly factory. When the hatch is on and in full swing, brown trout the color of weathered barn boards, as Henry often said of them, will leave their dark and secret hideouts and feed on large, clumsy duns and spinners like chubby-cheeked kids in a candy store. At the peak of their debauchery the pool will resemble a shallow puddle in a hailstorm, and the fish will stuff themselves openly and without regard for anything, including me.

The sun is nearly behind Morgan Meadows, and the sky is streaked with licks of fiery red and deep orange. A peacefulness envelops the river and pool, and it won't be long before the first trout begin to show in saucer-size riseforms. Until then, however, I am content to sit and thumb through the late afternoon. A belted kingfisher streaks down-river, and its loud, rattling call penetrates the stillness and startles me. I look for it against a background of hemlock and spruce but don't see it until it's fifty yards away. From the deeper woods comes a rustling sound—a deer coming to drink, no doubt, and I look for a game trail along the opposite bank.

The sun leaves the surface of the pool with the ease of a trout slipping from sunlight into shade. In the brief afterglow comes a period when everything contiguous to the pool becomes somber and as still as a house at dawn. The air cools and the warm scent of pine mulls with the damp riverbank. I look at other boulders in the pool, and in the fading light they appear somehow lifelike, as if they were cattle grazing on a distant plain.

There is another stirring beneath the pines on the other side of the river. Life is in there and whatever it is, it sees me. I scan the opposite side and try to pick out some part of a whitetail. I cannot, though, and lose interest when from off in the distance comes the sound of a camp bell, tolling campers in to supper. I saw the camp's battered green bus on my way here, at the village pharmacy, where it leaves off and picks up campers from downcountry cities. The kids leaving were laughing and pushing each other, whereas the kids arriving were silent and cautious and kept to themselves.

There is a small rise at the head of the pool. Then another. And another. So it goes for half an hour. They are small fish, though, and I decide to wait, which to my surprise is not hard to do. Usually I want to catch them, to feel them pull against me and know that even if I don't land the Fat Lady's thigh, I've still caught something. Henry loved small trout and would always go after them first. He claimed they were ante for the pot and would bring them in and then release them, to raise the stakes. With each one he released, he would say, "There you go. I raise you one more." And when he thought the stakes were significant, he would sit back and light a cigar and wait for the big boys to show their hands.

The stars and a thin sliver of yellow moon show themselves just as the first mayflies come off the pool's surface. The water is now without definition, the boulders become only faintly visible, and the pines bordering the river become shapeless and loom as an impenetrable wall of darkness. I check my rod, my leader and tippet. I check the knot on my fly, a size 8 Michigan spinner, and then stand up slowly. My joints snap and creak, and I feel the granite through the soles of my sneakers. I hold the fly rod, strip off a few lengths of line, and then flip the leader onto the surface next to the rock. I look down to see how the large fly is floating but have trouble picking it out in the darkness. I squint, stare, jerk the fly to create discernible movement. I finally settle for thinking I see it, and then lift the tip of the rod up and swing the leader into my left hand. In minutes I'll hear the rises of the large browns. I stare at the pool and now find it harder to wait.

155

The ephemerids take over the air above the pool and appear through the moonlight like paratroopers on a night mission. Their emergence triggers the browns' debauchery, and they disrupt the pool's surface like enemy ground fire. And streaking through it all are bats, phantom fighters knocking off the paratroopers left and right. All hell is breaking loose, and I suddenly wonder how Milly, our golden retriever, is making out with my wife. I wonder if she remembered to pack Milly's shot card before she left.

I tell myself to forget about things that no longer matter and lecture myself until I realize I'm not even fishing. I find myself standing around like a man waiting for a bus. I swear out loud and false-cast blindly into the air over the pool. I watch as my fly line reaches out and disappears into the darkness like a mysterious tendril. In the dark, I hear and feel my casts more than I see them. I listen to the fly line whipping through the air, feel it in the rod's guides, sense the power of the rod as it responds to the motion. When I let go, line shoots out; the fly whips past my ear and lands on the surface fifty feet away.

My plan to cast only to the loud rises is forgotten in my haste to begin fishing. And it's a mistake. Without a specific plan to follow, I feel disconnected, as if I had just arrived and had no sense of my surroundings. From waiting for a bus, I now feel like a man running after one.

I strip in the line and try to concentrate on the pool and all that is going on. I hear and see rises of small fish. They are weak, though, and sound like small hands slapping the water. The larger fish make a distinct sound that is deep and more like that of a cupped hand swiftly breaking the surface. I'm trying to think only of the pool and the browns and the mayflies. But it's impossible not to think of other things.

From behind I hear a loud and distinct *kerplonk*. It brings me back and I turn and start false-casting in the direction of the sound. I let go and hear another deep rise just as my line hits the water. I lift up on the rod and feel the fish on the fly. It's small, though, and I quickly strip in and release it. It's not the fish that made the deep sound I cast to. I can see part of the pool's surface in the moonlight and see the rises of the smaller fish. I cannot, however, see the rises of the larger fish. They seem to be just beyond the edge of moonlight.

I hear another loud *kerplonk* and false-cast in the direction of where I suspect the brown to be. I hope I don't snag one of the bats, which I have done before and pray I'll never do again. The line lands, the fly alights on the surface, out of sight, and I hear another *kerplonk*. I lift up on the fly rod and feel the brown on the end.

It's a good fish, strong and determined to be rid of the piece of steel that's embedded in its jaw. The brown races upriver, and I see the fly line stretching out across the pool to where I suspect one of the other boulders is. The fly line vibrates as it cuts through the surface, and I try to lead the brown away from the boulder. I cannot, though, and the brown breaks off just as I feel the line wrap around the unseen boulder. The fly line comes shooting back, and the fly rod suddenly relaxes and straightens. I strip in the line and feel in my vest for a box of flies. I am stunned by the loss. I hate losing good fish. They haunt me and make me wonder what went wrong. I have never caught a fish to equal the size and strength of those that get away.

Something is in the pines again. It's across the pool, opposite the boulder just ahead of me, behind the wall of darkness. It's watching me and fumbling among pine boughs and tripping over rocks and stumps. My pulse quickens, my stomach turns, and I stare to where I think it is. It could be a raccoon or deer or even a bear. But something tells me it's none of these.

I change my fly, holding a penlight in my mouth, and check the leader and tippet, most of which was lost to the brown and the boulder. I do not replace the tippet section and tie the fly to what's left of the leader. I strip off a few feet of fly line and false-cast. Now the entire pool is a hailstorm and fish are rising everywhere, even next to the boulder I'm standing on. I hear a loud rise and cast and hook a solid brown the instant the fly lands. I play the fish for several minutes and bring it in close to the rock. I get down on my knees and reach down to grab the fish, which I intend to kill and put in my vest. But just as I'm about to put my fingers around it, it shakes its head and thrashes and gets off. I have a feeling that I was born to lose fish.

Kerplonk! Kerplonk! I cast to where the brown must be. The brown pounces on the fly like a cur on a T-bone. And before I can react, fly line is slipping through my left hand and running through the guides and out into the darkness. My inner ear pounds and my rod hand trembles as if it were holding a divining rod over a well. The brown bulls up the pool, and I turn it from other leader-breaking boulders. Then it heads for the bottom, and I think I feel it rubbing the leader and fly against rocks. I lift the rod up and to the side as much as I think the line and rod will take before breaking. The brown comes off the bottom and heads for the right bank, where the current is faster and where large rocks and half-submerged limbs from blowdowns wait for the brown to wrap the leader around. I think I may have to get in the water and wade with the brown, to keep it clear of the debris and reduce the chances of it breaking off. I worry about my fly rod, wonder if I made a mistake in bringing such a fine one. Wading over and around rocks and other unseen obstacles is bad enough, but wading in the dark while trying to catch a large brown and protect an expensive fly rod at the same time may be downright foolish.

I fish with an old cane fly rod, a three-piece made by James Payne, and a Walker reel. Both were Henry's and are antiques. I never fished with the fly rod until my wife surprised me by having Orvis refinish it without my knowing. She sneaked it out of the house during the winter and had it refinished as a Christmas present to me. She told me that the man at Orvis had said it was very valuable but also very serviceable and that it would be a shame if I didn't use it. So I started using it the following spring (after I secretly called Orvis to confirm what she had told me) and now seldom fish without it.

I bring the brown back into the center of the pool, and it bulls its way upriver to where other minatory boulders lie in wait. All I can do is try to keep pressure on the fish and pray that my tackle holds up. The old fly rod arcs under the pressure, but feels strong and dependable. The fish is a big brown, and I think that maybe I'm going to catch it. I watch the fly line travel out from the tip of the rod and follow it until it disappears into the darkness. The line quivers, the rod pulsates, and for the first time that night I realize I'm sweating.

So I worry and sweat and try not to show it. I want to catch this brown very badly but work hard to hide my wanting. I want to catch this brown trout and feel it in my hands and never let it go. But if I let on how much I want it, I'll make a mistake and lose it. It's happened before. So I pretend it's just another decent brown, nothing special— but then the brown makes a deliberate, heavy move, and I know my ruse is absurd. It's the largest trout I've ever hooked and I'm scared that I may lose it.

I hear another noise in the pines and it's directly opposite me. I have an eerie feeling that someone is watching. Without taking my eyes off the spot where the brown is, I shout out, "Who's there?" But no one answers. My mind races with ideas as to what or who is making the noises. I shout out again, but still there is no reply.

The brown and I are engaged in a tug of war. It tries to bull one way and I the other. Actually, I'm just holding on, amazed that I haven't lost it yet. I know that so far I have been lucky and not skillful in avoiding snags, and I wonder how much longer my luck will hold.

The brown is making for the bank again, and I know now that I'll have to wade. I kneel and slide off the boulder while keeping the rod up and pointed in the direction of the brown. The water is much cooler than when I waded out earlier and it wraps around my legs like icy tongs. It's a strange, almost eerie sensation to be in the water. On the boulder I was above the river and could move about and manage the rod without difficulty. But now I'm only a few feet above the water and not only is my vision further reduced, but I'm disoriented and not sure of where I am in relation to the pool's boundaries. I feel like I'm in a large, dark closet. My sneakers dig into the sandy bottom, and I stick one foot out ahead of the other to feel for rocks. As well as I know this river and pool in daylight, I find I don't know it at all under darkness. Now my eyes are not enough. Now I have to rely on balance and touch as well.

I hold the rod high and inch my way across the river. I stumble, start to fall, regain my balance a dozen times. There are hundreds, maybe thousands of mayflies hovering around my head and clinging to my arms and rod. Some are even perched on the fly line like doves on a wire. They are also on the pool's surface and are either struggling to lift off or spent, their bodies motionless and wings outstretched. Bats skim the surface and dart through the air and come so close to my head that I duck and turn away, because I know that one is bound to hit me. All around me are feeding trout, some so close that I can reach out and touch the water they just parted. I am truly in awe of what's going on around me—*despite* me. That I have a large brown on the end of my line seems more a surprise than a fact, as if it's something unexpected and uncalled for.

When I'm across the river, the brown turns back in the direction I just came from. I turn and follow and feel it pulling the line along the bottom. I think it wants to swim into the shallows and out of the pool and make a break for it through the pines. I don't have a clue as to what it has in mind. I'm confused. It should be running for the boulders or any of the numerous snags along the banks. But it's running into the shallows at the tail of the pool, which doesn't make any sense at all. Fly line is coming off the reel, and I know that at any second I'll feel the knot that signals I'm into the backing. I decide to wade faster and see if I can regain fly line and not have to rely on backing that hasn't been replaced in years. I push through the water, and it rises up over my waist, and when I stumble and go down on one knee, I shift the fly rod to my other hand and keep going.

When I'm in the shallows, back in familiar territory, I finally see the brown in a thread-thin beam of moonlight. It's in less than a foot of water and appears as a silhouette against the sandy bottom. I hold the fly rod higher still and am surprised to see that I'm within twenty feet of it. I don't know why, but I imagined the brown to be still far away, in the dark, and maybe something I would never really see. But I see its long and thick back mooning through the surface, its broad tail working back and forth, and its head shaking from side to side. I think it's around twenty-five inches long and well over three pounds, maybe five. Now, however, it wants the deeper water, and its entire body strains against the rod and line to get there. My heart beats furiously and my pulse races. Rivulets of sweat run down the sides of my face and for a brief second I panic. I look at the brown and don't know what to do. This is where I usually lose the few very large browns I've ever had on the line. This is where I can almost touch them, and where my wanting them so desperately causes me to make a mistake and lose them.

It comes to me that there is only one thing I can do. I have to try to keep the brown in the shallows and get a few more feet of line on the reel. I have to walk carefully up on the brown and reel in at the same time. I have to do this while maintaining constant pressure and without spooking it by careless footfalls. Then I have to walk back along the bank and try to turn the brown on its side and pull and lift it up on the shore.

I approach the brown and get back almost all the fly line. I can see where the leader and fly line are joined, and I can see, though I don't want to, the large fly embedded in the corner of the brown's lower jaw. I step back as carefully as I can and try to lift up and to the side on the fly rod. I have to get the brown turned and its head above the surface. The brown turns slowly and comes in heavy and on its side. I continue stepping back until its head is on the sand. Then I walk up and around to the back of the brown while still exerting pressure from the front.

I straddle the brown and crouch down, expecting it to make a sudden move for the water behind it. But it doesn't. It lies there, and I slide it over small white stones until it's at the foot of the bank three feet away. I relax the rod, forget about taking the hook out of the brown's jaw, and stand up without taking my eyes off it. Its sides heave, its jaws and gills work slowly; its tail quivers. "Sweet Jesus," I whisper, "the Fat Lady's thigh."

★ ★ ★

"Great fish." I nearly jump out of my skin as the words hit the air.

"What? Who's there? Where are you?" I turn toward the voice and see the silhouettes of two people on the opposite bank. I look at them quickly and then turn back to the brown.

"Sorry to surprise you. We've been watching you for a while. That's some fish you have there. You and he have been thrashing around some, eh?" I look back at him as he and the other person climb down the bank and wade across the river at the tail of the pool.

They appear in the moonlight, and I make out their images. He is young and tall and has a beard and is wearing wire-rimmed glasses. She is almost as tall as he is and has long hair and is wearing dungaree shorts and a tee shirt with the camp's logo on the front. When they are within a few feet of me I see she is beautiful and I'm embarrassed and turn away.

"Why didn't you answer me when I called out before?" I ask. I say this not because I want to know but because I feel obligated to say something. Actually, I'd rather they wade back across the river and leave me alone.

"Didn't want to spook you," he says. "You had just hooked that fish when we came on the scene, and I thought we'd just sit and watch. It was something to see, too. You and that fish and the mayflies and the bats. Man, it was wild!"

My legs and arms feel rubbery and ache. I kneel down and touch the brown. I don't think it's over five pounds, but it *is* over three and maybe even four. I run my hand over its smooth and silky side and then work the fly from its jaw. The moonlight gives the brown a deep and rich luster that makes its side appear amber and its back ebony. Its head is huge and its jaws are dark and powerful-looking. It is, as Henry had always claimed, the color of weathered barn boards after a rain. I think I could look at the brown forever.

"It's beautiful," says the woman. "What will you do with it?"

But before I can say anything the man says, "I know what I'd do. I'd have it mounted—and I'd hang that beautiful fly rod right over it."

"It's so beautiful, though," says the woman as she looks at the fish. "What a shame to kill it after all it's been through." And I watch her as she kneels and gently runs her fingertips over the side of the heaving brown.

The man snickers, and I paw the sand with a sneaker. I look at the brown and then say to the woman, "You mean it would be a shame to kill something that's given me so much pleasure? And if I let it go maybe I'll catch it again, right?"

The woman raises her head and looks at me. She doesn't know what to make of my words. Then she says, "Yes. Why would anyone want to kill something that's given him so much pleasure?"

I bend over and pick up the brown with two hands and walk it into the shallows. I hold the brown under the water and move it slowly back and forth to force water through its gills. Its body starts to respond; its gills work rhythmically. I feel it strengthen in my hands. I let go, and the brown moves off into deeper water. The man and woman watch me, and when I'm back on the shore, the woman says, "I bet you catch it again."

"It doesn't matter if I do or don't." And it really doesn't matter. I suddenly feel full, as if I'd just satisfied a huge appetite or thirst, and now only want to lie down and slip into a sound and much-needed sleep.

"Man, I never would have let that fish go," says the man in a low voice.

"It's something you learn," is all I can say.

The Ice Fisherman

Thomas Williams

That morning he rose from his wife
As if he were not her creature,
Left his house with lines and auger,
And went to the white ice.

He had known the lake in summer,
All of its thin, swallowing water;
Now only the accident of weather
Keeps him from going under.

Coming across all that white distance
The wind is jawless but has hunger;
Without a bite it takes the sense
From his heels and turns them rubber.

The ice gives before his auger,
And the black water takes its place
To the edge of his thin counter,
Up from the darkness in one pulse.

Into that dark he feeds his line;
Down the fathoms of that thin
Extensor of his fearful touch
His hand is tender to a mouth.

Thomas Williams

The bait he serves to that deep dark
Is not his flesh, and yet the fool
Trembles and is trembling still.
He fears a mouth deep in the lake

Will take his offer and will bite
The steel hook inside the bait,
Will take the steel to get the meat
That we all are, that we must eat.

A
New
River

*Thomas
McGuane*

IN OCTOBER, I looked off the wooden bridge and into the small river I had come to like so well. It was nearly covered with yellow cottonwood leaves; they diagramed its currents as they swept toward each other around the framework of the old boxcar out of which the bridge was made. A cold wind eddied down the river into my face, and I was ready to decide that to everything there is a season and that trout season was over. Fall gives us a vague feeling that the end of everything is at hand; here I felt that when the snow melted in the spring my wonderful little river would be gone.

I don't know if it was literally the first time I saw that river, but it is the first time I remember seeing it: I came down the side of the basin riding a young mare. I could see, first, the tree line of the small river, then, here and there, flashes of its runs and pools as it made its way through the pastureland of its own small valley. There were a few bright and geometric lines where irrigation ditches made diagonals from its more eloquent meanders, and a few small flooded areas where the water had stopped to reflect the clouds and the sky. It was a river with an indifferent fishing reputation.

Young anglers love new rivers the way they love the rest of their lives. Time doesn't seem to be of the essence and somewhere in the system is what they are looking for. Older anglers set foot on streams,

165

the location of whose pools is as yet unknown, with a trace of inertia. Like sentimental drunks, their interest is in what they already know. Yet soon enough, any river reminds us of others, and the logic of a new one is a revelation. It's the pools and runs we have already seen that help us uncode the holding water: the shallow riffle is a buildup for the cobbled channel where the thick trout nymph with mirror flashes; the slack back channel with the leafy bottom is not just frog water but a faithful reservoir for the joyous brook beyond. An undisturbed river is as perfect a thing as we will ever know, every refractive slide of cold water a glimpse of eternity.

The first evening I fished the river, I walked through a meadow that lay at the bottom of a curved red cliff, a swerving curve with a close-grained mantle of sage and prairie grasses. It could be that the river cut that curve, then wandered a quarter-mile south; but there you have it, the narrow shining band, the red curve, and the prairie. Sauntering along with my fly rod, hope began to build in the perceived glamour of my condition: a deep breath.

"Ah."

There was a stand of mature aspens with hard white trunks on the edge of meadow and next to the water. The grass was knee-deep. White summer clouds towered without motion. As I crossed to that spot, I could make out the progress of small animals, fanning away from my approach. I hurried forward in an attempt to see what it was, and a young raccoon shot up one of the slick aspens, then, losing traction, made a slow, baffled descent back into the grass. By shuffling around, I managed to have four of them either going up or sliding down at once. They were about a foot tall, and something about their matching size and identical bandit masks, coupled with their misjudgment of aspens as escape routes, gave me a sense of real glee at the originality of things. The new river gurgled in the bank.

I walked in and felt its pull against my legs. Current is a mysterious thing. It is the motion of the river leaving us, and it is as curious and thrilling a thing as a distant train at night. The waters of this new river, pouring from high in a Montana wilderness, are bound for the Gulf of Mexico. The idea that so much as a single molecule of the rushing chute before me was headed for Tampico was as eerie as the moon throwing a salty flood over the tidelands and then retrieving it. Things that pass us, go somewhere else and don't come back, seem to communicate directly with the soul. That the fisherman plies his craft on the surface of such a thing possibly accounts for his contemplative nature.

167

I once thought that this was somehow not true of aircraft, that they were too new and lacked mystery. But I lived for a time in the mountainous path of B-52 nighttime traffic. The faraway thunder that arose and fell to the west had the same quality of distance and departure that trains and rivers have. One pale summer night, I made out the darkened shape of one of these death ships against the stars, and shivered to think of the freshness of the high prairie where I was living beneath that great bird and its eggs of destruction.

The only bird today was a little water dipper, one of those ousellike nervous wrecks that seem not to differentiate between air and water, and stroll through both with aplomb. I associate them with some half-serious elfin twilight, a thing which, like the raccoons, suggests that there is a playful element in creation. I began to feel the animal focus that a river brings on as you unravel the current in search of holding water.

The learning of this river corresponded with the waning of runoff. My casting arm was still cold from winter, and I waded like a spavined donkey. I am always careful to go as light as possible early on, knowing that any little thing will throw me off; and the matter of getting over round, slick rocks, judging the depth and speed of current—things like these start out tough. One feels timid. Later in the year, you make the long, downstream pirouettes in deep fast water that you'd never chance when you're rusty.

It is a matter of ceremony to get rid of stuff. The winter has usually made me yield to some dubious gadgets, and you're at war with such things if the main idea of fishing is to be preserved. The net can go. It snags in brush and catches fly line. If it is properly out of the way, you can't get at it when you need it. Landing fish without a net adds to the trick and makes the whole thing better. Make it one box of flies. I tried to stick to this and ended up buying the king of Wheatlies, a double-sided brute that allows me to cheat on the single-box system. No monofilament clippers. Teeth work great. Trifles like leader sink, fly-line cleaner, and geegaws that help you tie knots must go. You may bring the hemostat, because to pinch down barbs and make quick, clean releases of the fabled trout help everything else make sense. Bring a normal rod, with a five- or six-weight line, because in early season the handle you have on hatches is not yet sufficient and you must be prepared to range through maybe eight fly sizes. Weird rod weights reflect armchair fantasies and often produce chagrin on the water.

I began to have a look at the river. It went through hard ground but cut deep. It was like a scribe line at the base of sine and cosine curves of bank banded at the top with a thin layer of topsoil. The river bottom was entirely rocks, small rounded ones, and on either side were the plateaus of similar stones, representing the water levels of thousands of previous years. A few mayflies drifted past in insignificant numbers. I understand that mayflies bear a rather antique genetic code themselves, expressed in size and color, and my hope is that if things pick up, I have the right imitations in my box.

As I face new water, I always ask myself if I am going to fish with a nymph or not. Presumably, you do not walk straight into rising trout. Camus said that the only serious question is whether or not to commit suicide. This is rather like the nymph question. It takes weight, a weighted fly, split shot. Casting becomes a matter of spitting this mess out and being orderly about it. It requires a higher order of streamcraft than any other kind of fishing, because it truly calls upon the angler to see the river in all its dimensions. Gone are the joys of casting, the steady meter and adjustment of loop that compare to walking or rowing. The joys of casting are gone because this ignoble outfit has ruined the action of your fly rod.

Still, you must show purpose. American shame at leisure has produced the latest no-nonsense stance in sport, the "streamside entomologist" and the "headhunter" being the most appalling instances that come readily to mind. No longer sufficiently human to contemplate the relationship of life to eternity, the glandular modern sport worries whether or not he is wasting time. Small towns used to have a mock-notorious character who didn't feel this way, the mythical individual who hung the GONE FISHIN' sign in the window of his establishment. We often made him a barber or someone remote from life-and-death matters. Sometimes we let him be a country doctor, and it was very rakish to drift grubs in a farm pond against the possible background of breech birth or peritonitis. Finally, we took it as very American to stand up and be superfluous in the glaring light of Manifest Destiny.

In the shock and delight of new water, my thoughts were entirely ineffective. What is the relationship of the bottom to the water, to the landscape through which it flows, to the life of the air around it all and the vegetation that alters the wind and interferes with the light? In other words, should one fish that deep outer bank—shaded by a hedge of wild junipers—with a nymph, or would it be better to imitate the few pale morning duns that are drifting around but not yet inspiring any surface feeding? In the latter case, that glassy run below the pool is the spot. For a moment, I avoid the conundrum by turning into another river-object, a manlike thing with the unmoving fly rod. Because time has stopped, I really don't concern myself with an eager companion who has already put three on the beach.

Mortality being what it is, any new river could be your last. This charmless notion runs very deep in us and does produce, besides the tightening around the mouth, a sweet and consoling inventory of all the previous rivers in your life. Finally, the fit is so perfect that it gives the illusion that there is but one river, a Platonic gem. There are more variations within any one good river than there are between a number of good rivers. I have been fortunate in that my life-river has a few steelhead in the lower reaches, as well as Oregon harvest trout and the sea-run browns of Ireland; there are Michigan brook trout in the deep bends, braided channels in hundred-mile sections from the Missouri headwaters trout theme park; and here and there are the see-through pools of New Zealand. Fire and water unlock the mind to a kind of mental zero gravity in which resemblances drift toward one another. The trout fisherman finishes his life with but one river.

All this is getting fairly far-fetched; still, like the trout, we must find a way of moving through water with the least amount of displacement. The more we fish, the more weightlessly and quietly we move through a river and among its fish, and the more we resemble our own minds in the bliss of angling.

I came to a pool where a tree with numerous branches had fallen. Its leaves were long gone, and the branches tugged lightly in the slight current that went through the pool. A remarkable thing was happening: a good-sized brown was jumping among the lowest branches, clearly knocking insects loose to eat. Every three or four minutes, it vaulted into the brush over its window and fell back into the water. I knew if I could get any kind of a float, I would have a solid taker. I looked at all the angles, and the only idea I could come up with was that it was a good time to light a cigar. In a moment, the excellent smoke of Honduras rose through the cottonwoods. I waited for an idea to form, a solution, but it never happened. In the end, I reared back and fired a size 14 Henryville Caddis into the brush. It wound around a twig and hung in midair. The trout didn't jump at it suicidally. I didn't get the fly back.

Angling doesn't turn on stunts. The steady movements of the

habituated gatherer produce the harvest. This of course must be in the service of some real stream knowledge. But some fishing, especially for sea-run fish, rewards a robotic capacity for replicating casts, piling up the repetitions until the strike is induced. The biggest things a steelheader or Atlantic salmon fisherman can have—not counting waders and a stipend—are a big arm and a room-temperature IQ.

The river made an angular move to the south into the faraway smoky hills. In the bend, there was some workmanlike dry-wall riprap that must have reflected the Scandinavian local heritage. The usual Western approach would be to roll an old car into the river at the point of erosion. Instead of that, I found neatly laid cobbles that gave the impression that the river was slowly revealing an archaeological enigma or the foundations of a church. But for the next forty yards, the clear water trembled deep and steady over a mottled bottom, and I took three hearty browns that flung themselves upon the bright surface of the run. When I was young and in the thrall of religion, I used to imagine various bands of angels, which were differentiated principally by size. The smallest ones were under a foot in height, silvery and rapid, and able to move in any plane at will. The three trout in that run reminded me of those imaginary beings.

The river lay down at the bottom of a pencil-thin valley, and though I could see the wind in the tops of the trees, I could barely feel it where I fished. The casts stretched out and probed without unwarranted shepherd's crooks, blowbacks, or tippet puddles. I came to a favorite kind of stretch: twenty or thirty yards of very shallow riffle with a deep green slot on the outside curve. In this kind of conformation, you wade in thin, fast water easily and feel a bit of elevation to your quarry. The slot seems to drain a large oxygenated area, and it's the only good holding water around. Where had I seen so much of this? The Trinity? The Little Deschutes? It had slipped in the telescoping of rivers.

I couldn't float the entire slot without lining part of it. So I covered the bottom on my first casts, doping out the drift as I did, and preparing for the long float in the heart of the spot, one I was sure would raise a fish. The slot was on the left-hand side of the river and contoured the bank, but the riffle drained at an angle to it. I saw that a long, straight cast would drag the fly in a hurry. When the first casts to the lower end failed to produce, I tried a reach cast to the right, got a much better drift, then covered the whole slot with a longer throw.

The Henryville Caddis had floated about two yards when a good brown appeared below it like a beam of butter-colored light. It tipped back, and we were tight. The fish held in the current even though my rod was bent into the cork, then shot out into the shallows for a wild aerial fight. I got it close three times but it managed to churn off through the shallow water. Finally, I had it and turned its cold form upside down in my hand, checked its length against my rod—eighteen inches—and removed the hook. I decided that these were the yellowest, prettiest stream-bred browns I had ever seen. I turned it over and lowered it into the current. I love the feeling when they realize they are free. There seems to be an amazed pause. Then they shoot out of your hand as though you could easily change your mind.

The afternoon wore on without specific event. The middle of a bright day can be as mindless as it is timeless. Visibility is so perfect you forget it is seldom a confidence builder for trout. The little imperfections of the leader, the adamant crinkles standing up from the surface, are clear to both parties.

No sale.

But the shadows of afternoon seem to give meaning to the angler's day on about the same scale that fall gives meaning to his year. As always, I could feel in the first hints of darkness a mutual alertness between me and the trout. This vague shadow the trout and I cross progresses from equinox to equinox. Our mutuality grows.

A ring opened on the surface. The first rise I had seen. The fish refused my all-purpose Adams, and I moved on. I reached an even-depth, even-speed stretch of slick water that deepened along the right-hand bank for no reason: there was no curve to it. The deep side was in shadow, a great, profound, detail-filled shadow that stood along the thin edge of brightness, the starry surface of moving water in late sun. At the head of this run, a plunge pool made a vertical curtain of bubbles in the right-hand corner. At that point, the turbulence narrowed away to a thread of current that could be seen for maybe twenty yards on the smooth run. Trout were working.

I cast to the lowest fish from my angle below and to the left. The evenness of the current gave me an ideal float free of drag. In a moment of hubris I threw the size 14 Adams, covered the fish nicely for about five minutes while it fed above and below. I worked my way to the head of the pool covering six other fish. Quickly, I tied on a Royal Wulff, hoping to shock them into submission. Not a single grab. The fish I covered retired until I went on, then resumed feeding. I was losing my light and had been casting in the middle of rising fish for the better part of an hour: head and tail rises with a slight slurp. There were no spinners in the air, and the thread of the current took whatever it was down through the center of the deep water beyond my vision. This was the first time that day the river had asked me to figure something out; and it was becoming clear that I was not going to catch a fish in this run unless I changed my ways.

I was dealing with the selective trout, that uncompromising creature in whose spirit the angler attempts to read his own fortune.

I tucked my shirt deep inside the top of my waders and pulled the drawstring tight. I hooked my last unsuccessful fly in the keeper and reeled the line up. Then I waded into the cold, deep run, below the feeding fish. I felt my weight decreasing against the bottom as I inched toward the thread of current that carried whatever the fish were feeding on. By the time I reached it, I was within inches of taking on the river and barely weighed enough to keep myself from joining the other flotsam in the Missouri headwaters. But—and, as my mother used to say, "it's a big but"—I could see coming toward me, some like tiny sloops, some like minute life rafts unfurling, baetis duns: olive-bodied, clear-winged, and a tidy size 18.

I have such a thing, I thought, in my fly box.

By the time I had moon-walked back to a depth where my weight meant something, I had just enough time to test my failing eyes against the little olive-emergers and a 6X tippet viewed straight over my head in the final light. Finally, the thing was done and I was ready to cast. The fly seemed to float straight downward in the air and down the sucking hole the trout made. It was another short, thick, buttery brown, and it was the one that kept me from flunking my first day on that river. It's hard to know ahead of time which fish is giving the test.

Epstein's Conversion

Charles Gaines

WE FINALLY left the dock at Cozumel at 9:00 A.M. and were tossing around in the strait a thousand yards off the coast of Yucatan by ten. There was not a single trout angler in sight, and that was just fine with Epstein.

In fact, there wasn't any kind of fisherman in sight, though this was May and the middle of the annual sailfish run. A thirty-knot wind was blowing, there were eight-to-ten-foot seas running in the strait, and nobody but José wanted any part of it. All those fifty-foot Strikers and Merritts and Hatterases sitting back there at the dock like a meeting of the board of directors of the Bass Weejun Company, and every one of their captains with something else to do today but fish. Including the guy Epstein and I had chartered: Emilio.

"Ees too windy. Maybe mañana," he had said, and gone back to cleaning the already spotless cabin of the fifty-two-foot Egg Harbor he captained. It belonged to a man from Pennsylvania—a trout angler, Epstein was sure, who had instructed Emilio never to go fishing when the wind was blowing.

I had reminded Emilio that we had to leave *mañana*, and also that neither Epstein nor I had yet caught a sailfish on a fly rod. That was what we had come down here to do, but for the past two days we had let Emilio and the wind keep us from trying, and had settled for catching sail after sail on twenty-pound trolling tackle. Today was our last chance.

"Good-bye," Emilio had said to that, and closed the cabin door.

★　★　★

More seriously, it was fishing's last chance with Epstein. Epstein had given up fishing. Until this week he hadn't touched a rod since a July afternoon almost two years before, when a long simmering hatred for what he called "trout anglers" had finally boiled over.

We had been fishing emergers on a snobbish little brook in Vermont, the guest of George Talbot, a man I knew who was always talking about "riseforms" and his latest reading of Dame Juliana, but was otherwise, to my mind, okay. Not to Epstein's mind, however. He and Talbot had developed a strong antipathy for each other over the course of the two days we fished together, and I was much relieved at the end of the second day when it appeared that Epstein and I were going to get back to New Hampshire without any outright unpleasantness between the two of them.

Talbot and I had been taking down our rods, talking peacefully beside his car in the warm dusk with a bottle of Beam on the hood between us, when Epstein came splashing out of the brook, his forefinger through the bleeding gills of a large brown trout.

"Look at this," he shouted to me. "Do you believe this fish came out of this piss-ant little stream?" He tossed the trout at our feet, where it pitched feebly a couple of times in the dust. Talbot looked at the fish, then up at me, his face pale.

"Do you intend to kill this lovely fish?" he asked Epstein without looking at him.

"You bet, pal," said Epstein happily. "Kill it and eat it."

"I'm sorry, but I have to ask that you let me measure it first."

"Be my guest," said Epstein proudly.

Slipping to his knees, Talbot pulled a retractable tape from his vest, straightened the fish, and measured it. "She's not legal," he said. "We'll have to release her."

"What are you talking about?" Epstein demanded. "The limit is eight inches. That fish has to be over fifteen."

"Eighteen exactly," said Talbot. He was quickly constructing a little stretcher out of twigs. "I think she'll be okay if we can just get her back to the water without *touching* her anymore." He looked up at me, ignoring Epstein. "We have a regulation here that we kill only fish between eight and sixteen inches. Or, of course, anything over twenty inches . . ."

"*What?*" thundered Epstein.

"Of course, *most* of us haven't killed a fish of any size in years." Talbot slid the trout gently onto the stretcher he had made and stood up carefully. "I think she'll be all right, don't you?" he asked me.

"Well," I said, "it's bleeding from the gills."

"Let me get this straight," said Epstein. We were both following Talbot as he cat-walked toward the stream, holding the trout stretcher gingerly aloft. "That fish is two inches too long to be legal, and it's also two inches too *short* to be legal? Is that right?"

" 'Legal' isn't exactly the right word. It's just the way we all agree to do things here on the Passacowadee."

I hadn't liked the sound of Epstein's voice, so I said, "Look here, Talbot, I really *don't* think that fish is going to live. . . ."

Epstein interrupted me by suddenly hopping in front of Talbot and snatching the trout off the stretcher. "The way I see it," he said, looking from Talbot to me and back again, his eyes glittering, "we've got two classic trout-angler problems here. Number one"—he held up the fish by its tail—"is this fucker going to live or not. And number two, he's two inches too long for those of us here on the Passacowadee."

Talbot nodded without taking his eyes off his patient. He wanted the brown back and reached out. He was too late, though, because just then Epstein stuck the trout's entire head into his mouth and bit down. Holding the tail with both hands, he gnawed away furiously at the trout, snorting and huffing like a grizzly and spitting out trout blood and pieces of flesh, until finally he had chewed off the head—which he spat on the ground at the feet of the pale and hypnotized Talbot. Epstein grinned wolfishly. In his last civilized utterance of any kind to a trout angler, he said in a deceptively benign voice, "You see how easy it is to solve problems if we just put our heads together?"

Of course it was not everyone who fishes for trout who drove Epstein to give up the primary passion of his life, but only that percentage (growing daily, he believed) who qualified in his mind as trout *anglers*. Epstein's trout angler had rules to govern every pleasure, and that was what Epstein most despised about him. But he also hated the fellow's stuffiness and academic bent, his pipe and tweed hats, how vulnerable he looked in waders, his sheepish enthusiasm for following other trout anglers, his womanish sentimentality, the prissy way he ate and drank, his physical cautiousness, and his obsession with minutiae: little flies, little rules, little tools hung all over his vest, the invention of little tactical problems to make trout fishing seem harder than it is.

In the last year or so before he quit fishing, Epstein had begun to see trout anglers behind every bush and tree. In West Yellowstone and Ennis, in Oregon and Idaho, in Labrador and Ireland—everywhere he went they were waiting for him, pursing their lips over some local rule, wading cautiously in shallow water with the help of a staff, making flaccid little casts, spooking fish they never saw, lighting their pipes, and talking sentimentally. Talbot was just a merciful last straw. When pushed, Epstein would acknowledge that Talbot was not the most egregious trout angler he had ever met, just the last; and he would even express some regret at having thrown Talbot bodily into the Sundown Pool of the Passacowadee.

But however good or bad his motives, Epstein had sworn off all fishing that day in Vermont—and not fishing began to ruin his life. His marriage and his medical practice fell into shambles. He began to drink too much, and he developed an unnerving habit of picking fights with anyone wearing a uniform.

I happen to enjoy the company of people who are actively engaged in wrecking their lives over something they like or don't like, so long as they are not members of my immediate family; but one night at a party, Epstein's wife took me aside and asked me for help. She looked up at me with her great, dark eyes and asked me to "do something." We rarely saw the Epsteins socially, and I was moved. So I talked him into coming down to Cozumel with me. He had never done any salt-water fishing, and I was sure he would take to it. For the first few days, though, he found Emilio's pussyfooting delicacy about the weather and the cleanliness of his boat to be just other forms of trout angling. Fishing, it appeared, was about to lose Epstein permanently. And then we walked down the dock and met José.

José was sitting in a rusty lawn chair in the stern of a dumpy, homemade-looking thirty-foot boat called the *Gloria*. He knew no English, and Epstein and I little Spanish, but we worked out the essential details in a matter of minutes. Epstein and I were given to understand this clearly: We had found a skinny, barefooted Indian with a potbelly who didn't give a rat's ass how much wind was blowing.

The *Gloria* didn't have sonar or teak decks or a shower. Neither did she have a few more necessary accouterments to sport fishing—such as outriggers, a mate, or bait. But she did have an ice chest full of Dos Equis, and Epstein and I found a nice blue-skirted lure which we rigged without a hook on one of José's decrepit fifty-pound trolling outfits. As soon as we hit the straits, José turned upsea, cut the *Gloria* back to trolling speed, put on a Jimmy Buffett tape, and—holding a beer in one hand and spinning the wheel with the other, laughing and singing and hopping around to keep his balance like a potbellied parrot—he commenced to go fishing.

At first, Epstein and I couldn't stand up in the cockpit. But when we could, we let the lure out, and sailfish started jumping all over it. Everywhere we looked beyond the transom there were sailfish—herds of them, lit up and running over each other to get the lure. I gave Epstein the fifty-pound outfit and lurched toward the cabin for my fly rod.

"They're trying to eat the goddamn thing," Epstein shouted after me. All either of us knew about fly fishing for billfish was what we had read.

I staggered back into the cockpit holding the fly rod. "Just don't let them cut it off—it's the only lure we've got." Epstein was crouched at the transom, his legs locked under it, whipping the boat rod up and down and making the blue lure, thirty yards back, leap and plunge. Through the waves we could see sailfish diving and jumping all around it. I tried false-casting and couldn't because of the wind, so I dropped the big red-and-white streamer into the prop wash and let the boat's momentum carry it back about fifteen yards.

"I'd better go tell José what to do," said Epstein. "Here." He shoved the boat rod over to me. "I'll tell him to throw the boat out of gear when I shout."

"How are you going to tell him that?"

"Small, small problem, amigo," said Epstein. "Size of a trout angler's dick."

While he was gone, the boat quartered into a particularly big sea, yawed, and crashed into the next trough. Behind me I heard glass shatter and Epstein curse; then he was beside me again at the transom, grabbing back the boat rod.

"José is all set. I'm going to bring this fucker in."

I pulled the tip of the fly rod up into the wind to my right as far as I could without lifting the streamer off the water. Then I stripped some line off the reel and onto the deck and hoped I could make one good cast. Epstein was reeling fast, and the blue lure skipped toward us, hounded by sailfish. When the lure was about fifty feet away and still coming, Epstein said, "You ready?"

I nodded.

"*José!*" Epstein yelled, and just as the boat went out of gear, he yanked the rod up and backward over his head, lifting the lure off the

179

waves and catapulting it toward us. Confused, the sails milled forty feet off the transom. I lifted the fly rod's tip another inch or two and pushed it hard forward. The streamer picked up, caught the wind, and rode it out perfectly to the sailfish, pulling loose line off the deck. When it slapped down, I started stripping it back in foot-long jerks. The streamer hadn't traveled a yard before a sailfish charged in a quick, silver furrow of water and ate it. I let go of the underside of the transom with my knees, reared back to hit the fish, and slipped. Epstein caught me and held me upright. "Hit him again," he said, and I did, three times, and we watched the backing pour off the reel.

"Why is there blood all over the deck?" I asked Epstein.

"A window broke in the cabin, and I cut my leg on it."

"Isn't that an awful lot of blood?"

He was still holding me upright against the transom while I played the fish, and I could feel blood running down the backs of my legs.

"It's okay. Just don't lose that baby! Can you *believe this shit?*" Epstein whooped. The sail was tail-walking a hundred yards back, its lean, violet body snapping like a flag in the wind. "We have wasted our whole fucking *lives* fishing mudholes for guppies. I have just been made *whole*, goddammit. . . ." He added after a moment, "I have to puke now." His voice was still so delighted I thought he was kidding. He wasn't. Without letting me go, he turned his head and threw up violently on his shoulder and the deck. When he was finished, he coughed a couple of times and spat. "Deep-sea fishing!" he shouted hoarsely into my ear. "To hell with women and work!"

With Epstein holding me upright and with José handling the boat beautifully, I had the sail tired and circling just off the stern in eight minutes. When the fish moved under the boat, I yelled for José to go forward. Taking me to mean the fish was ready, I guess, he threw the boat into neutral and popped back into the cockpit like a jumping bean, gloved for billing the fish, thrilled to death with everything that was going on—even, it appeared, the unexplained blood and vomit all over his deck.

"Go *forward*," I yelled to him and pointed to the fly line running directly under the stern, which at that moment stopped and refused to budge. The fish had run the line around the prop.

"Shit," Epstein said and let me go.

"Aiyeee!" said José. He popped back into the cabin, reemerging in seconds in a mask and fins and, before Epstein or I could figure out what he was doing, he jumped overboard into the heaving sea.

Epstein and I looked at each other, then overboard. It was not a place anyone would have wanted to be. Between the fish and the fly line was a foot of fifteen-pound leader tippet. Though we didn't say it, neither Epstein nor I believed that the tippet had not already parted, either on contact with the prop or at the fish's first surge. But within seconds, the line came unstuck, and I felt it to be, miraculously, still connected to the fish.

Epstein pulled José back into the boat, and José got the engine going, and the boat turned upwind. Then he came into the cockpit and grabbed the sailfish by its bill. He pulled the fish half over the transom, and Epstein started clubbing its electric-blue head with a Coke bottle.

"Stop it," I said to him. "That's my fish, and I want to release it." Even before I had finished the sentence, I was sorry I had spoken it.

Epstein paused with his hand raised and looked at me. His face was set with a fierce new assurance, and his eyes had the same noncommittal savagery in them that you often see in animals' eyes.

"The hell it is," he said quietly. Then he clubbed the fish again with the bottle, and José let it slide dead onto the deck.

Both of them straightened up and grinned at me. Epstein had tied his tee shirt around his thigh, which had finally stopped bleeding. In real life he is a doctor, but he doesn't look like one. He is also an ex-college football player and wrestler, an enthusiastic fist fighter and skydiver—a big, trouble- and pain-addicted man. Later, back in Cozumel, not trusting Mexican clinics, he would disinfect and sew up his wound himself. It took thirty-five stitches to close the cut, and then we went out and drank a world of Cuervo Gold and said very little to each other.

One thing Epstein did say, late that night, was that he had found his religion. He said that very loudly at about three in the morning while staring unsteadily at a stuffed blue marlin hanging in the lobby of our hotel. And I suppose I believed him. I have not seen Epstein since that moment, but occasionally I hear about him and his fishing. A captain I know wrote me recently that he and Epstein took a Striker, a Morton's salt box full of cocaine, and two hookers down to Chile this past winter to look for swordfish, but spent all their time shooting sharks and getting laid in the tuna tower.

I have learned that very little in life is simple, even fishing. But there for a moment or two in the cockpit of the *Gloria*, standing astride his sailfish, shirtless and hairy, new-looking and sweating, and caked with dried blood and puke, Epstein was, I believe, simply a happy man.

After he had grinned at me for a long time, he picked José up and hugged him. Then he sat the little Indian carefully back down on the deck.

"Muchas gracias," Epstein told him.

José ran up to the wheel, cracked a *cerveza*, turned up the Buffett, and winked at us over the stained shambles of his boat. He put the throttle in the corner, and the *Gloria* heaved forward. "More fish now, sí?" he shouted.

Epstein squinted approvingly at him, as if trying to calculate just how many trout anglers the little fellow was worth.

Bonefish Revenge

David Simpson

TO THOSE who do not fish, angling is often seen as a moronic act, practiced only by drawling yokels in baseball caps. In reality, fishing can grow to a fearsome complexity quite unrelated to the rest of existence. The quixotic angler is most likely to become peevish about the promised benefits of civilization. He seeks wildness and an immersion near to that of the womb, with a passion that neglects employment, politics, and taxes. Something so keenly felt cannot be tipped into the cultural gutter. If football is metaphoric of the corporate miasma, then fishing is indicative of the secret, divergent life of the untethered soul.

The bonefish seems the perfect object of desire for this type of fisherman. Those who fly-fish for the vulpine apparition pursue something more on their travels than mere fish in the hand, the traveling being necessary because we have buggered our opportunities at home. Bonefishing does not require the physical preparation needed for some other fish, like the intimidating tarpon. The angler can go after them on his holiday and feel perfectly safe. He will also get his money's worth, for the bonefish is a miraculous creature that will streak off great hanks of line when hooked.

I do not mean to infer that bonefishing is easy. In most places these fish are spooky, and difficult to take on the fly. This snag can be overcome with a Zenlike and prayerful attitude, although the neophyte cannot see how he is going to fulfill his ardent desire without a sustained move somewhere south. On a one-week vacation, any great expectation is liable to leave him ready for the nuthouse.

The truth is, privation is rampant out there on the flats. Just getting in front of the fish seems a sizable obstacle. The angler is up against wind, tide, temperature, sun, commercial fishermen, local politics, tourists, famous golfers, outboard motors, bloodsucking insects, sea birds, surly guides, every kind of aircraft, strange intestinal flora, tropical disturbances, predator fish, and bonefish-eating natives. He soon learns to stand slightly to the side of this seething mess and watch for openings, when he can dash in and make connections. My own bonefishing career has been checkered with failure. Never one to reject the eternal verities of the sea, I would just as soon be catching more fish. If deprivation is what it takes to purge the spirit of its toxins, I say that it is time to take the boy off the emetic and put him on whole food.

In the past, the bonefisherman has had the Florida Keys as a spiritual home. Fish are still caught there, of course, but what angler can pretend that everything is right in the Sunshine State? Water problems and the concomitant decline of the snook population are enough to cause an initial mistrust. Florida is also a place where the cult of Disney crackles across the cultural synapse; where drug kingpins count laundered bank notes in the bluish, slightly unreal auras of swimming pools. In the Keys, legions of sun-wrinkled retirees, each with a pastrami-and-Swiss in a brown bag, go most days to glean the sea bottom of urchins and molluscs, the skeletons of which will eventually join the tourist tableau on the Overseas Highway. Still, the pull of the sea endures, and the fisherman who can just manage to stay somewhere below Biscayne Bay may still find some of what he seeks.

I went to the Keys on my first bonefishing trip, which began with a gruesome drive across the South in Robert McCurdy's Ford pickup. There were high points, including an enormous blind, penned alligator that was fed road-killed possums and armadillos. We ate soft-shell-crab po-boys, heavy on the mayo and Tabasco, beside a leaden Lake Pontchartrain. Standing on a bridge overlooking the dark and heavy Suwannee, I ignored suggestions of bass fishing, feeling a strong need to go, like the river, on to the sea.

Things began to go bad on the third day, as we reached the tourist foppery and environmental horror of the Florida orange country. On the western shore of Lake Okeechobee, a huge cumulonimbus squall swept down upon us. We had been drinking Scotch amid the orange groves and were unprepared for demonstrative acts of nature.

Instantly, the road was covered with three inches of water. It was then that I discovered we were at the hands of a driver who reacted to the aquaplaning of the tires by saying, "Another Scotch, with a little less water this time, please!"

It was this impairment of navigational systems that caused us to miss a turn, and, instead of running free down through the River of Grass, we were swept into the darkened bowels of Miami Beach. I'll admit I was at the wheel. We stared out with terror at the crowds of "seniors" wandering toothlessly through the orange glow of street-lights. This was bonefishing? It was when we drove by Joe's Stone Crab for the second time that we began to suspect we were victims of a Chamber of Commerce plot designed to have us cruise in circles on the palm-lined boulevards, buying expensive food and loud clothing until our money was gone.

We awoke the next morning in Key Largo, although I couldn't say how we got there. I felt poisoned. It was hot, and, from my pastel motel room, I could hear the creaking of terns and could smell the sea.

We moved down to Marathon, into cheap lodgings, and went fishing. Off Grassy Key, I cast to my first bonefish, a shadowy nimbus that drifted across a patch of clean sand. The flats streamed with a succession of sea life: sharks, spotted eagle rays, stingrays, barracuda, and turtles. Tarpon rolled and breached in the channels. I was astounded to see my first permit rise little more than a rod length from me, a luminous entity that hung in the swell and then vanished like windblown smoke. We paddled our canoe out to the channel flats off Tom's Harbor Key and took repeated shots at the typical Key bone-fish—huge, sophisticated curs that either ignored our flies or roared off the flats trailing vigorous wakes. One stormy evening off Burnt Point, we chased a school of tarpon while lightning wrinkled the ominous sky out over Florida Bay. We came in bug-bitten and feeling relieved that we hadn't hooked up and spent the night being towed toward Flamingo by some devil of a fish we couldn't see.

Each one of those days in the Key was one of unexpected magic. I lived in a state of perfect equipoise, wanting only to be balanced somewhere between sea and sky. I knew I had been waiting for this all my life. I felt whole and clean.

One month after my return from Florida, I flew down to Mexico to fish at a famous camp in the state of Quintana Roo. My companions and I were lured there by the promise of huge schools of naïve bone-fish. After considerable flying around in airplanes of various sizes, we were left on a mangrove-and-shell islet, where we met two skiffs, each manned by a swarthy little Mayan guide with a crooked stick for a push pole. In the boat, and running across Ascensión Bay, I easily stepped back up on the plane of tropical equipoise. The guide shut down and poled us up onto a turtle-grass flat and pointed. I assumed he meant to look for fish, so I tried to discern individual shapes against the dark bottom. The guide continued to gesture and make casting motions. Suddenly the entire bottom began to move; it was a school of *hundreds* of bonefish! I shot a cast into their general path and had an immediate hookup. The fish swam with its brethren for a moment and then tore off in two classical runs and circled the boat to the net. In the mesh lay a diminutive, three-pound Mexican bonefish, his vacant eye staring at the sky. He was big enough, and I was soaring.

My partner, a rank beginner, stepped up to the casting deck and had trouble seeing fish, but was soon into one anyway. We were giddy with the ease of it all and hopped around the boat with exaggerated en-thusiasm.

For two days, we cruised around the bay, picking up good numbers of bonefish, jumping big barracuda out of the holes, and getting shots at permit on the deeper flats adjacent to the channels. We stayed on a houseboat tucked into a protected corner of the bay and at night ate brilliant little lane snappers and spiny lobster. And even though I was recovering from a case of the trotskis, which I had contracted before Mexico, I had never felt more alive.

On the third day, an early tropical storm, far out in the Caribbean, began to pump clouds in, and the visibility and fishing went to hell. It was an event that rarely occurs in May. We moved back to the swampy flats at the main camp, where the fish were schooled and wary. I stopped catching fish. One of my friends caught a permit and repeat-edly bludgeoned everyone else with the story. Still, my desire to catch fish remained undimmed. I spotted tailers even before the guides. I made impossible over-the-shoulder casts to departing permit, which ignored my fly. I was in tune with the rhythms of the sea but couldn't even catch a snapper for dinner.

The pall of the storm approached with a frightening stillness. We flew out ahead of it, and could see Cozumel ahead of us, glowing in a pool of streaming, filtered church light. All I could think was that passion has a way of extracting its price. The only way out of this gloom, other than starting to catch fish, was to stop wanting to, and that was no choice at all.

We are at the Eastern counter, standing in an intense panel of raking sunlight. It is just after dawn on a September morning in Texas. When Robert tells the agent we are going bonefishing, she looks blank and says that the plane to Miami is on time. Robert replies, "It had better be, because I want to be drinking cheap rum by tonight!"

First off, I'm suspicious about the whole arrangement. We are headed for St. John, in the U.S. Virgins, which you could hardly call a bonefish destination. Second, it is not the season: September is the big hurricane month in the Caribbean. For the last two weeks, we have been hunched over the TV and tuned in to the Weather Channel. We're watching the radar screen, and great clots of clouds scud over the islands from their breeding grounds in the African Atlantic. What's more, there is really only one flat, although the previous April Robert found it intensely visited by bonefish and permit. Rumors of a fall tarpon run have finally atomized remaining doubt, and things at home have generally gone to hell anyway, so here we are again.

The journey itself is a little complex, but we have it laid out so that we'll be on the water twenty-four hours from now, to intercept permit tailing along the channels at first light. The idea is to fly to St. Thomas, take a taxi to Red Hook, the ferry to Cruz Bay, and finally meet a real estate agent with the jeep that goes with our rented house.

We begin by flying to Miami, where we spend an hour between planes, smoking Honduran cigars and viewing the Day-Glo tourist dreck sold in the airport shops. We then board a DC-10 with lots of other happy vacationers and take off into a tranquil sky. We forget about the storms. Far below, the Bahamas lie on a verdant sea, and puffy discrete clouds cast intense shadows on the shallows of the Great Bahama Bank. The flight is only slightly marred by the appearance of a crew of useless offshore types, headed for St. Thomas for a fishing tournament. Your mother will tell you not to type-cast folks, but these are types, and we know instinctively that they are the natural enemies of flats fishermen.

Sometime later, we are sitting on the tarmac at St. Croix, watching the palms being lashed over to oblique angles by wind and rain. This is not where we want to be, but St. Thomas is closed to jet traffic. An hour passes. We are then taken to San Juan, Puerto Rico, which opens an old wound for Robert, who always loses some item of his gear when passing through San Juan. We have paid an extra hundred dollars each specifically to *avoid* San Juan. At customs, Robert is summarily relieved of his lip gaff. The passengers are split into two groups and loaded onto selections from that strange catalog of aging aircraft that seem to gather in the tropics.

In St. Thomas, the luggage is slow in coming. Robert insists on retrieving his lip gaff. This business is all performed at three-quarter time, accompanied by a perspiration suite in the wet, heavy air. On the way to Red Hook, we are caught in a traffic snarl, and finally see the cause as a body laid out in the street, ringed by black faces. The taxi driver says, "Got *dot* one, mon!"

After dinner, Robert's drink (at exorbitant cost), a wet ferry ride, and meeting with a ruffled real estate agent, we take a jeep ride through a bizarre nightscape of tropical lushness. Despite having wanted it for so long, bed almost seems like a disappointment.

That tropical languor you hear about is real. We begin each day in bed, overcome by the sweet, intricate smell of the island. Mosquitoes drift languidly on the screens, and the ceiling fan revolves in lyrical circuits. Rising on one elbow, I can see the lights of St. Thomas across a void of gray space—sea and sky. It is too late to be on the flat at first light, so we pause to eat cheese toast and drink tea.

Each morning, the precise black sickles of permit tails emerge above the calm surface of our flat. The trades pick up, and the sun rises through glaucous clouds. We agree that nobody is exactly tearing the fish up. It rains. The heavy weather out in the Atlantic sends great cells of clouds over us. Still, there are a few shots at fish, and Robert catches a couple of bonefish and then has a permit on long enough to feel its resolute power before he is cut off on staghorn coral. I finally figure out the pattern for bonefish and seduce one, only to have it break off at the first insane surge.

The scenery is intense; we are fishing in a bowl of green, forested mountains. In the azure water outside the reef, pelagic fish cut into bait, sending them up in silver sheets that fall back to be consumed under the frenzied surface. We stand on one point of the flat, and mackerel swirl in the drop-off beneath our feet. The little amphibians of the Virgin Islands Seaplane Shuttle go to Tortola and back. The fast ferry *Bomba Charger* pounds through heavy seas, taking tourists to Virgin Gorda. None of this is a substitute for catching fish.

It rains. We spend part of each day reconnoitering for tarpon, with no success. One morning, rodless, I walk up the road from the flat to use the portable john (this is a national park) and watch a huge permit, looking powerful and malevolent, working the stony edges of the beach. By the second day, an afternoon nap becomes a necessary part of the agenda. It rains. After the nap, there is snorkeling—sporting with barjacks and mackerel off the rocks. On the fourth day, the winds intensify, and the pelicans move in from outside and begin to bomb the flat, effectively killing all the bonefishing. We still hope for permit, knowing that they are always the long shot.

At night, we concoct wild drinks of Cruzan rum and fruit juice, scheme, tie flies, and embark on repeated hunts for the ventriloquist tree frogs that carry on from the dripping vegetation. I begin to develop a speaking relationship with the tame anoles that live on the porch. Reading begins to seem like good entertainment. It is in the reading of some tourist propaganda that I discover that there is a little-known Virgin Island famed for bonefish. Enthusiasm returns. We burn up the telephone, trying to make connections in the three days we have left. We finally arrange a charter flight based on a hint from a park ranger. That, a night at the only hotel, and an afternoon with a "bonefish guide" will sop up the last of the money. No matter, we think, this is research for next time.

As we approach what we now call "Mystery Isle" from the air and circle the hotel, we look down at the flats and see two immense bonefish muds, each over a hundred yards long. Bingo!

We are soon introduced to our guide, Clinton, a sometime conch diver. Clinton is a regular fish hawk, all right, and holds himself very upright. Clinton is also very drunk on Heineken beer from the case he has in his icebox. He doesn't care much for fly rods. Out on the flat, the tides are at extreme height, and pushed higher by wind. The flats are too deep for sight fishing, but Clinton bulls around, showing us the departing silhouettes of acres of fish. Becoming disgusted, Clinton takes us for the standard mud run. We jump into chest-high choppy water and begin to cast into the head of the mud, where we can see the flashes of feeding bonefish. Robert is soon into bonefish. I finally hook up and discover that with hundreds of bonefish in front of me, I have caught a barjack.

It is then that a great yellow bastard of a shark shoots out from under my feet and everything stops. The piles of empty conch on the reefs seem strangely singular against a daiquiri sky. A tern floats over, and I can see through it, its frail bones an intricate tracery within a translucent body. I am having another of the transcendent moments that have come to me since my surfing days in Australia. Then I blink, and all is normal. My arms hang limp at my sides; my rod is under water. I feel like the man who, being deathly ill, has seen the face of God, only to remain ill. I am grateful for the awesome experience, but think that maybe right now I'd rather catch a bonefish.

The next morning, I am last to rise. Robert is out on the flat in front of the house, and as I lace my shoes, I hear him screaming like the Antichrist for his camera. Sprinting down the sea wall, I find him choking down a nice bonefish. He draws the fish out of the water, smiles wanly, and I shoot the classic trophy shot against a watercolor sky. I am big about this, being resigned to my fate.

That afternoon, we are taken to the airstrip, where we discover that our charter pilot has abandoned us and gone to see his girlfriend in San Juan. Rough weather is again looming, and the only other plane available to get us out is a hot ten-passenger turboprop flown by a grinning pilot with gold teeth and a black cowboy hat. The flight to Beef Island takes ten minutes and costs us one hundred and forty dollars, no extra charge for the vertical takeoff and one-wheel landing. Another hundred and fifty dollars gets us to St. Thomas, where buying cigars and rum does nothing to make me feel better.

Back on Eastern's big jet, we encounter the offshore types again, who tell us that they have been catching tarpon off the stern of their boat anchored at Red Hook, all week. This hurts me less than I might have expected. All I can do is sit at the window and think of bonefish revenge.

A Fly-Fishing Primer

P. J.
O'Rourke

I'D NEVER fly-fished. I'd done other kinds of fishing. I'd fished for bass. That's where I'd get far enough away from the dock so that people couldn't see there wasn't any line on my pole, then drink myself blind in the rowboat. And I'd deep-sea fished. That's where the captain would get me blind before we'd even left the dock, and I'd be the one who couldn't see the line. But I'd never fly-fished.

I'd always been of two minds about the sport. On one hand, here's a guy standing in cold water up to his liver throwing the world's most expensive clothesline at trees. A full two-thirds of his time is spent untangling stuff, which he could be doing in the comfort of his own home with old shoelaces, if he wanted. The whole business costs like sin and requires heavier clothing. Furthermore, it's conducted in the middle of blackfly season. Cast and swat. Cast and swat. Fly fishing may be a sport invented by insects with fly fishermen as bait. And what does the truly sophisticated dry-fly artist do when he finally bags a fish? He lets the fool thing go and eats baloney sandwiches instead.

On the other hand, fly fishing did have its attractions. I love to waste time and money. I had ways to do this most of the year—hunting, skiing, renting summer houses in To-Hell-And-Gone Harbor for a Lebanon hostage's ransom. But, come spring, I was limited to cleaning up the yard. Even with a new Toro every two years and a lot of naps by the compost heap, it's hard to waste much time and money doing this. And then there's the gear needed for fly fishing. I'm a sucker for anything that requires more equipment than I have sense. My workshop is furnished with the full panoply of Black & Decker power tools, all bought for the building of one closet shelf in 1979.

When I began to think about fly fishing, I realized I'd never be content again until my den was cluttered with computerized robot fly-tying vises, space-age Teflon and ceramic knotless tapered leaders, sterling-silver English fish scissors, and thirty-five volumes on the home life of the midge. And there was one other thing. I'm a normal male who takes an occasional nip; therefore, I love to put funny things on my head. Sometimes it's the nut dish, sometimes the spaghetti colander, but the hats I'd seen fly fishermen wear were funnier than either, and I had to have one.

I went to Hackles & Tackle, an upscale dry-fly specialty shop that also sells fish-print wallpaper and cashmere V-neck sweaters with little trout on them. I got a graphite rod for about the price of a used car and a reel made out of the kind of exotic alloys that you can go to jail for selling to the Soviet Union. I also got one of those fishing vests that only comes down to the top of your beer gut and looks like you dressed in the dark and tried to put on your ten-year-old son's three-piece suit. And I purchased lots of monofilament and teensy hooks covered in auk down and moose lint and an entire L. L. Bean boat bag full of fly-fishing do-whats, hinky-doovers, and whachamajigs.

I also brought home a set of fly-fishing how-to video tapes. This is the eighties, I reasoned, the age of video. What better way to take up a sport than from a comfortable armchair? That's where I'm at my best with most sports anyway.

There were three tapes. The first one claimed it would teach me to cast. The second would teach me to "advanced cast." And the third would tell me where trout live, how they spend their weekends, and what they'd order for lunch if there were underwater delicatessens for fish. I started the VCR, and a squeaky little guy with an earnest manner and a double-funny hat came on, began heaving fly line around, telling me that the secret to making beautiful casting loops is . . .

Whoever made these tapes apparently assumed I knew how to tie backing to reel and line to backing and leader to line and so on all the way out to the little feather and fuzz that fish sometimes eat at the end. I didn't even know how to put my rod together. I had to go to the children's section at the public library and check out *My Big Book of Fishing* and begin with how to open the package it all came in.

A triple granny got things started on the spool. After twelve hours and help from pop rivets and a tube of Crazy Glue, I managed an Albright knot between backing and line. But my version of a nail knot in the leader put Mr. Gordian of ancient-Greek-knot-legend fame strictly on the shelf. It was the size of a hamster and resembled one of the Wooly Bugger flies I'd bought, except it was in the size you use for killer whales. I don't want to talk about blood knots and tippets. There I was with two pieces of invisible plastic, trying to use fingers the size of jumbo hot dogs while holding a magnifying glass and a Tensor lamp between my teeth and gripping nasty tangles of monofilament with each big toe. My girlfriend had to come over and cut me out of this with pinking shears. I've decided I'm going to get one of those nine-year-old Persian kids they use to make incredibly tiny knots in fine Bokhara rugs and just take her with me on all my fishing trips.

What I really needed was a fly-fishing how-to video narrated by Mister Rogers. This would give me advice about which direction to wind the reel and why I should never try to drive a small imported car while wearing waders. (Because when I stepped on the accelerator, I also stepped on the brake and the clutch.)

I rewound Mr. Squeaky and started over. I was supposed to keep my rod tip level and keep my rod swinging in a ninety-degree arc. When I snapped my wrist forward, I was giving one quick flick of a blackjack to the skull of a mugging victim. When I snapped my wrist back, I was sticking my thumb over my shoulder and telling my brother-in-law to get the hell out of here and I mean right now, buster. Though it wasn't explained with quite so much poetry.

Then I was told to try these things with a "yarn rod." This was something else I'd bought at the tackle shop. It looked like a regular rod tip from a two-piece rod, but had a cork handle. You run a bunch of bright-orange yarn through the guides and flip it around. It's supposed to imitate the action of a fly rod in slow motion. I don't know about that, but I do know you can catch and play a nine-pound house cat on a yarn rod, and it's great sport. They're hard to land, however. And I understand cat fishing is strictly catch-and-release if they're under twenty inches.

Then I went back to the television and heard about stance, loop control, straight-line casts, slack-line casts, stripping, mending, and giving myself enough room when practicing in the yard so I wouldn't get tangled in my neighbor's bird feeder.

After sixty minutes of video tape, seven minutes of yarn-rod practice, twenty-five minutes of cat fishing, and several beers, I felt I was ready. I picked up the fin tickler and laid out a couple of loops that weren't half bad, if I do say so myself. I'll bet I cast almost three times before making macramé out of my weight-forward Cortland 444. This wasn't so hard.

I also watched the advanced tape. But Squeaky had gone grad school on me. He's throwing reach casts, curve casts, roll casts, steeple casts, and casts he calls "squiggles" and "stutters." He's writing his name with the line in the air. He's pitching things forehand, backhand, and between his wader legs. And, through the magic of video editing, every time his hook-tipped dust kitty hits the water, he lands a trout the size of a canoe.

The video tape about trout themselves wasn't much use either. It's hard to get excited about where trout feed when you know that the only way you're going to be able to get a fly to that place is by throwing your fly box at it.

I must say, however, all the tapes were informative. "Nymphs and streamers" are not, as it turns out, naked mythological girls decorating the high school gym with crepe paper. And I learned that the part of fly fishing I'm going to be best at is naming the flys: Wooly Hatcatcher; Blue Wing Earsnag; Overhanging Brush Muddler; Royal Toyota Hatchback; O'Rourke's Ouchtail; and PJ's Live Worm-'n-Bobber.

By now I'd reached what I think they call a "learning plateau." That is, if I was going to catch a fish with a fly rod, I either had to go get in the water or open the fridge and toss hooks at Mrs. Paul's frozen haddock fillets.

I made reservations at a famous fishing lodge on the Au Sable River in Michigan. When I got there and found a place to park among the Saabs and Volvos, the proprietor said I was just a few days early for the Hendrickson hatch. There is, I've learned, one constant in all types of fishing, which is: The time the fish are biting is almost but not quite now.

I looked pretty good making false casts in the lodge parking lot. I mean no one laughed out loud. But most of the other two thousand young professionals fishing this no-kill stretch of the Au Sable were pretty busy checking to make sure that their trout shirts were color coordinated with their Reebok wading sneakers.

When I stepped in the river, however, my act came to pieces. My line hit the water like an Olympic belly-flop medalist. I hooked four "tree trout" in three minutes. My backcasts had people ducking for cover in Traverse City and Grosse Pointe Farms. The only thing I could manage to get a drag-free float on was me after I stepped in a hole. And the trout? The trout laughed.

The next day was worse. I could throw tight loops. I could sort of aim. I could even make a gentle presentation and get the line to lie right every so often. But when I tried to do all of these things at once, it was disaster. I looked like I was conducting "Flight of the Bumblebee" in fast forward. I was driving tent pegs with my rod tip. My slack casts wrapped around my thighs. My straight-line casts went straight into the back of my neck. My improved surgeon's loops looked like full Windsors. I had wind knots in everything, including my Red Ball suspenders. And two hundred dollars' worth of fly floatant, split shot, Royal Coachmen, and polarized sunglasses fell off my body and were swept downstream.

Then, *mirabile dictu*, I hooked a fish. I was casting some I-forget-the-name nymph and clumsily yanking it in when my rod tip bent and my pulse shot into trade-deficit numbers. I lifted the rod—the first thing I'd done right in two days—and the trout actually leaped out of the water as if it were trying for a *Field & Stream* playmate centerfold. I heard my voice go up three octaves, until I sounded like my little sister in the middle of a puppy litter, "Ooooo that's a boy, that's a baby, yessssssss, come to daddy, wooogie-woogie-woo." It was a rainbow, and I'll bet it was seven inches long. All right, five. Anyway, when I grabbed the thing, some of it stuck out both sides of my hand. I haven't been so happy since I passed my driver's-license exam.

So I'm a fly fisherman now. Of course I'm not an expert yet. But I'm working on the most important part of fly-fishing technique—boring the hell out of anybody who'll listen.

Cowboys

Geoffrey Norman

JOHNSON CALLED to say he wanted to go fishing and was I available. I said yes . . . automatically, the way a society woman does when the clerk asks her if she'd like to charge it.

I assumed he meant to come down from the city for a day or two. He was big in arbitrage and never took much time off. I'd seen him get sweaty palms from spending a couple of hours away from the telephone.

But this time Johnson said he wanted to take a week. And he wanted to go back to the cabin that belonged to the club and stay there the whole time. I said it sounded like a fine idea to me; but since there was no telephone in that cabin, I wondered what was up.

I had a day to get ready, so I bought groceries and some beer. I inventoried my tackle and put what I thought I'd need into my four-wheel-drive wagon, which I gassed up and then checked out to make sure there was oil in the crankcase, water in the radiator, and air in the tires. I felt pretty well prepared when I went to the small local airport to meet Johnson's plane.

But I wasn't ready for the way he looked. Nothing could have prepared me for that. He'd lost a lot of weight and looked gaunt and weak. His clothes hung limply on him, and his face was the chalky gray color of cooling ash. I'd always figured him as a heart attack waiting to happen, but now I thought that maybe one of those fast-breeding cancers was just eating him up. I felt something growing in my throat, choking me, and I wasn't sure I'd be able to speak.

When we met, we gave each other the usual fractional embrace, shook hands, and said how glad we were to see each other. Johnson said I looked good and, without thinking, I said he did, too.

"Kind of you to say so," he said dryly, but he didn't elaborate.

We went to the baggage claim to wait for his gear. I was expecting a lot of it, since he'd come for the week. I'd seen him arrive with three big bags and a rod case just for an in-and-out trip. Johnson was on everyone's mailing list, and if the people at Orvis and Eddie Bauer didn't hear from him for a week or two, they'd probably assume he was dead.

"That's it," he said, and nodded at an olive-green bag coming our way on the conveyor. He lifted it without much effort and followed me out into the parking lot.

"Beautiful day," he said. "Just beautiful. You know, I wouldn't mind if October were a year long."

"I know what you mean."

He pitched his duffel in the back with the rest of the stuff, then took off his suit coat and threw it back there, too. He pulled the knot out of his tie and flung it in on top of the coat.

"All right," he said. "Let's get there."

"On the way."

"How far away am I from my first bass?"

"One hour," I said. "Hour and ten minutes, tops. It's faster since they finished the Interstate."

"I can remember when it took four hours to get to that camp," Johnson said. "Longer, if there was rain."

"You remember that time we got stuck so bad?" I said. "We'd been in that slough shooting wood ducks."

"Missed the homecoming dance."

"My love life has never been the same."

"Got a limit, though."

"Matter of fact."

"They call that 'having your priorities in order,' I believe," Johnson said and sighed. "Man, but I've had a lot of good times back in that swamp."

I nodded.

"Shot my first deer in there. Thanksgiving Day. I was twelve years old."

"I remember."

"Deer herd still in good shape?"

"From what I hear." I'd never been much of a deer hunter. They were just too big for me to feel good about killing them. That was the part Johnson liked, though. He'd been that kind of boy, and he'd grown up to be that kind of man.

"I haven't been deer hunting in . . . I'll bet it's been ten years."

"Season starts in another month. You could hunt the club as my guest."

"Kind of you to offer," he said. "But I think I'd better pass." Then he put his head back and closed his eyes. I couldn't remember seeing him sleep in a car. It was as shocking, in a way, as his appearance.

He woke when I turned onto the dirt road that led from browned-over farm country, through plantation pines, and into the big, dense cathedral of hardwoods that grew in the bottom land. It was cool and dim under the big trees.

"I believe this is the best-looking stand of trees in the state," Johnson said. "How much you figure the timber is worth?"

"Somebody offered eight million a couple of years ago."

"Don't take it," Johnson said firmly. "No matter how much they offer, don't ever let 'em cut these trees."

I parked in front of the cabin, and we took a few minutes to unload and change. Johnson's khakis hung loosely, like prison clothes, on his thin frame. He looked so bad that I couldn't help staring. When he caught me, I looked away.

"Let's get out on the water," Johnson said abruptly. "I need to be fishing."

We took an old juniper skiff that was beached at the head of a slough. I sculled from the stern, because I was so much better at it than Johnson. He always wanted to catch fish so bad that he couldn't remember to keep the boat under control. Me, I was lazier. I'd take a lick or two on the sculling oar, and when I saw the boat was lined up right, I'd make a cast. Johnson would have made a half-dozen by then.

We eased down the slough into a wide, shallow lake that had been formed by water backed up behind a matrix of beaver ponds. There were cyprus and gum trees growing up out of the shallow water and Spanish moss hung from the branches like crepe. Even though the day was hot, it felt cool under the trees. Johnson sat very still in the bow and didn't seem in any hurry to start fishing.

"There's more water in here than I remember," he said over his shoulder.

"More beaver. They're about to flood us out."

"You need to shoot a few."

"We try."

"You and I could have kept them under control," he said, without turning around. "With our Marlin .22s, remember? We were a couple of hard-shooting cowboys."

All this nostalgia was getting to me, or maybe I just didn't like where it was leading. Whatever, I changed the subject. "We're over an old creek bed here," I said. "Anywhere along that line of snags ought to be good."

"Right." Johnson worked his fly rod a few times, and when the loop was pushing forty feet, he dropped his deerhair Bug precisely at the base of a dead, bleached hickory tree. I'd never known a better caster. He'd saved and saved when we were kids so that he could buy a fly rod. Then he'd practiced endlessly in his back yard. It was the way true sportsmen fished, he said.

In later years, I was always getting letters from places like Isla-morada and Pez Maya with pictures of Johnson smiling and holding a big bonefish in one hand and his fly rod in the other. He went to tournaments and won trophies.

We worked down the old creek bed, casting to the snags that marked its flanks. True to form, Johnson made six casts for each of mine. But I kept the distance and enjoyed the feel of the blade of the oar as it sliced through the water. I had tried one of those trolling motors once—Johnson bought it—but I went back to sculling. I missed the feel of the oar and the delicacy of control I had with it.

Johnson caught the first bass. It hit the deerhair Bug in an oily surge of water, and Johnson shouted, "All *right*," when he set the hook.

The fish jumped three or four times and tried to go around a stump to break the leader, but Johnson controlled him with a firm hand and in five minutes he had him at the boat. He reached over the side and took the fish by its pugnacious lower lip.

"I believe he'll do for supper," Johnson said.

"Absolutely."

So he put the fish on a stringer and trailed it over the side. He rinsed his hand in the water, dried it on the leg of his khakis, and started casting again. I gave the oar a stroke to straighten us out and looked for a target to cast to. Except for all the questions, it felt like old times.

We fished through the afternoon, on into evening, when it started to get a little cool. We caught a good number of fish. Johnson caught three to each of mine, which was the normal ratio. We kept two fish for supper and threw the rest back. We cleaned the unlucky two at the bank where we beached the skiff. Johnson had a little folding filleting knife, and he took the slabs from the backbone with clean, efficient strokes and then took the pad of bronzed skin the same way. He carried our gear and the four white fillets back to the cabin.

I fried a slab of bacon for grease and then dusted the fillets with corn meal and black pepper and dropped them in the skillet. I boiled some greens, and Johnson fried potatoes in another skillet. When the fillets were pecan brown, I drained them on paper and put them on two old chipped white plates with the greens and potatoes. We opened two bottles of beer and went out to the porch of the cabin to eat. It was cool, and the mosquitoes were down.

"Good," Johnson said when he took his first bite of fish. "Real damned good."

"Glad you like it."

We ate, and the sun set, and Johnson went inside the cabin with the dishes and came back with two coffee cups full of bourbon. I figured the time had come. Johnson was going to tell me he was dying.

He was entitled to it, no question about that. We went back that far and had shared that much, anyway. But I didn't know what I could say to him, so I wished, in a way, that we were back in that cowboy world of ours with our Marlin .22s. In that world, you didn't complain when it came time to die. You didn't even mention it. I wanted to be wise enough, profound enough, to say something that would comfort him, and at that moment, when I realized there wasn't a chance in hell of that, I felt all my inadequacies more keenly than ever before. So much easier to be a cowboy and let the silence pass for meaning.

But Johnson didn't say a thing about dying. He sipped his whisky and identified it as Black Jack and then told a long story about how he and a bunch of the boys in his fraternity had gone to Lynchburg in an open Army-surplus jeep one December to visit the Jack Daniel's shrine. It was a good story and it didn't make any difference that I'd heard it before.

When he'd finished telling it, and our cups were empty, Johnson said, "What's on for tomorrow?"

"More of the same, I suppose."

"You know what I'd like to do?"

"What's that?"

"I'd like to catch some crickets and dig some worms. Then rig up a couple of cane poles and go sit on a brim bed somewhere."

"Little early for that."

"Seems like we found 'em this time of year before," Johnson said. "Anyway, let's give it a try."

"Sure," I said. I hadn't ever expected to see Johnson using a cane pole again. It would be like seeing Jackie Kennedy with her hair in pigtails.

But in the morning, after we'd eaten eggs and bacon and brewed a pot of sawmill coffee on the old wood-burning stove, we went out in back of a crumbling stable where the camp mules had been kept years ago and dug worms from a mound of old manure and leaves. It was alive with night crawlers, and in half an hour we'd filled a coffee can. We pulled a loose board from the floor of another crumbling building and uncovered hundreds of crickets. We put three dozen in an old mayonnaise jar.

There were some old cane poles stored under the camp house. We pulled two out and dusted off the spider webs, then rerigged them and put them in the skiff. We didn't even take our fly rods.

I sculled us down past the beaver pond to the main lake. We jumped a few teal along the way, and I said something about how it was a shame duck season hadn't opened.

"Didn't come to hunt ducks," Johnson said, as though duck season was too far in the future even to contemplate. Actually, it was only a month off.

So we did what he apparently had come to do, which was fish for bluegills with crickets and worms.

We found a bank where the water dropped off to eight or ten feet very rapidly, and when we could see small, gleaming white patches on the bottom, we dropped anchor. The white places were stone and shell that had been exposed when the fish fanned away bottom silt for spawning. When you were over a bed, you could smell it. It smelled like the mound of leaves and old manure out behind the mule barn.

"God," Johnson said when we'd anchored, "what a beautiful smell."

He caught the first fish, as usual. "Look at this little sumbitch *pull*, would you," he said happily, as the fat bluegill ran in strong tight circles, bending the limber cane pole and making the monofilament sing. When he got that fish in, he baited his hook again, quickly, and went back for another.

"Believe we have found us the spot," he said. "Come on and help me catch some."

The sun was warm and high by the time we started back for the landing below the cabin. We'd caught at least fifty bluegills, but, even so, Johnson was plainly sorry to be quitting.

"What a great morning," he said, stretching and looking up at the sky. "What an absolutely great goddamned morning."

I thought there was a tone of regret in his words, as you would get from a man who didn't expect to see many more mornings. But then, maybe it was my imagination.

We had kept six of the little fish and we had them for lunch, fried, with cornbread and beer. After lunch, we went to different rooms in the old cabin and took naps.

I dreamed hectic dreams, as I always do when I sleep in the afternoon. One of the dreams ended in metallic sounds, which woke me. After a minute, I realized the noise came from inside the house. I put my feet on the floor and walked until I reached the room where Johnson was working.

"Sorry," he said. "I didn't mean to wake you up."

"I'd slept too long, anyway," I said. "What are you doing?" He was up to his knees in old coffeepots, campstools, riding tack, and other such junk that had accumulated over the fifty-year life of the camp. It all looked forlorn and worthless.

"Looking for a gig."

"A gig?"

"Thought it might be a good night to paddle around and look for some bullfrogs. We'll need some kind of light, too."

It was a little late for bullfrogs, but I didn't say anything, since it had been a little early for bedding bluegill, too. Instead, I helped him go through that locker and two others. In the end, we had one rusty old gig and an old miner's hat with a battery-powered lamp. The battery, miraculously, was not dead.

When the sun had set, we took the skiff out into the swamp. It wasn't as good as it would have been in July, but we did find seven or eight big bullfrogs by the hot glow of their eyes. I eased in close, and Johnson speared them neatly with his needle-sharp gig. On the way back, we saw a small gater. Its eyes were six inches apart and shone like chunks of charcoal.

We had frog legs for dinner.

Johnson had found an old bolt-action .22 in one of the lockers, so the next morning nothing would do but to go out in the swamp and kill some of the beavers that were damming the creeks and flooding the timber. We did it just the way we did when we were kids, except we didn't have our old imitation saddle rifles.

We also skinned out the few beavers we shot, even though the pelts were worthless at that time of year. But Johnson seemed to think it had been a day well spent. We ate fried ham steaks that night and went to bed early. Johnson had an appetite and he didn't seem to tire quickly, the way you would if you were sick. I couldn't make sense of his behavior as I lay in the dark listening to a nearby owl and wondering what had brought me here, to the camp, with my old friend.

Johnson hadn't told me anything. He hadn't even tried to sell me on any of the investments he handled, the way he usually did. I had told him, once, that I didn't trust New York paper—news or commercial. That hadn't stopped him from trying, except this time. He hadn't talked about anything this trip except the old days.

The next morning, he wanted to go dove shooting. There were a couple of old rusted Fox doubles in one of the lockers and a few boxes of bird loads. We cleaned the guns and in the afternoon hid around a small patch of browntop that would have taken ten men to stand properly. Even so, we shot birds. Johnson got a limit—twelve birds—and I got half that many.

"Did you bring some onions?" he asked me on the way back to the cabin.

"Sure."

"Potatoes?"

"Yes."

"Well, let's make that hash we used to eat. You wouldn't believe the number of times I've dreamed about that hash. And the places where I've had those dreams."

We plucked birds for an hour and a half. I made the hash in a cast-iron stewpot, and we ate at the kitchen table.

"Delicious, as always," Johnson said. It was probably my imagination, but he looked like he'd gained weight and taken on some color. He sure didn't have the appetite or the disposition of a dying man.

"Glad you like it."

"One thing I'm sorry about," he said in an offhand fashion, "is that my son never got to see any of this." Johnson had been married long enough to have one child before a mean divorce. His wife got custody and promptly took off for California. She had remarried, and the boy had been adopted by her new husband. Johnson never saw him or mentioned him . . . until now.

I didn't say anything.

"He'll grow up short on memories," Johnson said. "He won't have anything like this dove hash to fall back on when everyone is raving

206

about the latest poached fish in kumquat sauce. You know what I mean?"

"Sure."

"I thought about kidnapping him once. I really did. I was going to bring him right here. They'd find us, eventually. When they did, he'd go back to California and I'd go to jail. But we'd both have something to carry us."

"What happened?"

"Lost my nerve."

I nodded again. Stupidly.

"My great regret," Johnson said with a lean smile, "is that my boy never got to eat your dove hash."

We shot squirrels and snapping turtles the next day, and ate squirrel and dumplings for supper. I decided that Johnson was definitely dying but that he wanted to spare me any talk about it. He was still a good cowboy that way. And I made up my mind to follow his lead. So, if he wanted to shoot squirrels, the way we had when we were still too young to shave, then I would shoot squirrels and do it with enthusiasm just like I had back in those days.

Without the phone and without any other men around, it was easy to slip back into the mood of those days. Once, while I was waiting for a fat, copper-colored fox squirrel to come in range, I found my hands trembling.

We made soup from a big, surly snapping turtle that had been sunning itself on an old snag when Johnson shot it squarely in the head. The turtle was rank, but the soup was delicious. "Better than the Four Seasons'," Johnson said.

We rigged a trotline and baited it with scraps from the turtle. In the morning, we had nine shiny channel cats and one blue. We skinned them and fried the fillets with hush puppies.

That was the last night of our week at the camp. Johnson hadn't said anything about leaving, and I figured that was up to him. So I waited while we sat out on the porch and watched the sun go down over the river bottom. Waited for him to say something.

It took a while.

"Well, I've enjoyed it," he said. "And I feel better than I've felt in a long, long time."

"That's good."

"I wasn't in the best shape when I got here."

"No."

"This has been great for me. I appreciate all you've done." His voice was husky and final.

"I haven't done anything," I said. "I've enjoyed it myself."

"Hard to believe, sometimes, the way things happen," Johnson said, and paused. I had the nervous feeling that he was about to say something profound. What could I answer? That I'd miss him? That the river bottom would be here after he was gone? That I'd be along after a while? If there was a suitable thing to say, it was beyond my knowing it. I waited.

"Well, I guess we ought to leave early," he said. "I don't want to miss my plane and get stuck in that airport."

"No."

"I'll see you in the morning."

"Right."

With that Johnson went inside to his room.

I waited, feeling relieved and a little cowardly, and then I went inside, too.

We packed up and got out early, and neither of us said much on the drive back. Johnson looked far better than he had when I'd picked him up, and his silence seemed content and satisfied. I didn't want to break in on it.

After he'd checked his bag and been assigned his seat, we walked down to the security checkpoint. Before he went through the detector, Johnson shook my hand in a way that indicated this wasn't just one more temporary parting.

"Take care of yourself," he said.

"You too."

"And thanks for not asking. If I'd told you, it would have put you in a box. You'll know what I mean in a couple of days."

I didn't get it, but he didn't give me a chance to ask any questions. He turned and went to his gate. I waited until the plane took off.

Two days later, the FBI called. It seems Johnson was involved in some kind of big insider scheme. I told the agent that I'd been fishing with Johnson and that I'd put him on a plane. He got the date and the flight number, thanked me, and said he'd be in touch.

He never called again. But I heard a lot about Johnson from people who called. Some were old mutual friends. Some were his own new enemies. I also heard from a lot of reporters. One of them tried to get me to show him where Johnson and I had spent our week fishing together. I refused. Politely, I think. I wanted to tell him I wouldn't take him back there unless I planned on using him for gater bait.

I read the stories that came out until they all started repeating each other. They all had one or two little things wrong, the way all of those "in-depth" stories do. In one of them, we had gone into the swamps to hunt for deer and in another we were "bait-casting for bass."

I didn't recognize the Johnson they wrote about. The five-million-dollar apartment. Place in the country with horses. The women.

It seemed like he had gotten hooked on the money the way other addicts get hooked on their drugs. Having it wasn't all that great, but not having it was unendurable. So he kept raising the stakes until he got caught.

He was in Costa Rica, according to some sources. Other people had him in Chile. I didn't know and didn't expect I ever would, but both were plausible. There was good tarpon fishing in Costa Rica and excellent trout fishing in Chile. Either way, Johnson would be all right. In some ways I felt bad for him. From now on, he could give up even hoping he'd ever see his son again.

But every time I thought about Johnson, I had to smile. He'd actually made it back to his hideaway one last time. And when he went down, he didn't take his sidekick with him. The way I saw it, that meant he was still a good cowboy.

Thousand Moon Lake

Dan Gerber

There are Indian mounds, two or three,
said to border this lake,
but I haven't found them,
rain that fills the trees,
earth that holds them spongy,
remnants of ancient barbed wire
grown halfway through their trunks.

In winter it seems a frozen pasture.
Only its flatness and irregular shape
would make you suspect
that under the snow, there's more.

Except for a silo on the hill
above the trees on the western shore,
almost obscured by leaves,
or a jet dividing the sky
at noon,
the Indians, one hundred years
before Christ, had yet
to build their mounds.

Birds feed and die at its edge,
herons nesting in tamarack,
a snake crawls into the nest
or dangles from the claw of a hawk,
the soft aggressive slither,
the heron gliding at sunset.

This spring, two horses drowned,
great children plunging
through the fluted ice,
the splash and struggle;
the broken water reforms,
clouds part, the sun appears,
a kingfisher flies low
and rattles out his call.

I drift in my boat
with no story,
connected to nothing but the shore.

Wind flues in the pines overhead,
dapples the face of the water,
alters my line
as I cast to small fish,
dreaming
on beds of old leaves.

And catch the image of the fisherman,
no more observer than observed,
no more observed than rings
pooling at the exposed roots
of the maple where a life has risen
to dance with the bones of my wrist.

Small Wonders

Bill Barich

I THINK of the pond most often in autumn for reasons that are entirely unclear to me. I have not seen it now for about five years, but it remains fixed in my memory the way few things are. It was on a fourteen-acre estate north of San Francisco, where my wife and I once rented a house. The house was a trailer, actually, with a leaky roof and shag carpeting the color of mustard, but we stayed in it for a long time because it was cheap and gave us access to the country. A doctor owned the estate, but he was in Africa doing charitable work and had put it up for sale, so for a while we had the run of the place. There was another house on the property, an old Colonial with an arbor and a fieldstone porch, and sometimes in the evening we would sneak up there with a bottle of wine and watch twilight fall through the vineyards, imagining that we had finally been delivered to our proper station in life.

Although I never bothered to measure the pond, I am sure that it couldn't have been more than thirty yards across at its widest point. Its source was a little creek that somebody had dammed in the distant past for a purpose no one in Alexander Valley could remember anymore. As for its depth, I once tested it by some judicious wading and found that nowhere did it rise much higher than the top of an average man's head. The water in the pond was often murky and opaque, tinted an unpleasant green-brown from all the algae swirling about. Toward the end of summer, when the valley was parched and dusty, it gave off an odor that spoke of creatures dying beneath its surface, hidden in the gloom. But there were other times when it was as inviting as a scene from a Manet pastoral. In spring, the cottonwoods and willows along

213

its banks were thick with bloom, and the bay laurels smelled of pepper. Later on, there were blackberries growing in a scraggly patch, drawing finches and starlings in flocks. And in autumn, we had the turning of the leaves; and then a few orange persimmons on the bare branches of a tree.

In my adolescence, I had read stories in outdoor magazines about fishing in farm ponds, so I was not unaware that my own might be worth investigating. Probably I would have explored it sooner if the trailer hadn't overlooked the Russian River. The Russian is an abused stream, burdened with everything from raw sewage to Budweiser flotillas, but in the winter months, when the mouth is open and the rains are heavy, it still has a certain grandeur. By December, steelhead trout have usually entered the river and begun to spawn, and because my dreams are as sweeping as anybody's, I spent my first winter chasing them. What I lacked in technique I tried to compensate for in determination, but steelhead, like the purest forms of art, are indifferent to the energy you expend. There is a magic in the spawning flux, and you interrupt it at your own risk, becoming subject to chills, fever, and several varieties of the common cold. For every fish I caught I put in countless hours, so that at night, as I nursed a whisky by our wood-burning stove, I would debate with myself over my sanity, winning about as often as I lost.

In March, when the weather turned warmer, a fresh run of smaller steelhead came into the Russian. The fish weighed no more than five or six pounds and were more brilliantly silver than most of the steelhead in earlier runs. In my part of the valley, they were known as bluebacks, perhaps because of a slight darkening along the spine. I went out to fish for bluebacks one morning and had no luck, and as I made my way back from the river, strolling through a meadow where the first poppies were beginning to show, I passed by the pond. It was almost noon, the temperature was close to seventy, and I decided to strip off my flannel shirt and take a rest in the sun.

Within minutes, I saw that I was not the only one who'd been sucked into basking. There must have been a hundred frogs near me on the shore. They lolled in the mud, jumped through the reeds, and performed spirited dives off rocky platforms. Some of them just croaked in happiness, high and dizzy on the first flies of the season. In the water, on a willow limb, two turtles were riding along with their ancient heads sticking out of their shells, like bits of gristle. I heard bees buzzing and a red-winged blackbird trilling its electrical trill.

Possibly, too, the sounds of growing plants were conveyed to me, along with the tunneling of earthworms and moles. In the midst of such abundance, I might have believed almost anything.

I can't say exactly what it was that made me throw a cast into the pond. Maybe it was a memory of fishing in a pond in Maine on a childhood vacation, or those old articles in magazines. The rod I was carrying was heavy, designed to cope with the steelhead I hardly ever hooked, and my spinning reel was strung with twenty-pound-test line, but I tied on a small Mepps spinner anyway and tossed it out. On the retrieve, I worked the lure quickly, hoping it would do its job as described in advertisements and imitate a darting minnow. I could see that even in the murk it was giving off flashes, just as scales do when the sun strikes them.

On my fourth or fifth cast, I felt a very light tug and continued my reeling, assuming that the blades of the lure had dragged through some moss. But soon I felt another tug, equally light, and realized that the resistance was deliberate, not accidental. I had a fish on. I knew that it couldn't be a trout—the pond was too warm in most months to support them—and figured instead that it must be a carp or a catfish or some other undistinguished type. One of the most exciting moments in random angling occurs when you pull your catch from the water, fearing in a primal part of yourself that you're about to confront a monster, so I was glad to find a shiny little bass on the end of my line, dangling before me in the air.

Where had the bass come from? Whenever I wanted answers to such questions in those days, I hiked across the road to visit my neighbor, Jack Stritzel, who lived on a pretty spread near a redwood grove that belonged to the Campfire Girls. He was in his seventies and had a broad Germanic face and bright-blue eyes. During his working years, he had managed a supermarket, been a drummer for a door-to-door photographer in the Pacific Northwest, and looked after vineyards and orchards for absentee owners. His health was robust, and he liked to bowl and go dancing and attend banquets put on by the Fraternal Order of Eagles. In town, he frequented the Bullshot Saloon. He was an absolutely cutthroat cribbage player. His dog, a miniature terrier, did tricks and was rewarded with peanuts.

I enjoyed Jack's company because he was among the last old-timers around. There were signs of gentrification on our road, and property values had climbed so high that only wealthy émigrés from metropolitan areas could afford to buy land. But Jack ignored most changes and lived his life as he had always done, minding the calendar and taking care of his seasonal chores. The garden had to be Rototilled and seeded every spring, and in summer he had to cut and stack wood, at least four cords of oak. After the first good rain in October, I would go with him to a cattle ranch owned by two bachelor brothers from Italy—they were eighty and eighty-four—and comb their pastures for meadow mushrooms, *Agaricus campestris*, which Jack called "pinkies" on account of the delicate pink fluting beneath the caps. He had no time to pause and admire the beauty of the valley, because he was *in* it and *of* it, joined to it as I could never be.

When it came to fishing, Jack was very selective. Steelhead were his favorite quarry, and he had introduced himself to people along the river in order to get access to private preserves. His main tactic was to imply that if he were let in, he would act as a guard and keep everybody else out—better one licensed intruder than an army of trespassers. The only other fish he deemed worthy of his effort was the trout. Once a year, he took a trip to a lake in the Sierra Nevada with his inestimable pal the Swede, who hailed from the baked flatlands around Lodi. I never met the Swede, but from Jack's heroic tales I formed an image of him as a Nordic drill instructor, crew-cut and muscular, whose capacities were twice as great as any other man's. When the Swede fished, he *really* fished, hauling them in by the dozen; and when he hunted, he *really* hunted. . . .

At any rate, after I caught my bass, I asked Jack about it, and what he said went something like this.

"Hell, yes, I know you have bass in that pond! The family who owned the place back before Doc bought it used to run a sporting club. Fellows from all over would come out to the property to fish, and the family would charge them a price for the privilege, but I never had to pay a cent since I was friendly with their grandson, Herbert, who's the fellow in the blue baseball cap you see me fishing with sometimes.

"Well, the deal was that they stocked the pond for the club members. They put in bass and bluegills and maybe some catfish. And everything went along fine until they sold out, after which nobody bothered to check on the water level during dry spells, and a lot of fish went belly up. So I can't predict what's left in there, although a couple of five-pounders must still be swimming around. Those fellows from the club, they don't come out here much anymore, but they were a good bunch of boys, except when they got to drinking, which happened every now and then. They'd get loud and rowdy and start roughhousing, and one morning after they'd been out somebody found one of them face down in the pond, as dead as he could be. The sheriff had to cart him away, and we were never sure if he'd drunk too much and drowned, or if he'd committed suicide because he was splitting up with his wife. A person with a broken heart, you know, he's liable to do most anything."

When the steelhead runs were over that April, I began fishing the pond regularly. I would walk down to it from the trailer along a path that led by stalks of new fennel and a tall, elegant stand of pampas grass. While I much preferred fly fishing, I had trouble doing it, because the shore was brushy and offered only a few spots that were clear enough for an unimpeded backcast. So I had to confine myself to close-in stretches I could easily reach. I tried hair flies first, but they seemed not to appeal to the bass. Instead, I caught hundreds of bluegills. They were voracious feeders and attacked the flies as if they were after revenge as well as sustenance. If a bluegill got swept up on my hook, the other fish around it were not upset; they kept right on attacking. Sometimes, I'd catch a bluegill, throw it back, and then catch it again immediately, shaking my head at its stupidity without ever reflecting on how often I repeated *my* mistakes.

In the heat of these frenzies, I would occasionally reel in a bass like that first one, perhaps five inches long and built compactly. I kept a sample one afternoon to see if I could tell what species it might be. The bass in most farm ponds are largemouths, and that proved to be the case with mine. I noticed that the fish had a greenish color that differed from the shades of brown and copper I'd observed on smallmouths in the Russian. A smallmouth may flourish in a stream, but a largemouth likes to hunker down in water that barely moves. Every variety of fish has a distinct personality, and if I were to portray the largemouth's in the style, say, of a classic tavern painting of dogs shooting pool, I would dress it in a ratty old bathrobe and show it refusing to return a ball that a child had hit into its yard.

Apart from its nasty temper, the largemouth is famous for its bulk. When I found a reference in a fishing book to a Florida subspecies that can weigh as much as twenty pounds, I became even more eager to pursue a trophy. I abandoned my fly rod eventually, admitting that I could not cover the necessary ground, and switched to an Ultralite spin rod equipped with a tiny reel and four-pound-test line. The problem of which lure to use raised, in turn, all the eternal problems, and I wound up toting around fifteen different kinds, including the legendary Rapala from Finland and a one-eyed thing in chartreuse called Bob's Buzz-O-Matic.

Largemouths are supposed to be on the prowl for food both early and late, so I got up at dawn one morning and went to the pond. The day was foggy and damp, without a hint of sunshine, and as I approached the water I heard a terrible screech and immediately saw a great blue heron take flight. The bird was so surprised and outraged by my presence that for a few seconds it seemed to lose its balance. It did not rise with any majesty but instead made an awkward ascent, flapping its prodigious wings, screeching again, and almost colliding with a tree. When it corrected itself at last, it gained altitude with astonishing speed and soon fell into a steady gliding pattern that had a look of relaxation about it, a general easing of tension.

I failed to catch any fish that morning, but I kept at it over the next week and learned that the heron was not alone in making forays to the pond. In envy, I watched belted kingfishers swoop down from cotton-wood boughs to capture fingerlings, signaling their success with a rattling cry. There were egrets that stood in the shallows and had such a pure, ghostly whiteness that to stare at them was to taste the madness of Ahab. Somewhere nearby lived a raccoon that conducted its raids by night, bringing along a family of coonlets, and once I saw an osprey hover above the water, studying it in the leisurely fashion of somebody reading a menu, before sinking its talons into a bass that met the specifications of my fantasy.

But then I had my breakthrough. On a May afternoon, as I was retrieving a Hawaiian Wiggler, a largemouth splashed up and swallowed it. After a single leap, it sank to the bottom of the pond and refused to be budged. I thought it had sprouted roots. With my flimsy tackle, I was reluctant to apply any pressure, and I cursed the person who had conned me into giving the bass a sporting chance. The truth was that I didn't care anymore about notions of fair play. I wanted to land this fish and be celebrated for my labors. The largemouth had other ideas, though, and streaked toward a pile of deadfall, wrapping my line around a sunken branch and trying to tear free. I tightened my drag, lifted the tip of my rod, and did my best to control it; and—against my expectations—something in the fish began to quit, and it drifted upward as resolutely as it had once clung to the depths.

All my civilized instincts told me to release it, but I pulled it to shore, hit it with a rock, and carried it home. It was very fat through the middle. Its stomach bulged, and it must have weighed three pounds. When I laid it on a kitchen counter and carved some fillets, they were moist and white and glistening. I cooked them simply, in butter and oil, and we sat down to eat. Never have I experienced such awful flavors. The pond was in the fish the way the fish had been in the pond, infusing its flesh with algae, slime, tadpoles, dragonflies, and beetles. With every bite came a pondy essence, a little sliver of the murk.

That largemouth was the only big fish the pond ever yielded to me. In time, I discovered that the bass were not very active, except in spring. This had to do, I think, with their spawning cycle. While they were depositing and fertilizing their eggs, they seemed hyperconscious of everything around them, tuned in to hatching bugs and constantly alert to predators who might threaten their fry. The aggression I had first seen in bluegills was also characteristic of them. Often I felt that they struck at my lures more out of annoyance than hunger. If I saw a good bass roll, I would cast to it again and again, making no pretense that I was fooling it. I could have been banging garbage-can lids or playing my stereo full blast; and though I got a few responses, they were never quite what I desired.

   In time, too, my affection for the estate grew, so I was very disturbed when I heard that it had finally been sold. I still get angry when I think how we got the news. My wife and I had put in a hard morning in our vegetable garden, turning over the soil and spading in manure from a neighbor's corral, and we were resting on our deck, as filthy as coal miners just up from the shaft, when an unfamiliar car pulled into the drive. Inside was a skinny old realtor with the meanest face imaginable. He took a look at us, clucked his tongue, and addressed us in the bullying, imperious tone of voice that the blindly fortunate sometimes use. It is a tone that mocks and then takes a smug self-satisfaction from the mockery. Waiters know it, and so do servants, cleaning women, and anybody who has been poor.

   What the realtor told us was that we had to be gone in thirty days, because the new owner, another doctor, wanted no part of trash like us. Outraged, I replied that he was violating several laws, but it was Jack Stritzel who ultimately saved us from being evicted. Some relatives of the doctor's had a place in the valley, and he visited them on our behalf and delivered a pitch that was similar to the one he had perfected while

219

plying ranchers and farmers. If the doctor's family had never lived in rural isolation before, he said, they might be lonely and apprehensive, and it would be nice for them to have a decent, honest, mature couple on the property. This couple—Stritzel would vouch for them—could water the lawn when the family went on vacation and also fend off the many thugs in Alexander Valley who robbed unguarded estates.

So we were granted a reprieve. The doctor, his wife, and their young son moved into the main house. They were appalled by the realtor's behavior and assured us that we could stay on as long as we liked. They were kind to us, and we became friends and sometimes had drinks or dinner together—and yet nothing was the same for me anymore. As the doctor went around the estate making repairs, I could feel him taking possession of it, gathering in the river, the hills, and the mountains. That was natural enough, of course, but it deprived me of the illusion that I was lord of the manor. I had to see myself for what I was, broke and struggling, a bad provider, and I wasn't happy about it at all.

And then the doctor put ducks in my pond! There were about ten of them, domestic mallards, male and female, cute but dumb as stones. A fox killed two right off the bat, and I was not among the mourners. Now when I left the trailer with my rod, I ran into a circle of webbed feet and quacking beaks. What a racket they made! Quack-quack-quack—as if I had a knapsack full of stale bread! They would swim after my lure, and I'd have to yank it away from them. If they were napping on the water, I had to cast around them, although a few times I was tempted to give them a scare. When a persimmon dropped from the persimmon tree, they kicked it around, pecked at it, even sat on it and tried to hatch it. Yes, I was losing my turf, watching my world be compressed and foreshortened. Okay, you ducks, I thought, this is where we draw the line.

I can remember my last walk to the pond. After five years on the estate, it was time to leave trailer life behind. Up at our house, a moving man was loading furniture and boxes of books into his truck. I had to get away, because the trailer in its nakedness revealed its many flaws, and I found it hard to believe that we had ever lived there. All I had left of the romance was a panoramic view of the valley that we got through our windows. By a creek that emptied into the river, there was a row of Lombardy poplars; beyond the trees, on a hillside, I saw a vineyard where new shoots and leaves were creeping over trellised stakes.

At the pond, I sat down on the ground and sent frogs into their diving routine. The ducks offered their usual salute. Of the original brood only a few were left, and the others had been replaced by more exotic species, so that the flock now had interesting colors and textures. I watched dimples form on the water as the mouths of bluegills took in insects. Somewhere near the shadowy bottom bass were lurking, and I had a moment of wonder when I considered how many hours I had spent fishing for them. Wasted time, I thought. The pond was so small, so infinitesimal compared to the future I was beginning to imagine that a day would come when it would have no hold on me. My mind would be clear, I believed, and I would be free of such attachments.

Jiggermen

Ted Williams

WHEN ALDERS along wild river tops are burned with frost and the brook trout pair off and hover under scarlet maple leaves, when the Great Bear walks through pine spires and New England slouches from the sun, lesser anglers sip bourbon by black-cherry fires, wax mellow about the season past, and clean and store their tackle. Jiggermen sip bourbon by black-cherry fires, wax mellow about the season past, and *set up* their tackle. For them, fishing never ceases and northern winters never are long.

Of course, I am not so pretentious as to claim that I am a jiggerman. At forty, I am far too young, and I haven't quite mastered the lingo or attained the proper stance or gut. But I am striving, making fair progress. I have been told that I have potential. At fifty and with new false teeth, Adamona is closer to it than I. He talks like Fess Parker, which helps, but, at six foot three, he looks like him as well; and he doesn't even have gray hair. He has far to travel. Knowles, beefy, grizzled, fluent in clipped Cape Codese, seventy-eight and a master curmudgeon, has everything he needs to be a jiggerman except a proper chisel. He chops with some bent, spoon-billed K-Mart contraption that I cover with a slicker when it must repose in the back of my truck. It saddens me to see such potential squandered.

Anyone can jigger, but few can become jiggermen. It takes monumental dedication, and there are rigid qualifications. First, one must be a Yankee. (A friend of my brother once said his barber knew a jiggerman from New York, but I never believed it.) For those who would delete the "er," referring to the art as "jigging," there is no hope whatever. He who catches pickerel on purpose by any means will never amount to anything more than an ice fisherman—the sort who builds fires on shore, sits on bait buckets, skims his holes, and drills instead of chops. Jiggermen pursue yellow perch, and only yellow

223

perch. They have it right when they observe that tilts are cowardly devices more accurately called "traps," and that fishing with them is to winter angling what cut-rate prostitution is to holy matrimony.

In my state, Massachusetts, there are perhaps a hundred jiggermen, if one counts apprentices. Most know each other. They meet only on ice, and their conversations consist mainly of grunts and nods. None can quite match the Russian. Paunchy and ancient, he fishes every day of the year, and never more ardently than when the ponds are walkable. Ten or twenty years ago, he realized that somewhere in some season his wife had stalked permanently from the house—maybe, he idly hypothesizes, because he had turned the cellar into a personal bait concession and didn't pay enough attention to all the dead stuff. When lunchtime arrives, the Russian does not go to the sandwiches; the sandwiches go to the Russian. While eating, he places his jiggerstick between his knees and maintains jigger action with pelvic thrusts.

Food is apt to fly from our forks, so twitchy are our wrists by mid-December. Then one night the wind drops and the unlit moon shows plain around its bright rim—too big, it seems, to fit. The geese leave Glen Charlie before midnight. We know that by dawn there will be shuffling ice, so-called because we shuffle over it and reach way out with our chisels so the jagged silver fractures don't quite radiate to our feet. One chop, and we are through.

At times such as these, people summon the police to rescue us from our folly. I suspect that they are the same souls who, when I worked for the Massachusetts Division of Fisheries and Wildlife, would try to muster me to the aid of ducks who hadn't moved in such a long while that their feet "obviously" had frozen fast to the ice. When the cops arrive, they ask if they can talk to us. If Knowles is present, he'll holler, "Sure, come on out." And the cops, who know nothing of ice or jiggermen and have tried to order us off ponds that were not just walkable but drivable, will splutter and tell us that they prefer to remain on shore, that they have received reports that the Three Stooges were stumbling around the skimmed-over pond, and that they just want us to know that they are there to fish us out, animate or otherwise. So far, only Adamona has required fishing out—half a dozen times, perhaps—and always he has attended to it himself. He drives to a Laundromat, runs his clothes through the drier twice, while robed in a tarpaulin, and is back fishing inside an hour. Knowles and I have been through a few times, but only to our waists.

224

Until the ice frosts over or the snow falls, our normal, shallow beats are off-limits. There the perch can see our every motion. Sometimes we glimpse them as they flash away or see the green weeds shudder. So now we fish deep water. Even twelve feet down we can spy our jiggers dancing. When the jigger is motionless, the bead wiggles to a stop, and it is then that the perch eases in, moving only its pectorals, and takes: twitch, twitch, flutter, flutter, stop . . . *bump*. I snap my wrist; the three-foot fiberglass jiggerstick dips, and the drag on the taped-on spinning reel slips half a turn. I crank the fish up, watching it dash around under my feet, turning its lovely black-and-golden bars toward the sun. Then it is on the ice, twisting and glistening. A good perch, maybe nine inches, its pelvic fins redder than any brook trout's.

A week later, the real cold settles from an azure sky. Now blue wood smoke rises straight from the cottages along the stark shoreline, and in the low, bright sun the ice chips fly like welding sparks to Adamona's chin. Jiggermen by nature cannot effervesce about how the *thunk, thunk-keyoo* of good steel on hard ice so stirs their blood or why they find clean, precise, efficient chopping almost an end in itself. You do not hit the ice in the same spot each time, but, rather, you work gradually toward your foot, so that the cut—preferably in the ice—is chisel width and four or five inches long. One chop for each inch of ice—unless, of course, you are equipped in the fashion of, say, Knowles, in which case you may count on at least ten. Sludge is not skimmed; it is shunted to the sides by holding the shaft still for three seconds, then extracting it in slow motion like a screwdriver used to mix paint. Usually, the perch fit through okay; you don't care about the pickerel or bass. A jiggerman may be tracked by his hole trail.

Today the kids are skating and passing pucks. One, a ten-year-old who says his name is Bryan, advises us to chop over air pockets, because he has heard that fish frequent them to obtain additional air. Also, he says that we should note the way the perch were swimming when we haul them up, so that we can determine the direction of the school. I tell him that if he is not careful he will grow up to be an outdoor writer. Bryan doesn't like the cracks that start at one end of the pond and howl and groan along its length. But we explain that it is the sound of safe and thickening ice, the music of the jiggerman.

Why, Bryan wonders, are we wasting our time with little fish when we could be catching great big ones like his uncle does down the lake. Adamona sighs an indulgent sigh and smiles a patient smile, a smile born of nearly half a century of plodding the frozen surface water of this tired old planet. He knows, as I do, that it's no good explaining. Bryan—as does the society to which he still is affixed—places a premium on sheer bigness. With luck, he one day will spring from that society like the free-swimming medusae of pond anemones, but for now he is anchored to the muck.

I am trying to raise Scott and Beth to be jiggerpeople, but I know that I will never live to see the fruition of my work. For them, too, the words "bigness" and "quality" are nearly interchangeable. Like Bryan, they have this perverse fascination with pickerel and "loudmouth bass," as Beth calls them. Long ago I told them that I would take them jiggering only if they asked politely. But they never ask, so I have to force them to come, and always they require constant herding and fetching. Once, though, I dealt with them in a harsh and fitting manner.

It was one of those days in mid-February when the springtails hop in corn snow and little pods of crane flies dip and bob and hang around at head level. We were at the "Big Lake," where all three of us learned most of what we know that is worth knowing.

"How about we go jiggering?" I inquired, picking up my chisel.

"Nah," said Scott and Beth.

"I'm gonna walk around the island, though."

"Nah," said Scott and Beth.

"All right then. This is your last chance. I'm going right now. I'll leave you here. I really will. Do you want me to go without you?"

"Okay," said Scott and Beth.

So I struck out "all alonely," as Beth says. It is five miles around the island. When I reached Rhinoceros Rock, a tiltman accosted me. "Do you like pickerel?" he asked.

"No," I announced, firmly.

"Weeell," he declared, kicking at the wet ice, "you might as well take these heah."

"Why?"

" 'Cause I ain't goin' ter."

"You mean you don't like pickerel *either*?" I asked in disbelief.

The tiltman shook his head and dropped his jaw, so that he looked like a dental patient posing for inspection.

"Then why do you kill them?" I asked. "Why are you out here? Why are you going to all this trouble?"

The tiltman looked surprised and hurt, dropped his jaw farther, then said he didn't rightly know. So I took off my Bean's belt and strung up his pickerel. There were five—bright, fat fish all more than two pounds. The fangs left long white trails down the linseed-darkened leather.

Now and then I'd catch a perch. I breathed deeply of the fresh, warm air, fragrant with pine needles and pond water. I shucked off my shirt and let the vitamin D soak into my winter itch. I didn't even have to chop, because there were plenty of old tilt holes, all connected with boot prints and ringed with cigarette butts, shiner parts, and muddy wisps of kabomba weed. It was a fine morning to be alive and jiggering in.

Between the bridge and Muskrat Island, snowmobiles shrieked and tore back and forth across the ice. How colorfully, how thoroughly Knowles would have cursed them and their operators had he been at my side. "Don't it frost your ass," Knowles would have said had he been there. Presently, a snowmobiler paused and, leering at me from the saddle, asked if I would watch his tilts for him while he raced. Lacking Knowles's quick, acerbic tongue, I could think of no more appropriate comment than "No."

I regarded the snowmobiles as they flickered through the heat waves, fantasizing that the Big Lake opened like a pickerel maw and sucked them in. And, lo, as I stood there, *it did*. At least, it sucked in one. It happened beneath the bridge, where the current flows even in the dead of winter. First the hat bobbed to the surface, then the snowmobiler. With that, the racing ceased.

At the head of First Perch Cove, a tiltman hollered at me. I couldn't comprehend him across the wide expanse of ice, but I thought I knew what he wanted. When I came abreast of him, he asked if I liked pickerel.

"No," I said, sternly.

He had eleven, all big fish. I better take them, he explained, because otherwise he was going to feed them to his neighbor's hogs. *Not even his own hogs.* He had a long piece of clothesline, so I shook the pickerel I was carrying off my belt and threaded the line through sixteen sets of gills. Now there was no carrying the pickerel; I had to drag them the way Knowles used to make me drag stripers off dawn-washed Nantucket beaches, leaning far forward, with the cord cutting into my shoulder. I struggled toward camp, cogitating all the while: If I was going to go to all the trouble of making pickerel chowder and if tiltmen gave away their pickerel, I might as well do it up big.

So I went around to all the tiltmen in view, soliciting pickerel. I collected two more and two potbellied loudmouth bass. And when I gained our beach and moved up the path like a Clydesdale hitched to a stone-boat, Scott and Beth dropped their plastic sleds and goggled at my load. I left it by the turnaround circle, wiped the sweat from my forehead, and proceeded nonchalantly onto the porch. Still, they did not speak.

I opened a beer, stretched out on the davenport, and flexed my little jiggerstick.

"Fair jiggering," I intoned. "You should have come."

More than anything, jiggering is a philosophical state of being, but to reach it one first must master the simple mechanics. Therefore, brief tackle instruction is necessary. If Knowles, for example, would only pay attention to it, he could be a journeyman jiggerman in a week.

The jigger: a willow-leaf spinner blade filled with solder that embraces, at the hole end, the eye and one-quarter inch of shank from a clipped perch hook and, at the other, the rest of the hook. It takes a good man to keep it all straight with a nail and a pair of needle-nosed pliers while blowing on the hot solder. Adamona insists on building his jiggers backward, so that the solder is on the outside. You do not want to do this, because, among all sorts of other things, the hook hinders polishing of the brass. The trouble with Adamona and Knowles is that they carry their Yankeeness to preposterous extremes. They are too stubborn, too set in their ways, and too opinionated. They have these notions about jiggering, of which virtually all are wrong.

But, to get back to tackle talk. At least Adamona is correct when he observes that a proper jigger is like a piece of fine jewelry, and he is offended when one is treated otherwise. A former friend of his, whom he had presented with a brace of jiggers, actually took sandpaper to them; a decade later, Adamona still tells the story.

Let me hasten to explain that we are not snobbish. We feel that, on occasion, it is perfectly acceptable to bait a jigger with a worm or perch eye. But "the bead" is far more sporting and, usually, equally effective. By the bead we mean red, pea-sized glass beads with holes through the center. Once, I spent a whole day trying to find beads. "You get them from women's necklaces," Adamona had instructed. But, as usual, he was wrong. All the women I phoned said they didn't have any (although I will say that they sounded a little brusque, giving me the impression that they hadn't hunted very hard). At length, I unearthed a batch from the chaotic bowels of Paul's Tackle Shop in Worcester, Massachusetts, where supposedly they were to be strung onto spinners. One threads the bead onto a common pin, clips the point and, with a combination of fingers and pliers, wraps it twice around the jigger hook so that the bead is tight up to the metal and so that it wiggles seductively but does not slip off the barb. Believe me, it takes a good man; even the Russian doesn't do it on his first try.

The chisel: again, not acquired at a store. Nothing that is sold commercially is remotely usable by real jiggermen. One makes one's chisel or has it made. The head is hardened steel, no wider than the shaft and steak-knife sharp. Off ice this is protected by a cowhide sheath (best made by a cobbler), so that sharpening is never necessary. The shaft, to which the head is welded by a professional versed in attaching hard steel to soft, must be solid stock with a milled aluminum cap three and a half inches in diameter and machine-pressed onto the top (to catch in the ice if, God forbid, you drop your chisel). A quarter-inch hole is drilled in the shaft just under the cap, and through this is inserted a length of quarter-inch nylon cord tied off in a loop, so that should the chisel slip to the bottom despite the cap, it may be retrieved with a treble hook wired to a bamboo rug pole. You can stick your hand through the loop, too, although jiggermen rarely do this. A jiggerman must chop with one hand, so take care that the shaft is not too long.

Boots: felt lined.

Clothing: wool pants and parka. Stripeless snowmobile suits are acceptable if sufficiently grimy.

"High pressure," grunts Adamona, meaning that it is cold and clear and the perch "won't eat," as he puts it.

"They could of et Thursday in the rain," I remark.

"Could of," allows Adamona.

But then my jiggerstick bends sharply and my hand is taken to the hole. The drag clatters. Stalemate. I fear a pickerel. Slowly, carefully, I argue the fish to the ice. It sticks in the hole. I increase the pressure.

"Want my gaff?" inquires Adamona, referring to the length of curtain rod, one end of which he has smashed with a hammer around the eye of a barbless striper hook.

The jigger rips out and orbits my head.

With my knees, I pull off the slime-darkened glove from my right hand and gingerly probe the hole. Joyfully, I feel toothless perch lips. I pinch one between thumb and forefinger and pull. Nothing. I pull and wiggle, feeling tissue rip. I get my index finger under a gill plate, and out she slides—a bright, foot-long cow.

"Gawd, ain't that *beautiful*," cries Adamona.

I insert my hand in my armpit, feeling the blood sear back into my fingers. Then I put the glove back on and swing my arm around. The big perch arches and lies still; within seconds, her rigid fins turn white with frost.

By 2:00 P.M., I am toting seventeen perch, better than I had expected with the bad jiggering weather. About a dozen more—all Adamona's—are scattered over the ice. I never can get Adamona or Knowles to put their perch promptly in their jiggering bags (over-the-shoulder canvas affairs made by wives). Instead, they leave them where they fall, the way kids leave gum wrappers on living-room rugs, and they pay for it, because when they finally get around to picking up after themselves, they find that the gulls have assisted them. Knowles, who has much in common with gulls and long has identified with them, always yells at them to "get the hell off my fish"; but they obey only when he shakes his jiggerstick and lumbers after them like a baited bear.

I would as soon leave woodcock around a birch run as yellow perch around ice. Nothing in fresh water rivals them as table fare, certainly not their larger, coarser cousins—the saugers and walleyes about which so much fuss is made—and certainly not the much-flapped-about and mushy salmonoids. To clean perch properly, one must: slice off head, angling toward pelvic fins so that these and head and guts rip away in one unit. Slice off front dorsal. Slit hide to tail. Flip. Slice belly to vent. Slit hide from vent to tail. Peel hide off left flank. Peel hide off right flank. Pull—never cut—back dorsal and anal fin. Scissor out rib cage. I've been cleaning perch this way for thirty-five years and am now down to twenty seconds per fish. Adamona, on the other hand, insists on filleting perch, wasting time and meat. As I said, he is set in his ways.

Because I tend to forget important details, I keep a fishing journal, and if the following details seem important to you, too, then you have potential as a jiggerman. Thus far, I have related them only to Knowles, Adamona, and the League of Women Voters, which I frequently find meeting in my living room when I return from jiggering. The members listen politely but seem unimpressed, and I frankly doubt if any has much potential. Anyway, my entry for the next outing reads as follows:

Jan. 29—Sunny, 10 degrees but warming fast. To Caragrimseg at 8:15. Got in with only two-wheel drive. Saw red grouse in road. Guy waiting for his son and setting up tilts. He had loud beagle. I found partly cooked chicken, with feathers still on, frozen into ice among burnt logs. Mist from waterfall had made hoarfrost on tree. Beautiful in sun, but melted fast. Ice getting thicker, but still good chopping. After 40 minutes got perch on bead. When I broke his neck and took eye he threw up live mummichog. Didn't know they were in here. I put it in hole but it was hurting. Ruggles pissed on tiltman's sled and got yelled at.

I remember telling Ruggles that I, too, looked down on tiltmen, but that this time he had gone too far. At this point, I suppose, I ought to explain that Ruggles is my jiggering dog. When the popples are yellow and the milkweed blows, he doubles as a Brittany spaniel, pointing woodcock and bringing the dead ones halfway back to me. When I pick up my chisel and ask him if he wants to go jiggering, he responds by spinning and yelping and biting at my pants cuffs. While jiggering dogs help a lot, they are not absolutely essential to the sport. They are used mainly for barking at fish, investigating cottages, retrieving discarded ice chunks, participating in hockey games, sniffing the crotches of fellow jiggermen, running around, and, especially, saluting all matter that breaks the gray monotony of a winter pond: logs, sleds, tilts, bait buckets, radios, Thermos bottles, jackets—everything. Ruggles, for example, has accomplished the herculean task of teaching Knowles and Adamona actually to adapt an aspect of their jiggering routine; he has conditioned them always to wear their jiggering bags.

On this day, because no other jiggermen are abroad, I do something that otherwise would betray the cub in me. I chop a big hole, rake out the chips with my fingers, get down on my belly, and study what is happening beneath me. The chill water feels wonderful around my nose and upper lip; it rides up with the surface tension, smelling of swamp and summer. It is clear but even now flecked with suspended bits of protoplasm that drift like stars in some grand and imperceptible pattern. The universe beneath the ice comes into focus when I cup my hands. Browning coontail undulates over lush green bottom moss. The white spot becomes a wound on a pickerel's beak. I wiggle the line, and he regards the jigger with wicked, reptilian eyes, then flattens his head, flares his gills, and snatches. But I do not set. I get him to strike four times before he loses interest. Three perch, one a good one, materialize and hang around the jigger as if from a mobile. Tails motionless, they fan their pectoral fins and arch their needle-ridged dorsals. Suspiciously, coyly, they drift toward their comrade's ghastly, wrinkled, fluid-drained eye, peck it, and drift back. Twitch, twitch, flutter, flutter . . . *bump*. I yank the line, and, incredibly, the perch is on. Not the big one, though. I slide him onto the ice and break his neck. Soon there are eight perch, surrounding the eye like wagon spokes. They move in and out and will not take. I watch them, hypnotized.

"Hey! Hey!" Someone is yelling at the north end of the pond. It is the tiltman, who has been joined by his son. He is wondering if I am dead. I wave, and he sits down again. The shadow of a red-tailed hawk sweeps across the ice, and the timeless fluting of jays drifts from the woods. I roll back onto my stomach and return to my voyeurism. Ruggles whines and prods me in the neck with his cold nose. Jiggering dogs won't let you die without noticing them first.

I decide not to let another season slip by without finding Sandy—the semimythical pond, discovered by the Russian, that Adamona fished in the distant past. All he remembers is that it was somewhere north of Caragrimseg, deep in the woods, and that a troop of hippies had set up a commune there, getting the place posted. Unaware that there haven't been any hippies anywhere for a good long while, he never went back.

So, on this misty March morning we find ourselves trudging a tote road through the pine barrens of southeastern Massachusetts and the feral, forgotten cranberry country they embrace. Pitch pine. Scrub oak. Wintergreen. Bull brier. Old burns. Cranberry bogs. Sand. The sun cuts through. Water beads sparkle on teaberries and pine needles and unshed oak leaves. The air is heady with the scent of pine and wet earth.

"This ain't right," says Adamona, backtracking and striking off on another tote road. "It oughta be over this next ridge." I recall how colossal is the quantity of next ridges in my life that were supposed to have worthwhile things in back of them and didn't. Here is yet another.

Finally, though, the right ridge gets in our way, and Adamona is wild with excitement, which, for a jiggerman, means grinning and saying, "Theah, b'Gawd." The pond even looks mythical. The woods around it and the sky over it are clear and bright, whereas it remains shrouded in mist with the tops of drowned cedars poking through. A forty-foot band of open water obliges us to harpoon an ice raft and ferry ourselves to main ice, poling with our chisels, watching the bow and stern slip under the surface and the water rise almost to our boot tops.

"This is worse than when you drug me onto Turnpike," I observe, referring to the time I'd been fishing alone at Turnpike Pond with a spinning rod and bobber in April. Adamona had shown up and, with great disgust, asked why I wasn't jiggering. I'd laughed. But then he had fashioned a bridge out of planks and picnic tables, and we had drifted around the pond all afternoon on a tiny ice floe. Such is the attitude that keeps his business with Laundromats so brisk.

There is no need to chop. Rain has swirled out holes everywhere. The ice is punky and honeycombed. We move over it, probing with our chisels as through a minefield. Sometimes, in the darker sections, we can push our chisels through. The perch come slowly, but they are lovely cows. There are just enough to give us unquiet dreams through summer nights.

"Next week this'll all be prayer ice," declares Adamona, as if that which we are standing upon were something else.

With a sound like French police cars, two mute swans beat through the mist and scull off toward Caragrimseg, now open. Redwings, perched on blushing swamp maples, are shouting "Oklaree," and in the pitch pines a chickadee chants "Feebee." We can hear the ice sputtering and popping in the sun. It is going. At noon we are driven off.

Adamona sighs. "Spring," says he, "always comes so fast."

Last Voyage of the Bismarck

W. D. Wetherell

BUOYANCY IS a quality I have always admired, but always from afar. To be carried along on the choppy froth of things, bouncing, floating, skipping, held above the turbulence by an unquenchable welling up—these seem to me in my leadenness the happy pinnacles of joy. Swamped as I am by bothersome detail, weighed down by brooding, ballasted by doubts, it is all I can do to manage a rough treading water, let alone actually float. And though I have never had it tested, I suspect my specific gravity corresponds to that of granite. Solid, Wetherell undoubtedly is. Buoyant, Wetherell definitely is not.

I feel the lack most tangibly when I'm fishing. An awkward enough wader at knee depth, I become positively enshackled when I venture into waters above my waist. The wader fabric clings to me like one of those heavy rubber suits the pearl divers were wont to drown in; my wading shoes send up vibrations frighteningly similar to those produced by ball against chain. What makes it worse is my aspiration. Not content with the shallow, easily wadable stretches, I'm always reaching out for more—reaching so far that my right hand furiously false-casts a rod held aloft like a sinking Excalibur, while my feet—touching nothing—pedal back and forth like an inebriated duck's.

The ultimate futility of this struck me quite forcibly one morning

235

several years ago when I was on Franklin Pond. As usual, I was up to my shoulders in ice-cold water, casting to brook trout that, as usual, rose a teasing yard from my best efforts. I went through double-hauls and triple-hauls and hauls for which no name exists, but they had no effect whatsoever, except to chase the trout out even farther: I could cast forever and not catch a fish. And though the long-term solution was obvious, it penetrated my waterlogged brain very slowly, as if having to course the same slow evolutionary furrows up which it dawned on prehistoric man.

A boat. Of course. Something to float me out to where the trout were feeding. Eureka!

For a moment, I let the thought of it carry me away. As always, the effervescence of that first inspiration quickly sank into something heavier and dull: the writerly poverty in which I dwelled. For if I was going to acquire a boat, it would have to be a modest one. No flashy runabout with gleaming outriggers, no cedar skiff with loving overlaps—these were unquestionably too dear. Nor did the "belly boat" have any appeal for me, that weird bastardization of waders, inner tube, and fins that makes a fisherman resemble a cross between a hanging tenpin and one of the lumpier peapods in *Invasion of the Body Snatchers*. No, what I needed was an actual craft of some kind, maneuverable, portable, lightweight, and cheap.

It was in the flash of that first dawning notion that the solution lay. For if I was aping prehistoric man in the similarity of our ends, so, too, could I ape him in the actual means. Man did not make his first leap from shore in a Ranger bass boat with dual Merc outboards, nor did he shove off in an Old Town ABS canoe. He made the first timid venturing on a raft made of hippo bladders, a glorified and bubbly balloon.

As it turned out, our local sporting-goods store had three of the latest models. Inflatable rafts, two, three, and four-man versions, propped next to each other on the wall like siblings of steadily increasing plumpness and height. They weren't made of hippo insides, but plastic—plastic that had all the quality and thickness of a ninety-nine-cent beach ball. So although I'd had visions of myself coming home with the kind of durable Avon favored by Jacques Cousteau and amphibious commandos, it was apparent that I was going to have to settle for something considerably less grand.

I examined the rafts more carefully. For something so simple, there was an amazing proliferation of reading matter stenciled across the sides, with extravagant claims of weight-bearing capabilities contradicted by repeated cautions about life jackets. That the rafts were made in Taiwan didn't bother me; the Chinese were an ancient people, and hadn't they invented the junk? The price was reasonable, too, with the two-man model selling for the same price as a dozen bass bugs.

It was the two-man model I finally chose. With a weight-bearing capacity of four hundred pounds, it could carry Celeste and me with freeboard to spare. The coziness of the actual *sitting* room bothered me (I estimated its measurements at roughly three by five), but I let the box illustration override all my doubts. Pictured were *four* bikini-clad models riding the two-man model in what appeared to be not only comfort but also outright joy. Convinced, I went over to the shelves and pulled a box out from the bottom. The actual purchase, for something that was to become so lifelike and personal, seemed anticlimactic and crass. The see-through wrapping, the smell of newness, the exchange of cash. It smacked of buying a child.

I unswaddled it gently when I got home, worried lest any stray pins or splinters puncture it at birth. Spread across the carpet with the flat whiteness of pita bread, it was slow to inflate. (Indeed, the inability of any of a dozen pumps to inflate it in anything less than half an hour was the Achilles heel of the whole enterprise; the slow *press press press* of foot against bellows was the monotonous cadence of its life.) Only gradually did it grow into a delightful roundness and buoyancy. And round and buoyant is how the raft looked when inflated, with the swelling billow of a magic carpet yearning to be airborne. The contrast between the loftiness of its ambition and the modesty of its means suggested the name. By the time I called Celeste into the room to marvel at what air had wrought, she was *Bismarck*, and *Bismarck* is what she remained.

Her maiden voyage came that very evening. There's a remote lake on the height of land behind our home that is so wild and lovely I hesitate to even whisper of its existence. Lightly visited and seldom fished, it harbors a fussy population of largemouth bass, some running to size. An old jeep trail runs up to it, but there are no launching ramps, and it would be a long, brutal portage for a canoe. Various rowboats and runabouts have been carted in over the years; their stove-in wrecks dot the shallows like huge planters deliberately installed for the propagation of lilies.

It was, in short, the perfect place to let *Bismarck* do her stuff. At nine pounds, she was a delight to backpack, and in no time at all Celeste and I were standing on a granite shelf that sloped into the lake, alternating steps on the air pump. Celeste *oohed* and *aahed* over the scenery; I *oohed* and *aahed* over *Bismarck*'s squat lines.

She looked good in the water. Alert, stable, round. Damn good. Even Celeste thought so.

"Why, she's pretty," she said. She rolled her jeans up, to wade out to her, then suddenly hesitated. "Uh, how do we get in?"

As usual, she had gone right to the heart of the matter. For *Bismarck*, lovely as she was, was a maddening, ornery, downright impossible bitch to board. The very buoyancy I admired would make her shy away at the slightest ripple, so that approaching her required all the stealth and caution necessary in mounting an unbroken colt. By holding onto the side and bracing my feet against some rocks I was able to boost Celeste into the stern, followed quickly by our fly rods, picnic supper, and wine. By the time all was settled, there wasn't much room left for me.

Correction: no room at all.

"Good-bye," Celeste yelled, reaching for the oars.

"No, wait a second," I said. "Can't you just . . . scrunch?"

Scrunch is what we did. Celeste tucked up her legs to make a space, I turned sideways and heaved myself up perpendicular to the inflated thwarts, then by judicious wiggling we managed to wedge me in. My first remark was the obvious one.

"It's a good thing we're married."

With our arms intertwined about fly rods, our legs jutting out around each other's chest, I suppose we must have looked like a pornographic carving on a temple dedicated to piscine love. I reached for the oars and promptly stroked them into Celeste's chin; she, experiencing a cramp in her right leg, stretched it toward my throat, tipping off my hat. Our fly lines immediately became entangled; the overturned picnic basket leaked pickle brine down over our knees. *Bismarck*, feeling the breeze now, drifted out from shore.

"You sure this is the two-person model?" Celeste asked.

I thumped the lettering "Here, read for yourself. Two people. Two intimate, acrobatic, contortionist dwarfs. And there," I said, pausing dramatically, "is our bass."

A school of them was tearing apart the lily pads on the far shore in pursuit of—what? Frogs? Shiners? Or was it just their own sheer compacted joy in their bassness, the tremendous joy and lust for existence I sense whenever I have one on the end of my line? We rowed over to find out.

It was a long row. A very long row. *Bismarck*, filled to the gunwales, was not a happy sailor. Halfway there, I fell back in exhaustion; Celeste took over, and by the time we were actually in casting range, collected sweat had added another few inches to the bilge beneath our bottoms.

But that's the sad part of the story. Not another negative word will I inscribe beside *Bismarck*'s name, for once we got to the lily pads we caught bass aplenty, the largest weighing in at over four pounds. *Bismarck*'s good qualities were evident on every one: the stealth and silence of her approach; her low water line, with its canny view into the bass's own plane; her stability; the ease with which a hooked fish slithered in over her side. By the time we left that night, *Bismarck* had more than justified her existence, and plastic though she was, I already felt that sentimental affinity that can make a boat the most precious and dearly loved of man's things.

Though Celeste and I continued to play this funny twosie the rest of the summer, it was as a solo craft that *Bismarck* really came into her own. Alone, I nestled into her bottom as if into a soft and yielding waterbed, casting from a comfortably horizontal position, my neck pillowed by the air chamber in the stern. When I was alone, *Bismarck* became a delight to maneuver, responding so quickly to the oars that I often spun her around and around in mad circles just for fun. She rowed quickly and steadily, and seemed to skip under all but the strongest breezes with enough freeboard to keep me reasonably dry. Her lightness and airiness were constant sources of amazement. There were days when I had fish on that towed us halfway across the lake, so that I felt like Ishmael on a miniaturized Nantucket sleigh ride, my mouth dropping open in delight.

What impressed me even more was *Bismarck*'s sturdiness. I fished her hard that summer and autumn, then again the following spring, often taking her out five or six times a week. One of the smaller air chambers developed a leak, but the other three were enough to float her, and I began deliberately seeking out tougher water, to see what she could do. The wide Connecticut in a northwest chop, *Bismarck* bouncing along like a stubby tugboat; huge Newfound Lake, where powerboats threatened to swamp us with their wakes; remote trout ponds, where briers scratched the plastic but punctured her not. . . . We fished them all. There was even one magic afternoon when I found some white water for her—the mouth of a trout stream that empties into the Connecticut. She did well, of course. I backed down the current stern first, and she went bouncing off the rocks like an exuberant pinball, impervious to harm. Confidence expanding, I took her to salt water and tried her out on a windy bay; I took her to a lake in deep autumn when a capsize might have finished us both. *Bismarck* met every new challenge with aplomb.

And the two of us caught fish. Smallmouth that showered her bottom with spray; trout that scissored back and forth near her bow like escorting dolphins; a pike that threatened to puncture us; big walleyes that towed us farther than any bass. Viewed simply as a fishing tool, *Bismarck* proved herself many times over, and I was surprised never to encounter another fly fisher so equipped. Occasionally, I would see sunburned, angry teenagers paddling along in similar craft near shore, but I never saw one being seriously fished, and most of the time I had to myself whatever body of water I was exploring.

Our partnership remained intact for three full seasons. I had originally thought of her as little more than a disposable boat, to be used several times, then discarded like a tissue. Now, her durability proved, I began making the opposite mistake: thinking of her as something permanent and fixed. If I did picture her end, it was always in some cataclysmic happening that would send us both to the bottom in style: a spectacular collision with a spear-shaped rock; a pike big enough to disembowel us; a foot too heavy on the air pump, blowing her to smithereens. That she might die more slowly and subtly never occurred to me at all.

The truth is, she was dying—dying from neglect. By the time that fourth spring rolled around, I had forsaken her exuberant chanciness for the firmer rhythm of a canoe—a fifteen-foot Old Town with a separate beauty all her own. *Bismarck* sailed less and less; for long months altogether, she remained in the backpack, her plastic folds stiffening from nonuse. Occasionally, I meant to take her out, but my back was always aching too much to carry her, or it was too windy, or . . . But why make a list? Excuses count for nothing, not in love affairs, not in boats. She was the apple of my eye, then one day she wasn't, and it's as simple and sad a story as that.

And yet we were to have one more day together after all. It was in May, a weekday afternoon when I felt weighed down with a leadenness that went beyond mere fatigue and as flat as one of those leftover leaves one finds on the forest floor. That I desperately needed a filling of water, sky, and trout was obvious. I started to pull the canoe out of the barn, then—motivated by a sudden, overpowering instinct—went back into the mud room and grabbed the backpack instead.

Fifteen minutes later, I was hiking up the trail toward Franklin Pond, a bundled *Bismarck* perched high on my shoulders like an eager baby spotting out the terrain. The morning sun had given way to ominous yellow clouds, and I hiked faster than usual in order to stay warm.

The pond sits tight against the slopes of the one legitimate mountain our town has. It's about five acres in extent, stocked occasionally by helicopter, and unfishable without some sort of raft. So miniature is it, so silver and round, that the usual analogy is to a gem, though I tend to see it as a bowl instead—a punch bowl cradling the liquified granite essence of the surrounding hills. Trees reflect on its surface; a breeze will ripple the tops of the surrounding spruce, then drop to strum the water, so that the two waves are never quite synchronized, and the dual shimmers shimmer continuously. So pure is the water, so generous the reflection, the casting into its depths gives the sensation of casting into midair.

I unrolled *Bismarck* on the rough tent platform that is the only man-made structure on its shores. Again, I went through the old familiar ritual of making her waterborne. The slow accordion press of the air pump; the furious shutting off of valves; the precarious launching and more precarious boarding; the quick assembly of oars. It was good to return to something I had loved and find it unchanged. Unchanged except, that is, in one important respect. As I stroked my way toward the far shore, feeling her generous and yielding tug, I realized with what can only be described as a sinking sensation that *Bismarck*, my neglected *Bismarck*, was sinking.

Slowly sinking. The long winter in the mud room with its constant freezing and thawing had opened *Bismarck*'s seams. Water seeped in through a dozen thin cracks—my butt was already numb from icy pond water collected in the stern. It was obvious that *Bismarck* was on her way out, and yet . . . well, it wouldn't happen immediately. The two air chambers that formed the hull were already empty, but a quick check showed that the largest chamber, the outer one, was still partially filled. With luck—if I handled her carefully—*Bismarck* had an hour's float left.

Risky, sure, but there was a compelling reason not to return to shore at once: the trout. Between one moment and the next, as if on an invisible maestro's dramatic cue, they had begun rising on all sides. I

241

worked out some line and immediately caught four brookies in a row on a small Gray Wulff. The lower *Bismarck* sank, the easier it was to slide them over the side, until finally it was hard to determine where pond ended and boat began, and the trout bubbled around my stomach in perfect contentment as I twisted free the fly.

I don't remember how many trout I finally caught. The flies were hatching so fast on the water that the pond literally boiled. A hungry swallow flew down from the mountain, then another, then a third, until finally the air seemed just as thick with darting birds as it did with lazy insects. There were swallows everywhere, coming in squadrons, peeling off, strafing the surface, jetting away. It was a miracle I didn't snag one on my backcasts, but they seemed to be deliberately toying with the line, ducking under it like girls jumping rope. They were teasing me—inebriated with the same airy exuberance as the rising trout and the hatching flies.

Then it began to snow.

Huge snowflakes, falling faster than their size should warrant, tumbling down over the swallows and the flies and the trout until everything became jumbled together in a world where there were no separate planes or spheres or perspectives, but everything was one. Was I casting for flies or for trout or for swallows? Was I fishing water, snow, or sky? Man, trout, bug, or bird? It was dizzying, but I was sinking in it, and I began rowing *Bismarck* toward shore, not from self-preservation, but simply because I needed the ballast of the oars to keep my soul from flying away. As I neared shore, a brown shape glided beneath *Bismarck*'s hull in a rush of fluid and backward-flowing fur: a beaver, and it was too much for me. I realized for the first time what those nineteenth-century writers meant when they wrote the word "swoon."

I didn't, of course. I didn't turn into a swallow, and I didn't swoon and, more important, I didn't sink. *Bismarck* and I reached shore together, though by now all that was left of her was a thin plastic pressure against my bottom, her last cradling gasp. She boosted me onto a flat rock within stepping distance of land, then made a final expiring sigh and sank away in bubbles. By the time I pulled her up on shore, her seams were open from bow to stern.

I folded her up more carefully than I ever had when she was whole, then started back down the trail to my car, zigzagging through snow-flakes that spread apart into sun. My thoughts were inflated by the miracles I had just witnessed; I walked so fast and with such light-footed sureness that it was almost as if I had inherited *Bismarck*'s very air. I was . . . yes, there was no mistaking it. I was buoyant. Buoyant at last.

Bismarck. June 14, 1982–May 5, 1986.

She was a lot more than a toy.

Children

Richard Ford

CLAUDE PHILLIPS was a half-Blackfeet Indian, and his father, Sherman, was a full-blood, and in 1961 our families rented out farm houses from the bank in Great Falls—the homes of wheat farmers gone bust on the prairie east of Sunburst, Montana. People were going broke even then, and leaving. Claude Phillips and I were seventeen, and in a year from the day I am going to tell about, in May, I would be long gone from there myself, and so would Claude.

Where all of this took place was in that remote part of Montana near the Canada border and west of the Sweetgrass Hills. That is called the Hi-Line, there, and it is an empty, lonely place if you are not a wheat farmer. I make this a point only because I have thought possibly it was the place itself, as much as the time in our lives or our characters, that took part in the small things that happened and made them memorable.

Claude Phillips was a small boy with long arms who boxed in the same amateurs club I boxed in—up in Sweetgrass and across the border in Canada, wherever we could box. He was ten months younger than I was, but he was hard-nosed and had fight courage. His real mother was his father's first wife, and was Irish, and Claude did not look like an Indian—his cheeks wore more color in them and his eyes were gray. His father had later married another woman—an Indian, an Assiniboin, named Hazel Tevitts—who Claude did not talk about. I didn't know much about their life then, only that it didn't seem much different from mine. You did not learn much of other people in that locality, and though Claude and I were friends, I would not say I knew him very well, because there was no chance for it.

Claude's father had stayed the night in the motel in town and called Claude in the morning and told him to come down there at noon. On the way Claude stopped at my house—just out of the blue—and said I should come along. We were due to be in school that day, but my father worked on the Great Northern as a brakeman in Shelby, and was usually gone two nights together, and my mother was gone for good by then, though we didn't know that. But I did not go to school so much, as a result, and when Claude drove up in the yard, I just got in with him and we rode to town.

"What're we going in for?" I said when we were out on the Nine Mile Road, riding across the tops of the wheat prairie.

"Sherman's brought a woman in," Claude said. He was smoking a cigarette clenched in his teeth. "That's typical. He likes to put something on display."

"What does your mother think about it?" I said. We referred to Hazel as Claude's mother even though she wasn't.

"She married a gash hound. She's a Catholic," Claude said. "Maybe she can see the future. Maybe she thinks it's superior." He shook his head and put his arms up around the steering wheel as if he was thinking about that. "There might not be actual words for what Hazel thinks, yet. This ought to be funny." He grinned.

"I'll still have a look," I said. "I'll do it."

"Sure you will. Then you'll just have to give her a pumping, right?" Claude flexed up the muscle of his right arm.

"I might have to," I said.

"That's typical, too," he said. Claude was wearing the yellow silk jacket his father had brought back from the war, one with a red dragon coiled around a map of Korea on the back, and *I died there* embroidered under it in red. He reached inside it and brought out a half-pint bottle of Canadian gin. "Rocket fuel," he said. "Sherman forgets where he hides it." He handed the bottle over to me. "Fire up your missile."

I took a big drink and swallowed it. I didn't like whiskey and had not drunk it much, and when it went down I had to look out the car window. The wheat fields running by were two inches up and green then as far as you could see. The only trees alive were the olive breaks planted in rows on the rises and out distant, alongside some house or a Quonset where a farm still ran. The little town of Sunburst was ahead, lower than where we were driving. I could see the grain elevator and the narrow collection of houses down one side of the railroad spur.

Claude said suddenly, "Maybe Sherman's going to give her to us." He held the bottle up and took a drink. "He doesn't care what happens. He's been in Deer Lodge twice already. Twice *I* know of."

"For what?" I said.

"Stealing and fighting. Then fighting and stealing. He stole two cows once, and they caught him there. Then he stole two trucks and beat a guy up for fun. He went down for that."

"I don't need to beat anybody up," I said.

"There's Mr. Conscience talking now," Claude said. "Have another drink, Mr. Conscience." He had another drink of the gin, then I took another one, then he threw the bottle in the back, where the seat of his Buick had been torn out and the floor boarded in with plywood. Two fishing rods were rattling back in the dust.

"Who is this woman," I asked, feeling the gin tightening my scalp.

"He brought her over in the caboose last night from Havre. He deadheaded her in. She's Canadian. I didn't actually catch her name." Claude laughed, and we both laughed about it, and then we were down among the first poor houses of Sunburst.

Sunburst had one paved street, which was the Canada highway, and the rest dirt streets. There was the elevator, a café, an implement company, a sawdust burner, one bar, and the motel. It was the show-up for the Shelby crews that worked the GN going south. A switch engine hauled in a caboose and three cars two times a day, switched out the elevator spur, and took the crews back and forth to the main line. A green bull-pen shack was across the tracks, and my father's brown truck sat parked beside it with other crew trucks.

The motel was a little cottage camp across the highway—six white cottages and a skinny gravel lot. The closest cabin had a sign on top that said ROOMS FOR TOURISTS, and there was only one car, with an Alberta plate, parked at the cabin nearest the street.

Claude drove in the lot and gunned his engine. I saw a woman look out through the blinds of the office cabin. I wondered if she would know me if she saw me. Claude and I did not go to school in this town, but at the Consolidated in Sweetgrass.

Claude honked the horn and his father stepped out of one of the cabins. "Here comes the great ladies' man," he said. "The big Indian." Claude grinned. We were both a little drunk now. He revved the engine again and kicked out gravel.

Sherman Phillips was a large dark man with a big belly. He walked bent forward and took very small steps. He had on a long-sleeved white shirt, and his black hair was slicked back and tied in a long ponytail. He wore glasses and a pair of bedroom slippers with no socks. I didn't see how any woman would like how he looked. He drank a lot, is what my father said, and sometimes he had been seen carrying a loaded gun.

"Clear conscience is no conscience," Claude said to his father out the car window. He was still smiling.

Sherman leaned on the car door and looked in at me. His big face had pockmarks, and a scar below his left ear. I had never been this close to him. He had narrow eyes and he was clean-shaven. A pack of cigarettes was in his pocket, and I could smell his aftershave.

"You two're drunk as monkeys," he said in a mean way.

"No, we're not drunk at all," Claude said.

I could hear Claude's father breathe in his chest. The lines in his face behind his glasses were deep lines. He looked back over his shoulder at the cabin. Behind the screen in the shadows, there was a blond woman in a green dress watching us, but who didn't want us to see her.

"I've got to get home right now," Claude's father said. "You understand? Hazel thinks I'm in Havre."

"Maybe you are," Claude said. "Maybe we're all in Havre. What's *her* name?" He was looking at the cabin door where the blond woman was.

"Lucy," Sherman said, and breathed in deeply. "She's a nice girl."

"She likes you, though, I guess," Claude said. "Maybe she'll like us."

Sherman stood up and looked down the row of cabins to the office, where a phone booth was outside. The woman was gone from the office window, and I thought that she probably knew Claude's father because he had been here before, and that probably she knew all the railroad men—including my father.

"I'm going to bring her out here," Sherman said.

"You going to give her to us as a present?" Claude said.

And Sherman suddenly reached his big hand through the window and caught Claude's hair in the back and twisted it. Claude's hair was as short as mine, for boxing, but Sherman had enough of it to hurt. He had a big silver-and-turquoise ring on his index finger that pushed into Claude's scalp.

"You're not funny. You're clucks. You're stupid clucks." Sherman forced Claude's head almost out the window. He seemed dangerous to me, then—just suddenly. He was an Indian, and I wanted to get out of the car.

Sherman opened the door, pulled Claude out by his hair and away from the car, and put his big face down into Claude's face and said something I didn't hear. I looked the other way, at my father's Dodge truck parked over beside the bull-pen. I didn't think he would be back until late tonight. He stayed in Shelby in the bars sometimes, and went home with women. I wondered where my mother was right at that moment. California? Hawaii? I wondered if she was having a good time.

"Okay now, wiseass?" I heard Sherman say. "How's that, now?" He still had Claude's hair, but had raised his voice as if he wanted me to hear, too. Claude was much smaller than his father, and he had not said anything. "I'll just break your goddamn arm, now," Sherman said and grabbed Claude up closer, then pushed him away. Sherman glared over at me in the car, then turned and walked back toward the cabin he'd come out of.

Claude got back in the car and turned off the engine. "So fuck him," he said. His face was red, and he put both his hands in his lap. He didn't try to touch the back of his head, he just stared out at the Polar Bar, beside the motel. A little red polar bear sign was shining dimly in the sunlight. A man came out the side door wearing a cowboy hat. He looked at us sitting in the car, then walked around the side of the building and disappeared. No one else was in town that I could see. I didn't say anything for a few moments.

Finally I said, "What're we doing?" The car engine was ticking.

Claude stared ahead still. "We're taking her off somewhere and bringing her back tonight. He doesn't want her out in the street where people'll see her. He's an asshole."

Behind the cabin screen I could see Claude's father in his white shirt. He was kissing the woman in the green dress, his big arms wrapped around her. One leg was hooked behind her so he could get all of her against him and hold her. I could hardly see the woman at all.

"I think we should kill her," Claude said, "just to piss him off."

"What *will* happen to her?"

"I don't know. What's going to happen to you? Maybe you two'll get married. Or maybe you'll kill each other. Who cares?"

The screen opened and Sherman came out again. He looked bigger. He walked in his short steps across the lot, the sun gleaming off his glasses. He had dollar bills in his hand.

"This is shut-up money," he said when he looked in the window again. He stuffed the bills down in Claude's shirt pocket. "So shut up." He looked across at me. "Go the hell home, George. Your old man's cooking dinner. He needs you home."

I didn't smile at him, but I did not talk back either.

"I'll take him home," Claude said.

"He'll spew this."

"No, he won't," Claude said.

"I don't spew anything," I said.

Claude's father glared at me. "Don't talk toward me now, George. Just don't begin that."

I looked at him, and I wanted him to know what I was thinking: that I was sorry Claude had to be his son. I wanted the woman inside the cabin to come with us, though, and I wanted Sherman to leave. I knew Claude would not take me home.

Sherman motioned toward the cabin door, and for a few seconds nothing happened, then the screen opened and the woman came out. She closed the cabin door behind her and walked across the lot carrying a paper sack. She was wearing a man's sunglasses and was thin and flat-chested and wore green high heels. I wasn't sure how old she was. Claude and I watched her while Sherman policed up and down the street to see who was watching us. The woman in the office was not at the window. A car drove by the motel going north. A switch engine had started shunting grain cars out to the elevator, and I could smell diesel. Nobody was paying attention to any of this.

"So, all right now," Sherman said when the woman arrived. I could see through the window that she wasn't a woman but a girl. She was older than we were, but not by very much. "This is Claude," Sherman said. "He's my son. This is his close friend George, who's not going. Claude's going to take you fishing." He looked across the street at the switch engine. "This is Lucy."

The girl just stood there, holding her folded paper sack. She was tall and pretty and pale-skinned, and she didn't seem happy.

"You don't want to go fishing with us," Claude said. He had not made a move to let her in.

"Let her get in," I said. "She wants to go."

The girl bent and looked in the back where there was no seat. A crate was there with a jack, the two rods, and a jumper set.

"I'm not riding in that back," the girl said, and looked at me.

"Let her in front," I told Claude.

I don't think he wanted the girl in the car. And I didn't know why, because I wanted her in. Maybe he had thought his father had an Indian woman, and he wasn't sure what to do now.

Claude opened the door, and when he stood up I could see that the girl was taller than he was. I didn't think that kind of thing mattered though, because Claude had already whipped boys with his fists who were bigger than he was.

When the girl got in she had to pull her knees up. She was wearing stockings, and her green shoes were the kind without toes.

"Hello, George," she said, and smiled. I could smell Sherman's aftershave.

"Hello," I said.

"Don't cause me any fucking trouble, or I'll break you up," Sherman said. And before Claude could get in, Sherman was starting back to the motel in his bedroom slippers, his ponytail swinging down his back.

"You're a real odd match," Lucy said when Claude had gotten in the driver's seat. "You don't look like each other."

"Who do I look like?" Claude said. He was angry.

"Some Greek," Lucy said. She looked around Claude as Sherman disappeared into the motel room and closed the door. "Maybe your mother, though," she said as an afterthought.

"Where's she now?" Claude said. "My mother." He started the car.

The girl looked at him from behind her glasses. "At home. I guess. Wherever you live."

"No. She's dead," Claude said. "Are those my father's glasses?"

"He gave them to me. Do you want them back?"

"Are you divorced?" Claude said.

"I'm not old enough," the girl said. "I'm not even married yet."

"How old *are* you?" Claude said.

"Twenty, nineteen. How does that sound?" She looked at me and smiled. She had small teeth and her breath had beer on it. "How old do I look?"

"Eight," Claude said. "Or maybe a hundred."

"Are we going fishing, today?" she said.

"We talk about things we don't intend to do," Claude said. He hit the motor then, and snapped the clutch, and we went swerving out of the lot onto the hardtop, heading out of Sunburst and back onto the green wheat prairie.

Claude drove out the Canada highway eight miles, then off on the county road that went between the fields and past my house toward the west mountains a hundred miles away, where there was still snow and it was cold. My house flashed by in back of its belt of olive trees— just a square, gray two-story house, unprotected toward the east.

251

Claude was driving to Mormon Creek, I knew, though we were only doing what his father had told us to and not anything on our own. We were only boys, and nothing about us would interest a woman, or even a girl the age of this girl. You aren't ignorant of that fact when it is true about you, and sometimes when it isn't. And there was a strange feeling of suspense in me then—that once we were there I did not know what would happen and possibly nothing good would.

"That's a pretty green dress," Claude said as he drove. The girl had not been saying anything. None of us had, though she seemed to have her mind on something—getting back to the motel maybe, or getting back where she'd come from.

"It's not for this season," she said, staring out at the new fields where the air was tawny. "It's already too dry to farm."

"Where are you from?" I said.

"In Sceptre, Saskatchewan," she said, "where it looks just like this. A little town and a bunch of houses. The rest knifed up with these farms." She said *house* the way Canadians do, but otherwise she did not talk that way.

"What did your family do?" Claude said. "Are they a bunch of cheddar-head Swedes?" He seemed to expect everything she said to make him mad.

"He farmed," she said. "Then he worked in a tractor shop in Leader. In the fall he cleans geese. He's up to that right now."

"What do you mean, he cleans geese?" Claude said. He smiled a mean smile at her, then at me.

"Hunters bring geese they shoot. It's just out on the open prairie there. And they leave them at our garage. My father dips 'em to get the feathers out, then guts 'em and wraps 'em. It's easy. He's an American. He's from Wyoming. He was against the draft."

"He plucks 'em, you mean—right?" Claude said, driving. "Is that what you mean he does?"

"They smell better than this car does. I wouldn't have known you two were Indians if it wasn't for this car. This is a reservation beater is what we call these."

"That's what *we* call them," Claude said. "And we call those motels where you were at whorehouses."

"What do you call that guy I was with?" Lucy said.

"Do you think George looks like an Indian?" Claude said. "I think George is a Sioux, don't you?" He smiled at me. "George isn't a goddamn Indian. I am."

"An Indian's a bump in the road to me," she said.

"That's true," Claude said. And something about her had made him feel better. I didn't believe that this girl was a whore though, and I didn't believe she thought she was, or that he did. Claude's father did, but he was wrong. I just didn't know why she would come over from Havre in the middle of the night and end up out here with us. It was a mystery.

We started down the steep car path to Mormon Creek bottom, where the water was high but not too muddy to shine. Across the bridge and a hundred yards downstream was a sawmill that had made fence posts but been wrecked. Behind it was a pitch clay bluff the creek had cut, and beyond that were shallows and a cottonwood swale. On the near side was a green willow bank and a rusted car body that had been caught in the willow roots. It was a place Claude and I had fished for whitefish.

"Not much of a lumber place," Lucy said.

"That's why the sawyers did so great," Claude said.

"Which way's west?"

"That is," I said, pointing to where the white peaks of mountains could just be seen above the coulee rim.

She looked back the other way. "And what're those mountains back there?"

"Those're hills," Claude said. "We keep them separate in this country."

"It is a nice atmosphere though," she said. "I like to be oriented to the light."

"You can't see light with those glasses," Claude said.

She turned to face me. "I see George here. I see well enough. He's nicer than you are so far. He's not an asshole."

"Why don't you take those glasses off?" Claude said. We were crossing the low bridge over Mormon Creek. The Buick clattered and shimmied on the boards. I looked down. I could see through the clear surface to gravel.

"Where does *this* water go?" Lucy was looking around me.

"Up," I said. "To the Milk River. It goes north."

"Did Sherman bust you, is that the trouble?" Claude said. He stopped us right on the bridge, and grabbed at the glasses, tried taking them off Lucy's face. "You got a big busted eye?"

"No," Lucy said. And she took off the glasses and looked at me first, then Claude. She had blue eyes and blond eyebrows the color of her

253

hair. And what she was hiding was not a black eye, but that she had been crying. Not when she'd been with us, but when she woke up, maybe, and saw where she was, or who she was with, or what the day looked like ahead of her.

"I don't see why you have to have them on," Claude said. Then he drove off the bridge and turned onto the post mill road downstream, the Buick bucking and rocking over the bumps.

"It's too bright," she said and pulled the hem of her dress over her knees. It was a wool dress, as green as grass, and it felt hot against me. "What's the fun out here," she said. "That's a well-kept secret."

"You are," Claude said. "The blond bombshell. You're our reward for being able to put up with you."

"Good luck for that party." She clutched her paper bag. Her fingers were short and pink, and her fingernails were clean and not bitten, just a regular girl's hands. "Where's *your* mother and father?" she said to me.

"His old man runs the rails. He's a gash hound, too," Claude said as we drove in under the cottonwoods that grew to the creek bank. "His mother already hit the road. This is wild country up here. Nobody's safe." Claude looked at me in a disgusted way, but he knew I didn't like that talk. I didn't think that was true of my father, and he did not know my mother—though what he said about her was what I thought. It was not unusual that people left that part of Montana. She had never liked it, and neither my father nor me ever blamed her.

"Are you boys men now?" Lucy said and put her glasses back on. "Am I supposed to think that, now that we're out here?"

"It doesn't matter what you think," I said. I opened the door and got out.

"At least somebody accepts truth," Lucy said.

"George'll say anything to get on your pretty side," Claude said. "Him and me are different. Aren't we, George?"

But I had already started toward the creek and couldn't hear what the girl said back, though she and Claude were in the car together for a little while. I heard him say, "Hope means wait to me," and laugh, and I heard his door slam, with her left inside.

Claude took his casting rod to the creek bank with his jelly jar of white maggots, and tied up a cork-and-hook rig, then went to the shallows where sawdust from the mill had laid a warm-water bottom and a sluice down the center of the creek. Sometimes we had caught fifteen whitefish in a school there, when they'd fed. One after another. You could put your bait where they were and bring one back. They were big fish and steady fighters, and Claude liked them because they were easy to catch.

It was three o'clock then, and warm, but I did not want to fish. I did not like the waiting of fishing. I'd hunted for birds with my father, walked them up out of the rosebush thickets. But I did not care so much for fishing, and not for whitefish at all.

Claude had taken off his yellow jacket, and the girl had brought it back up—walking on the toes of her shoes—and spread it in the sun, then sat facing the creek. She raised her dress to her knees and took off her shoes and stockings and pushed up her sleeves. She'd unbuttoned her front enough to let sun on her neck and leaned on one elbow, smoking a cigarette, blowing the smoke in the warm air.

"I wish I could play the piano," she said when I walked up from the bank. "Do you play one?"

"No," I said. My mother had played a piano when we'd lived in Great Falls. She played Dixieland in the house we'd rented there.

"Out here makes me think about that," she said. "I'd like to go in somebody's house and sit down and play some song." She blew smoke out the side of her mouth. She still had on Sherman's sunglasses. Her long legs were so white they looked gray, and thin enough that her calf bones stood out. She had shaved them above her knees, and I could see where the blond hair began. She looked at me as if she wanted me to say something else, but I had nothing else to say. "Do you ever have the dream that somebody you know is leading you into a river and just when you're knee-deep, you step in a hole and you fall under. Then you jump in your sleep, it scares you so much?"

"I have that," I said. "Sometimes."

"Everybody probably does," she said.

I sat beside her on the grass, and we watched Claude. He was casting out toward the car body and walking his bobber down through the sluice. Now and then he'd look back at us and make a phony gesture of having a fish on his line, and then he would ignore us. I could smell the cottonwoods and the sawdust air from the mill.

"Do you have a suitcase full of your clothes?" I said.

"Where?" she said. She was smoking another cigarette.

"I don't know. Someplace else."

"I just left," the girl said. "I wanted to take a trip suddenly—to someplace warmer. I'm not sure I had this in mind, though." She

255

looked at Claude, who had looked up at us again then turned around. Whitefish made little dimples on the flat water, seizing insects I could not even see. It was not a good sign for the rig Claude was using; though at any time fish can do another thing and you will begin to catch them. "His father's not so terrible," she said and touched her nylon stockings, which were in a pile on the grass. She lifted one up with her little finger. "You certainly wouldn't think he'd sit in the dark in the middle of the night and pray in a motel. But he does. He's nice, really. He's pretty big, too. His son's scrawny."

I tried to think about Sherman praying but couldn't think of what he'd want to pray for or hope to have come to him. "Where'd you meet him?"

"At the Trails End Bar in Havre, where I was too young to get in, or should've been. You get in odd situations sometimes."

"How old *are* you?"

She widened her eyes at me. "You're now a criminal. I'm just sixteen, though I look older than that, I know it. Someday I'll regret it." She reached for her paper sack and brought out a can of beer, a cold hot dog, and a red transistor radio. "I've accumulated this much so far."

"When did you leave home?"

"Exactly one night before last," she said. "I didn't think I could trust anybody up there—maybe I was wrong. Who knows?" When she opened the beer it spewed up her arm. She took a drink and handed it to me, and I drank some. "Drinking distances you," she said. "I *would* like to see the Space Needle, still." She picked up the little radio, leaning on her elbow, and stared at it. "Batteries are my next assignment. For this thing." She thumped it with her finger as if she wanted that to turn it on. "I'm not going to eat *this* either." She picked up the hot dog and tossed it in the grass.

"You didn't want to come out here, did you?" I said.

"I didn't want to stay back in that room. Sunburst? Is that what that place is called? You accept help where you get it, I guess."

"Uh-oh, now. Uh-oh," Claude shouted. His rod was curved over, and his line was cutting around the water this way and that. "Here, now. Here he is," Claude said, and looked over his shoulder and wound in on the reel. "This is the big whitefish," he yelled.

Lucy sat up and watched. Claude had walked into the shallows in his shoes, holding his rod up as the fish toured around him. "Look how excited he gets," she said and took a drink of her warm beer. "A monkey could catch a whitefish. They're trash fish. He's stupid."

I saw the fish shine through the surface, then turn down in the cold water. It was a big fish, you could tell by how deep it took the line. I knew Claude wanted to get it in to show.

"He's going to break that one off," Lucy said, "and I bet he doesn't have another hook." And I thought he would break it off myself. I'd seen him break off big fish before.

Claude brought his rod butt down then and struck it with the edge of his hand, struck it hard enough that the rod tip snapped. "They hate this," he shouted, and he smacked his rod butt again. "A fish feels pain."

The rod dipped, then rose. The line ran out toward the willow bank twenty yards away, then the fish turned on the surface, its white belly visible as Claude began backing it out, and I saw that the fish was falling in the current, losing distance.

"That trick works," Claude shouted at us. "Pain works. Come see this thing."

I walked down to where he'd waded back onto the mud bank. The fish was already on its side, finning sideways in the shallows. "It's huge," Claude said, hoisting the fish up with his rod. And it was a huge fish, long and deep-chested and silvery as it touched up out of the silt. "You can't catch this fish every day, can you?" He was sweating and jittery. He wanted Lucy to see the fish. He looked around, but she'd stayed sitting, smoking her cigarette.

"Great," she said and waved a hand at him. "Catch two more and we can all throw one away."

Claude smiled a mean smile. "Get it off," he said, and dragged the big fish back onto the grass where it lay with its gills cupping air. It was not a pretty fish. It was two feet long, and scaly and silver-white. "Use this," Claude said. He pulled his black spring-knife out of his pocket and clicked down the blade. "Just cut the hook out."

And I got on my knees in the grass, held the fish across its cold body, and cut up right through the bottom of its gill, using the point of the blade. I opened the cut out, pushed under the hook and dug it loose. The fish made a strangled sound when I put my weight on it, but it didn't move.

"Hooked in the gills," Claude said, watching the fish begin to bleed where I'd cut it. "It'll eat good."

I stood up and gave Claude his knife. The fish still breathed, but it was too badly cut to live in the water again. It was too worn out and too big. It wouldn't have lived, I didn't think, even if I hadn't cut it.

Claude pinched the hook between his fingers and the knife blade, straightening the point. "I'm going to catch a bigger one," he said. "They're out there in rows. I'll catch every one of them." Claude looked over his shoulder at Lucy, who was still watching us. He bit his bottom lip. "You're into something, aren't you?" He said this in a whisper.

"I hope so," I said.

"She's a sweetheart." He closed his knife on his pants leg. "Things can happen when you're by yourself, can't they?" He smiled.

"Tell secrets, now," Lucy said and looked up at the sky and shook her head.

"It's not a secret," Claude yelled. "We don't have any secrets. We're friends."

"Great," she said. "Then you and Sherman are all alike. You got nothing worth hiding."

I went back up and sat beside Lucy. Swallows were appearing now, hitting the creek surface and catching the insects that had hatched in the afternoon air.

Lucy was at her red radio, thumbing its little plastic dial back and forth. "I wish this worked," she said. "We could get some entertainment in the wilderness. We could dance. Do you like dancing?"

"Yes," I said.

"Do you have a girlfriend, too?"

"No," I said, though I did have a girlfriend—in Sweetgrass—a half-Blackfeet girl I had not known very long.

Lucy lay in the grass and stared at where a jet was leaving a trail of white cloud, like a silvery speck inching westward. She had her green dress a little farther up her legs so the sun could be on them. "Do you understand radar, yet?"

"I've read about it."

"Don't you see things that aren't there? Is that right?"

"They're still there," I said, "but they're out of sight."

"That's the thing I liked about fishing when my father used to go with me," she said, gazing up. "You only saw half what was there. It was a mystery. I like that." She pursed up her lips and watched the jet going east. To Germany, I decided. "I don't mind feeling lonely out here." She put her hands behind her head and looked at me through Sherman's dark glasses. "Tell me something shameful you've done. That's an act of faith. You already know something about me, right? Though that wasn't so bad. I've probably done worse."

Claude yelled from down in the creek. His rod was bent and he had it raised high in both hands, the line shooting upstream. Then suddenly the rod snapped straight and the line fell back on the surface. "There's his long-line release," Claude said, then laughed. He was in better spirits just from fishing. "If I didn't horse 'em, I'd catch 'em," he said and did not look where we were.

"He's a fool," Lucy said. "Indians are fools. I'd hate to have their kids."

"He's not," I said. "He's not a fool."

"Okay. I guess I'm too hard on him."

"He doesn't care."

She looked at Claude, who was beginning to rebait his hook, standing to his knees in the creek. "Well," she said, "you'll never see me after today, either. What have you done that's shameful?"

"Nothing," I said. "I haven't done anything shameful."

"Lying is it, then," she said. "That's shameful. You lied because you're ashamed. There isn't any out to this. It's a game, and you lost it."

"You're not ashamed of anything, are you?"

"Yes I am," she said. "I'm ashamed of leaving home without saying anything to anybody. And of spending the night with Sherman in that motel. That's just two days of things. I'll give you a second chance. Are you ashamed of being out here with me—whatever kind of person I am? That's easy, isn't it?"

"I haven't done anything to you I'm ashamed of," I said, though I wanted to think of something I might be ashamed of—that I'd hurt someone or hated them or been glad a terrible thing had happened. It seemed wrong to know nothing about that. I looked at Claude, who was throwing his line onto the current, his bobber catching the sluice and riding it. In forty-five minutes we would lose daylight, and it would be colder. After that we'd take Lucy back to the motel for Claude's father, if he remembered. My own father would never even know I had been here, wouldn't know about this day. I felt on my own, which was not so unusual. "I was glad when my mother left," I said.

"Why?" Lucy said.

"We didn't need her. She didn't need us, either." Neither of those things was true, but I could say them, and it didn't bother me to hear them.

"Where is she now?" Lucy said.

"I don't know," I said. "I don't care."

Though just from her voice then I could tell this didn't matter to her. Shame didn't mean any more to her than some other way you could feel on a day—like feeling tired or cold or crying. It went away, finally. And I thought that I would like to feel that way about shame if I could.

Lucy took her sunglasses off. She reached over and put her hands on my arm and kissed my arm above the wrist. It was a strange thing for her to do. "What he said about your parents was a lie," she said. "It was too harsh. If they're happy, you'll be the same way. I bet my parents are happy I'm gone. I don't even blame them." I didn't say anything, because I didn't know what kind of people they could've been—some man who'd gone across the border to stay out of the war. "Why don't you kiss me?" Lucy said. "Just for a minute?"

I looked at Claude. I saw he had another fish on but wasn't yelling about it. He was just pulling it in.

"He can see us," she said. "I don't care. Let him." She pushed her face up into my face and kissed me. She kissed me hard and opened her mouth too wide and put her tongue in mine, then pushed me on the grass and onto her stockings and her shoes. "Just do this," she said. "Kiss me back. Kiss me all you want to. I like that."

And I kissed her, put both my arms around her and felt her skinny back and her sides and up to her breasts and her face and her hair, and held her on top of me, pushing against me until my heart beat hard and I thought my breath would stop. "You boys," she whispered to me, "I love you boys. I wish I was staying with you tonight. You're so wonderful."

But I knew that wasn't what she meant. It was just a thing to say, and nothing was wrong with it at all. "You're wonderful," I said. "I love you."

"You're drunk," I heard Claude call out. "You're both fuck drunk."

I was on my back and my mouth was dry. Lucy pulled away from me and looked at him. "Don't act jealously," she said, then reached for her can of beer and took a drink.

"I'm down here fishing," Claude said. "Come look at this. It's a great fish."

"Let's let him have something," Lucy said and stood up, though I didn't want her to leave but to kiss me again, to stay. But she got up and started down barefoot to where Claude was kneeling in the grass. "Let's see your poor fish," she said.

Claude had another whitefish in the grass. The one I'd killed was dry and lying beside it, and the second one was smaller, but it was bright and bending in the grass. Claude had his hand on it and his spring-knife ready to pry out the hook himself.

"It's smaller," he said, "but it's prettier. It's livelier."

Lucy looked down at the fish. She said, "That's a picture of helplessness, I guess, isn't it?"

"It's a whitefish," Claude said as the fish tried to twist free under his hand. "They're the best. And it's helpless. Right. You bet it is."

"What a surprise that must be," Lucy said, watching the fish struggle. "For the fish. Everything just goes crazy at once. I wonder what it thinks."

"They don't. Fish don't think," Claude said.

"Don't they have little perfect spirits?" Lucy looked at me and smiled. She didn't care about any of this. I could tell.

"Not this one," Claude said.

He moved his hand around to the top of the fish to make a better grip so he could use his knife, but the fish twisted again, and with its top fin it jabbed Claude's hand into the meat below his thumb.

"Look at that!" Lucy said.

And Claude let the fish go and wrung his hand and flung blood on the fish and on his face and on Lucy. He dropped his knife and squeezed his hand where the fish had cut him, his jaws set tight. "Son of a bitch thing," he said. He put his hand in his mouth and sucked it, then looked at it. The wound was small and narrow, and it had begun to seep blood on his wet skin. "Fucking thing," Claude said. "Fucking fish is dangerous." He put his hand back in his mouth and sucked the cut again. He looked at Lucy, who was watching him. And for an instant I thought Claude would do something terrible—say something to her or do something to the fish that would make her turn her head away, something he would later be sorry for. I had seen that in him. He was able to do bad things easily.

But what he did was take his hand out of his mouth and stick it in the grass and lean hard on it to stop the blood. It might've been an Indian way. "Who cares," he said, and he seemed calm. He pushed his hand harder in the grass. The blood had dried already on his face. The fish was still twisting in the grass, its stiff gills trapping air, its scales growing dry and dull. "This is your fish," Claude said to Lucy. "Do something with it. I don't want it." I knew his hand hurt him by the way he talked so quietly.

Lucy looked at the fish, and I thought her body, which I was close to, became relaxed somehow, as if something that had been bothering her or that was hard for her suddenly wasn't.

"Okay," Lucy said. "My fish. Let me have that knife."

Claude picked the knife up and handed it to her, the blade forward in the dangerous way. "This is sharp," he said, and as she reached for it, he jabbed it at her, though she only moved her hand out of the way and did not take a step back. "You think we're handsome?" Claude said. "Us two?"

"You're the most handsome boys I ever saw," Lucy said, "in this particular light." She put her hand back out for Claude's knife. "Let me have that."

"We could kill you, right now," Claude said. "Who'd know about it?"

Lucy looked at me and back at Claude. "That woman in the motel would probably be the first one. I had a talk with her this morning before what's-his-name came back to life. Not that it matters."

Claude smiled at her. "You plan to kill me when I give you this knife?"

I could see Lucy's toes twitching in the grass. "No. I'm going to kill my fish," she said.

"Okay," Claude said, and handed her the knife by the blade. Lucy stepped by him and, without getting down on her knees, leaned over and pushed the knife down straight into the fish Claude had caught—pushed it through in the middle behind the gills that were still working, and on into the ground. Then she pulled the knife back far enough to get it out of the ground, picked the fish up by the handle, and flung it off the blade into the Mormon Creek. She looked at Claude in a casual way, then threw his knife out into the deep water, where it hit with hardly a splash and disappeared down among the fish.

She looked around at me. "There you go," she said.

And Claude was smiling at her because I think, he didn't know what else to do. He was sitting on the ground in his wet shoes, and he wasn't squeezing his hand anymore. "You'll do anything, won't you?" he said.

"I always commit the wrong sins," she said. "I thought we'd have fun out here. That must prove something."

"I bet you'd fuck a pig in knickers," Claude said, "you Canada girls."

"You want me to take my dress off?" she said. "Is that what you mean? I'll do that. Who cares. That's what *you* said."

"Do that, then. I'll watch it," Claude said. "George can watch.

That'll be okay." I thought about kissing her then, sitting on Claude's jacket in the grass, and I was ready to watch her take her dress off.

And that's what she did, with Claude on the ground and me standing close to the side of Mormon Creek. She unbuttoned her green dress front, reached down, crossed her arms, and pulled her dress over her head so that she was only in her loose petticoat. And you could tell from her face that she was occupied by something—I don't know what. She pulled the loose straps off her shoulders and let her petticoat drop off of her so that she had on only a pink brassiere and pants that looked like the cotton pants I wore. Her legs and her stomach were white and soft and a little fat, and I didn't think she looked as good as when she'd had her dress on. Not as good as I thought would be the case. There were red marks and scratches on her back and down the backs of her legs, which I thought were the marks Sherman had made on her. I thought of them in the motel in Sunburst, under some blanket together, making noise and rolling and grabbing at each other in the dark.

And then she took off the rest. The brassiere first and then the cotton pants. Her breasts were small and up-pointed, and her ass was hardly even there. I didn't look much at the rest of her. Though I could see then—or so I thought at the time—how *young* she was by how she stood on her pale thin legs, with her thin arms, and how she turned only at the waist and looked at me, so she could be sure I saw her, too. Like a girl. Younger, maybe than even I was, younger than Claude.

But it did not matter because she was already someone who could be by herself in the world. And neither Claude nor I was anything like that, and we never would be, never if we lived to be old men. Maybe she was born that way, or raised to it, or had simply become that in the last two days. But it embarrassed me at that moment—for myself—and I know I looked away from her.

"What's next?" she said.

"What do you think you're good for now," Claude said, sitting in the grass, looking up to her. "Everybody thinks they're good for something. You must think you are. Or are you just good for nothing?" And he surprised me, because I didn't think he was taunting her. I think he wanted to know the answer, that something about her seemed odd to him, maybe in the way it seemed to me.

"A lot of this seems a lot alike to me," she said and sighed. "You can take me back to the motel. I've had all the fun I'm going to." She looked around at her clothes on the ground, as if she was trying to decide what to pick up first.

"You don't have to act that way," Claude said. "I'm not mad at you." And his voice seemed strange to me, some soft voice I hadn't heard him speak in—almost as if he was worried. "No, no," he said. "You don't." I watched him extend his hand and touch her bare ankle, saw her look at him on the ground. I knew what was going to happen after that, and it did not involve me, and I didn't feel the need to be there for it. Claude had a serious look on his face, a look that said this was for him now. And I just turned and walked back toward the Buick at the edge of the cottonwoods.

I heard Lucy say, "You can't ever read other people's minds, can you? That's the trouble." Then I quit listening to them altogether.

I will say how all of this turned out because in a way it is surprising, and because it did not turn out badly.

In the car I didn't wait a long while for them. They were not there long. I thought I wouldn't watch them, but I did, from the distance of the car. I happen to think it is what she wanted, though it might seem she wouldn't have. In any case I don't think she knew what she wanted from me. What we did, I thought, didn't matter so much. Not to us, or to anyone. She might've been with me instead of Claude, or with Claude's father, or another man none of us knew. She was pushing everything out. She was just an average girl.

I turned on the car radio and listened to the news from the Canadian station. Snow and bad weather were on their way again, it said, and I could feel the evening grow colder as it went to dark and the air turned blue. Trout moved against the far willow bank—swirling, deep rises that weren't like other fish, and created in me a feeling of anticipation high up in my chest. It was that way I had felt early in the day, when we'd driven down to this very place to fish. Though the place now seemed different—the creek, the tree line, the mill shed—all in new arrangements, in different light.

But I did not, as I waited, want to think about only myself. I realized that was all I had ever really done, and that possibly it was all you could ever do, and that it would make you bitter and lonesome and useless. So I tried to think instead about Lucy. But I had no idea where to begin. I thought about my mother, someplace far off—on a *flyer*, is how my father had described it. He thought she would walk back into our house one day, and that life would start all over. But I was accustomed to the idea that things ended and didn't start up again—it is not a hard lesson to learn when that is all around you. And I only, at that moment, wondered if she'd ever lied to me, and if so, what about, wondered if she was someplace with a boy like me or Claude Phillips. I put a picture in my mind that she was, though I thought it was wrong.

After a while the two of them walked back up to the car. It was dark and Lucy had her shoes and her stockings and her sack, and Claude had his fishing rod and his one fish he put behind the seat. They were drinking another beer, and for a minute or so they were quiet. But then Lucy said, just in a passing way, straightening her green dress, "I hope you aren't what you wear."

"You *are* judged by it, though," I said. Then that tension was over, and we all seemed to know what was happening to us.

We got in the car and drove around over the wheat prairie roads at night, drove by my house, where it was still dark, then by Claude's, where there were yellow lights and smoke out the chimney, and we could see figures through the windows. His father's truck was parked against the house side. Claude honked as we passed, but didn't stop.

We drove down into Sunburst, stopped at the Polar Bar, and bought a package of beer. When Claude was inside, Lucy said to me that she hoped to rise in the world someday. She asked me in what situations I would tell her a lie, and I said not any, then she kissed me again while we sat waiting in sight of the dark train yard and the grain elevator, ribboned in its lights, and the empty motel where I had seen her first that day. The sky was growing marbly against the moon, and she said she hated a marble sky. The air in the car was cold, and I wondered if Sherman was already on his way to town.

When Claude came back with the beers, we all sat and drank one, and then he said we should drive Lucy to Great Falls, a hundred miles away, and forget all about Sherman. And that is what we did. We drove her there that night, took her to the bus station in the middle of town, where Claude and I gave her all the money we had and what Sherman had given him as the shut-up money. And we left her there, just at midnight, going toward what and where neither of us knew or even talked about.

On the drive back up along the Great Northern tracks we passed a long train coming north, sparks popping off its brakeshoes and out its journal boxes, the lighted caboose seeming to move alone and unaided through the dark. Snow was beginning to mist in the black air.

"Sherman wouldn't have come back." Claude was watching the

265

train as it raced along beside us. "She wanted to stay with me. She admitted that. I wish I could marry her. I wish I was old."

"You could be old," I said, "and it could still be the same way."

"Don't belittle me now," Claude said. "Don't do that."

"No," I said. "I'm not."

"And don't belittle her." And I thought Claude was a fool then, and this was how you knew what a fool was—someone who didn't know what mattered to him in the long run. "I wonder what she's thinking about," Claude said, driving.

"She's thinking about you," I said. "Or about your old man."

"He could never love a woman like I can," Claude said and smiled at me. "Never in his life. It's a shame."

"That's right. He couldn't," I said, even though I thought that shame was something else. And I felt my own life exactly at that instant, begin to go by me—fast and plummeting—almost without my notice.

Claude raised his fist and held it out like a boxer in the dark of the car. "I'm strong and I'm invincible," he said. "Nothing's on my conscience." I don't know why he said that. He was just lost in his thinking. He held his fist up in the dark for a long time as we drove on toward north. And I wondered then: what was *I* good for? What was terrible about me? What was best? Claude and I couldn't see the world and what would happen to us in it—what we would do, where we would go. How could we? Outside was a place that seemed not even to exist, an empty place you could stay in for a long time and never find a thing you admired or loved or hoped to keep. And we were unnoticeable in it—both of us. Though I did not want to say that to him. We were friends. But when you are older, nothing you did when you were young matters at all. I know that now, though I didn't know it then. We were simply young.

About the
Editor

DAVID SEYBOLD is the editor of two anthologies: *Waters Swift and Still* (with Craig Woods) and *Seasons of the Hunter* (with Robert Elman). His stories have appeared in numerous magazines and anthologies. He lives in New Hampshire with his wife, Laurie, and daughter, Ashley.

About the
Illustrator

JOSEPH FORNELLI is a member of the Society of Animal Artists and an associate member of the American Watercolor Society. He has illustrated numerous books, and his work has been exhibited throughout the United States.